Delivering Digital Images

Delivering Digital Images
Cultural Heritage Resources *for* Education

The Museum Educational Site Licensing Project, Volume 1

EDITED BY

CHRISTIE STEPHENSON

PATRICIA McCLUNG

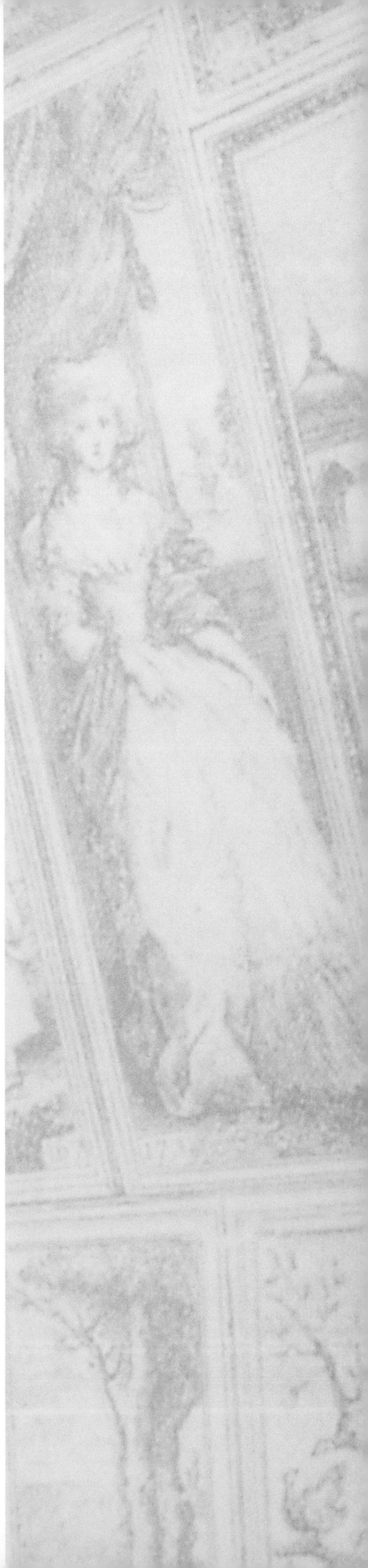

THE GETTY
INFORMATION
INSTITUTE

Printed in the United States of America

The Getty Information Institute
1200 Getty Center Drive, Suite 300
Los Angeles, California 90049-1680
310-440-7310
Fax: 310-440-7715
http://www.gii.getty.edu

Bridging art and technology, the Getty Information Institute provides leadership in networking cultural heritage information for research, education, and community enrichment. The Institute works internationally, nationally, and locally, and in concert with other Getty programs, to develop the model policies, tools, and methods needed to link cultural information globally.

Copyeditor: Linda Allen
Design and Production Management: The Left Coast Group, Inc.
Production: Loraine Hoonhout, Robin Williams at The Left Coast Group, Inc.
Printing: Typecraft, Inc.

ISBN 0-89236-509-9

Contents

Foreword

At this particular moment in history—as converging technologies bring images, sound, and text together for networked delivery—cultural institutions have a unique opportunity to shape their own destiny. The Getty Information Institute is dedicated to making information about our cultural heritage universally accessible. To this end, the Institute fosters demonstration projects that build on collaborative partnerships and capitalize on technological advances to strengthen the presence, quality, and accessibility of cultural information on emerging networks.

The Museum Educational Site Licensing Project (MESL) was undertaken in this vein, to explore the possibilities of electronic networks for increasing the availability of cultural heritage information. When it was launched in 1994, the MESL project had an ambitious agenda that resonated with the central vision of the Getty Information Institute. Its primary focus was to define acceptable terms and conditions for distributing museum images for educational purposes. Framed as a practical demonstration project involving 14 institutions, it necessarily encompassed much more. Before the project ended in the summer of 1997, participants grappled with a variety of issues from content selection, image capture, and standards for recording and transmitting data to systems interface design, faculty and student training in new technology, software tool development, use and impact studies, economic analyses, and intellectual property questions.

This report and its companion volume, *Images Online: Perspectives on the Museum Educational Site Licensing Project,* document as fully as possible the project's methodology, its central issues, and its lessons, including issues that were unresolved and need to evolve over time by trial and error in an iterative process. Consistent with its original central purpose, this report defines terms and conditions for distributing digital museum images via university campus networks. This important outcome was realized through a collaborative meeting of some of the best minds from among the universities and museums that participated. In addition to these legal and administrative issues, the report covers project findings on a variety of complex issues that were central to the experiment: content selection, technical infrastructure, use of the images and their impact, and economic considerations.

The project is indebted to the institutions that met the challenges it presented, and to the people in those institutions who made it happen, brought the critical issues to the surface, and wrote about them for this publication. Collaborations such as theirs require steadfast commitment, a daunting amount of hard work, and the determination to achieve consensus on crucial issues. Their efforts, documented here, demonstrate new ways to harness technology to make the world's cultural heritage more accessible. More importantly, they foreshadow many of the transformational benefits that in time both teachers and students will enjoy.

ELEANOR FINK
DIRECTOR
THE GETTY INFORMATION INSTITUTE

Preface

The Museum Educational Site Licensing Project (MESL) was launched in 1994 as part of The Getty Information Institute's Imaging Initiative, which was created to act as a catalyst in improving networked access to cultural heritage materials. MESL was conceived as a collaborative project rather than a research assignment, on the assumption that a real-world experiment—ambitious and bold though it was—was the best way to reveal and engage the primary issues. More importantly, we believed that the challenges impeding progress, particularly the legal, administrative, and technical ones, lent themselves to collaborative experimentation and problem solving.

As it turned out, the MESL project far exceeded our expectations, thanks to the creative energy that evolved among the participants over the course of the project. The MESL publication *Images Online: Perspectives on the Museum Educational Site Licensing Project* captures some of the individual voices of the MESL participants, and reflects the extraordinary talent and personal commitment to this experiment that became the hallmark of the MESL project. This companion volume, *Delivering Digital Images: Cultural Heritage Resources for Education,* covers the project's methodologies and essential findings.

I want to extend a special thanks to Christie Stephenson, MESL Project Director, and Patti McClung, MESL Project Manager. Through their hard work, personal dedication, and relentless professionalism, Christie and Patti were largely responsible for MESL's success. Their thoughtful guidance as well as their unwavering respect for the people and participating institutions nurtured the endeavor's progress and preserved the spirit of the collaboration.

KATHLEEN MCDONNELL
ASSOCIATE DIRECTOR
THE GETTY INFORMATION INSTITUTE

Participating Institutions

Museums

- Fowler Museum of Cultural History
- George Eastman House
- Harvard University Art Museums
- Library of Congress
- The Museum of Fine Arts, Houston
- National Gallery of Art
- National Museum of American Art

Universities

- American University
- Columbia University
- Cornell University
- University of Illinois at Urbana–Champaign
- University of Maryland
- University of Michigan
- University of Virginia

Sponsoring Institutions

- The Getty Information Institute (formerly the Getty Art History Information Program)
- MUSE Educational Media

All Web sites referenced in this publication were active as of April 1998. If electronic documents referenced in this publication are no longer posted on a Web site, contact the Webmaster for the site and request an archive document, if available.

Editors' Notes and Acknowledgments

The Museum Educational Site Licensing Project (MESL) was undertaken to explore ways to make museum images and related information available in an online environment for educational purposes. It set out to clarify the uncertainty surrounding intellectual property rights for images distributed on campus networks. It grew to include a full range of technical, pedagogical, economic, and policy issues.

From the outset, the project's participants and sponsors planned to document their experiences in order to share them as widely as possible. This volume, *Delivering Digital Images: Cultural Heritage Resources for Education,* serves as the official project report of our collective undertaking. Its outline was approved by the project coordinators and Management Committee; project staff as well as several project coordinators and Management Committee members reviewed and commented on drafts. It describes the purpose, process, and findings of the MESL project. The report is supplemented by a second volume, *Images Online: Perspectives on the Museum Educational Site Licensing Project,* which brings together a rich collection of individual and institutional perspectives on various aspects of the project.

The editors are grateful for the invaluable contributions of all those who supported the process of reporting on the MESL project: at the Getty Information Institute, Kathleen McDonnell, Michelle D'Amico, Nancy Bryan, Ben Davis, and Eleanor Fink; the other members of the MESL Management Committee—Maxwell Anderson, David Bearman, Howard Besser, Clifford Lynch, and Jennifer Trant; Diane Zorich, who reviewed the manuscript; and the design team at The Left Coast Group, especially Chris Schabow and George Kupfer. Finally, and most especially, we thank the authors, who gave their time to help us build the record of this ambitious undertaking, and all of the participants who contributed to the project's success.

CHRISTIE STEPHENSON
PATRICIA MCCLUNG

The Evolution of the MESL Project

CHRISTIE STEPHENSON

As networked access to digital images became increasingly feasible in the course of the past decade, the cultural heritage community began to raise a number of questions. Could digital access to their holdings provide a revenue stream for museums, a source of much-needed income in an era of declining public and private support? Should museums open up electronic access to their collections, using the network to build new communities of visitors, both actual and virtual? In universities, where sophisticated network infrastructures were already in place, some educators were beginning to look to new technologies to reach distance learners, revitalize their curricula, and gain access to new materials for their personal research. But early experience left them keenly aware of the paucity of authoritative data available in digital form, and concerns about intellectual property rights issues often paralyzed many who were ready to embrace new technologies enthusiastically.

In early 1994, a group of like-minded individuals came together and began to discuss these issues.[1] Over the next six months, the Museum Educational Site Licensing Project (MESL) was framed as a testbed demonstration project, designed to bring together representative museums and universities to explore the administrative, legal, economic, technical, and educational issues that would need to be resolved in order to realize the goal of networked distribution of museum content for educational use. The organizational phase of the project was supported by the Getty Information Institute (formerly the Getty Art History Information Program) and MUSE Educational Media.

The project was officially launched in September 1994 with the release of the initial call for participation in the MESL project, which included a project overview, objectives, timeline, and support and selection criteria.[2] Over 80 museums and universities submitted detailed applications, indicating their willingness and ability to participate. From those applications, the project's Management Committee[3] selected six cultural heritage repositories and seven universities to participate in MESL. Participants were notified in early December 1994.[4]

The cultural heritage repositories were:

- Fowler Museum of Cultural History
- George Eastman House
- Harvard University Art Museums
- The Museum of Fine Arts, Houston
- National Gallery of Art
- National Museum of American Art
- Library of Congress (invited to participate in February 1995)

These seven museums and libraries were chosen to represent a broad spectrum of organizational types—public and private, large and smaller, art and cultural history collections. The only absolute requirements were that the institution have existing automated collections information and access to electronic mail. Those selected were consciously chosen because of their wide range of experience in the networked environment. The National Museum of American Art, for instance, had an established core of material already available on the Internet at the time the MESL project began. The Museum of Fine Arts,

Houston, on the other hand, had barely begun to use e-mail, but had a strong institutional commitment to exploring the educational benefits of digital access to its collections.

The seven universities selected to participate were:

- American University
- Columbia University
- Cornell University
- University of Illinois at Urbana–Champaign
- University of Maryland
- University of Michigan
- University of Virginia

The seven universities chosen were judged to have the necessary technological expertise and infrastructure to support the project on their respective campuses. They were also selected on the basis of having expressed strong administrative support for the project and having faculty members willing to participate in the experiment by committing to using MESL data in their teaching. Each of the participating universities was required to assemble an interdisciplinary project team, drawing on librarians, technologists, instructional designers, and faculty members.

Over the course of the next two and a half years, the participants worked together to explore their collective agenda. Together they developed a methodology for investigating a broad range of legal and administrative, technical, and pedagogical issues. During the course of the project, the museums made 9,319 digital images and associated data records from their collections available to the universities to mount on their local networks for educational use. Throughout the project, the participants explored the legal and administrative issues that could define an ongoing system of providing cultural heritage images and associated information to educational institutions; discussed issues surrounding the scope of the content provided and its implications for both the current demonstration project and future efforts; explored and tested the technical issues involved in the production, distribution, and deployment of the content; and examined the impact of the experiment on their institutions and on users.[5]

The project's success rested on the commitment and contributions of project participants. Collectively, they struggled to understand the complex issues of licensing and rights administration and to define the technical parameters of the experiment, from data export and image production through distribution to campus delivery. They worked to bring new users to the material and to support those who were trying to incorporate it into their teaching. They endeavored to evaluate the impact on each of their own institutions and to speculate about future models that could build on this experiment.

▶ Legal and Administrative Issues

While the MESL project had many facets, one of its primary premises was that site licensing could serve as a model for providing museum cultural heritage content to educational institutions. The framers of the project speculated that educational licensing could provide access to museum documentation in digital form while relieving educational institutions from the burdens of trying to clear rights to use images, and that the educational missions of both museums and universities would be served by minimizing the legal and procedural obstacles associated with the use of cultural heritage images and information in digital form. They were also interested in investigating the economics of such a system of licensing, to explore the possibility of designing models that provided enough cost recovery to underwrite further digitization and documentation efforts.

The project itself was conducted under a jointly executed cooperative agreement rather than an actual license. No money changed hands between the participants, although many institutional resources were expended on all sides.[6] As a group, the participants sought to understand how to take the lessons they were learning under this agreement and transform them into a model site licensing agreement. Such an agreement might provide a modest cost-recovery income stream for the producers of information, while respecting the shared educational values of both the museum and the university.

Together the group explored in great detail potential terms and conditions for licensing museum digital content in an educational environment. Together the group negotiated definitions of user groups and acceptable educational uses of the content. Among the questions the participants grappled with were: Are alumni and donors part of the "university community" under terms of a site license? What about "distance learners"? Could a student download an image from the MESL database, include it in a paper, and put that paper in her own Web space for the world to see? Could a university development office copy an image from the MESL database to use in a printed fundraising brochure?

Over time, the group came to realize that within the scope of the project it would be impossible to develop a single model site license per se. To do so would require definition of a specific distribution mechanism and a much more detailed exploration of the nature and scope of a collective administrative body to administer content on behalf of museums. Instead, the group developed a set of model terms and conditions for educational licensing that reflects a collective exploration of participants' shared values within the MESL framework. The resulting model terms and conditions did not represent the language of a specific contract, but instead sought to define the nature of a new relationship between the museums and universities based on their mutual value exploration.

"One reason we wanted to join the project initially was this whole idea of a safety net. This was a prototype project and there were museums and universities exchanging information with each other in a closed group."

JEANNETTE DIXON
THE MUSEUM OF FINE ARTS, HOUSTON
Participants' Meeting

▶ Content Selection and Content Models

While the MESL project was not designed to focus on content per se, the issue of content selection was critical to the project's success. In addressing the issue of content selection, the participants confronted a number of issues that have broad implications as we move into the digital future. The nature of the experiment required faculty members at the participating universities to select from the available holdings of the participating museums to ensure that they could have access to significant content from which to teach or to design curricular units. The process was cumbersome and frustrating; in some cases, no match existed between those willing to teach using digital images and the content available. After the content was selected and mounted on university networks, it was difficult to characterize what was there in a way that users could comprehend. In some cases, there was breadth; in other cases, depth. Only those who had been actively involved in content selection or who had considerable knowledge of the holdings of the participating museums were able to approach the MESL data with reasonable expectations of what they might find.

Since it will no doubt be years before educators have access to digital versions of all of the images they might be accustomed to teaching with, or need for their research, how will we reach "critical mass," providing enough content in digital form to make educators look to digital resources as they now look to traditional print sources or local slide collections? If the works they are accustomed to using are not represented, why should they be motivated to use the licensed digital content? Will they remain wedded to 35 mm slides or work locally to digitize their personal canon under the doctrine of fair use?

On a higher level, will the presence or absence of particular images redefine the canon in ways that provoke new avenues of critical inquiry? Might the presence or absence of objects in the corpus of digital content mislead students, who may assume that the works available online represent the limits of what actually exists? These are the kinds of questions raised by the MESL project that we will need to grapple with during the protracted transition from analog to digital systems.

▶ Technical Issues

Although the MESL project was designed as an experiment and not as a system that would scale, the project provided many opportunities for highlighting and investigating technical issues that would need to be dealt with in the design of future systems. The MESL project's technical agenda was ambitious. Museums had about six months from the start of the project to export the first set of data from their collections management systems, map it to the project's data dictionary, and link it to independently created digital images. After receiving the data, the universities had only about a month to process the data, integrate it, and mount it on their networks before the semester began. At the outset, the group made a series of technical decisions that influenced many other later decisions. What could they learn from those decisions? What features would not move forward if the group were to speculate on a next-generation system? What kinds of difficulties did the implementers encounter by merging images and text data from diverse sources; how might the results be made more consistent and predictable?

Although the project focused on delivering digital images of museum objects, another important component of the experiment was its use of existing museum collections management system data about those objects. Unlike most libraries, museums have a longstanding history of disparate collections management systems and few standards in place for cataloging the objects in their collections. Participants were eager to explore the issues involved in exporting data from their systems, mapping it to a common data structure, and then creating a public access database out of the diverse data sets. How difficult would this process prove, and how could the resultant product be characterized and evaluated? A host of issues surrounding the repurposing of existing collections management data for the general search and retrieval environment were uncovered in the course of the project.

With respect to the images themselves, the group wrestled not only with the absence of clear standards but also with simple issues of terminology. They struggled with such questions as a common understanding of the term "high resolution," as well as more arcane issues such as whether it is possible to produce lossless JPEG files. Under the system as developed, universities received previously compressed images from the museums, then resized them for their local delivery environment by recompressing them. How does this process affect image quality, and what might it tell us about how to model future systems?

For a variety of reasons, the distribution model chosen was to have each museum export its data and create its own digital images, then ship them to a central distribution point, which would duplicate the data and ship it to each of the universities. The role of the central distribution point began as bit-shuffling, but grew to include quality assurance as it became obvious that some of the exported data did not adhere to the structure of the data dictionary as specified. The group was eager to learn whether economies of scale might be achieved through experience with data processing over time and to postulate how such a distribution point might work in the future, as it became clear that quality assurance would be critical to the success of future licensing arrangements. What lessons did we learn in the MESL distribution process that might inform the design of a production model?

Another of the decisions made at the outset of the MESL project was that each university would be free to mount the data on its local network in whatever way it chose. At the beginning of the project, proprietary image databases were more common than they are now, since the Web has become a more ubiquitous delivery mechanism. The decision to encourage heterogeneous implementation allowed the MESL participants to investigate whether there could be generalizable requirements for using images and documentation from museums. What could be learned from the deployment strategies at each site? How would implementation strategies affect acceptance by users, and what might that tell us about generic functional requirements for image delivery systems?

▶ Use and Impact : The Evaluation Process

As the participants continued to explore their collective agenda, they also began to evaluate the impact of this experiment on each participating institution. Could generalizations be made about the MESL project's effects on museums and universities? Were there lessons to be learned that might inform future projects?

The evaluation process centered on three survey instruments:

- *Faculty/student questionnaire:* A pencil and paper survey administered to faculty and students using MESL content in the classroom (questionnaires administered before and after participation).
- *Casual user study:* A Web-based survey mounted on each university's Web site, to elicit responses from those using MESL data in settings other than specific course support.
- *Attitude survey:* Two surveys administered to project participants at the project's beginning and end to study changing attitudes about the use of online images and text as well as observations about the MESL project as a process.

In addition, focused group discussions were used to elicit further reflections on institutional impact by asking the participants to respond to a number of questions: Did participation in the MESL project cause museums to think differently about the potential for generating income from licensing digital images? Were faculty and students ready to embrace the new technology and the new content? Did the availability of digital museum images and information make it possible to reach new audiences and new users? Was this project so difficult that it would be hard to envision continuing to participate in a similar scheme in the future? As the participants contemplated these and other questions of impact, much of the richness of their findings was revealed.

▶ Economic Issues

The MESL participants also struggled with some critical issues connected with evaluating the economic framework of this specific project and what insights the MESL experiment might yield for the economic modeling of future licensing administration. In group conversations, the participants discussed some of the larger economic questions, such as where the value resides in implementing a system for licensing museum content. Is it in the image, the structured data records, the additional texts such as curatorial or conservation notes, or the aggregation of all of these? Does the value reside with a single object or only in the aggregation of large numbers of objects? Would single works or an entire collection be licensed?

Should licensing income be distributed to participating museums equally, proportional to the size of their contributions, or based on the licensing or use of individual objects in their collections?

As the participants examined the value stream for the museums, they postulated that value may come from the broad support for their educational mission, with a modest income stream to support future projects, and the realization of economies of scale. For universities, value may come from the authenticity of the museums' data, the aggregation of large collections, and enhanced searching capabilities. These issues need further examination in order to posit an ongoing model that will attract additional participants from both museums and universities.[7]

An eighteen-month study funded by the Andrew W. Mellon Foundation, begun in 1996, is now examining the economics of networked access to visual information in more detail.[8] This study is being carried on independently of the MESL project but is closely allied with it, and much of the evaluative data was gathered for use in both the MESL evaluation efforts and the Mellon Study. The latter is looking at the costs of a system similar to the MESL initiative in three major activity centers (museums, central distribution point, and educational institutions), including both start-up and ongoing costs. It is also gathering information on the costs of existing image delivery systems from visual resources collections. Finally, it will examine not only costs incurred, but also costs avoided, by the choice of site licensing over other content delivery models. The final report of the Mellon Study is scheduled for summer 1998.[9]

▶ Summary of Project Milestones

After being selected in December 1994, the participants first assembled in early February 1995 for a three-day meeting to articulate a detailed framework for project activity. This was the first of six such meetings held over the next two and a half years, where participants gathered to discuss their collective agenda, review progress, and plan next steps.

The entire MESL project progressed at two levels: inter-institutional (the collective project agenda) and intra-institutional (each participating institution's internal agenda). To carry forward the intra-institutional agendas, each participating institution was asked to assemble at its site a project team headed by a project coordinator, who served as the primary "point person" for MESL activity. On the museum side, the project teams included staff from registrars' offices as well as the information technology, photo services, library, education, and curatorial departments. On the university side, teams included librarians, visual resources specialists, computing personnel, instructional technologists and designers, and faculty members.

This report focuses primarily on the inter-institutional project agenda. That work was carried on by working groups, many organized at the first participants' meeting, which focused on the major areas of project activity, including Terms and Conditions, Content Selection, Documentation and Distribution, Security and Monitoring, Evaluation and Base Measurement, Faculty Training and Support, and Communications and the World Wide Web. Each working group had an evolving task list, and electronic discussion lists were established to facilitate their work.[10] The Management Committee took a strong role in defining the project at its outset. In addition, a staff of approximately two full time equivalents (FTEs) oversaw and guided the progress of the working groups and facilitated the project's collective agenda.[11]

At the initial meeting, participants had their first discussions of the size, quality, and format of images the museums would supply to the universities. They began to explore the content and structure of the accompanying data. They discussed available options for distributing images and data from the museums to universities. They reviewed university capabilities for providing security for the data, and began to frame the definitions of users and acceptable uses that would form the basis for the project's cooperative agreement. Discussion of and decision making on these topics continued throughout the following months, largely by means of an electronic discussion list, MESL-L.

The following brief project chronology provides a framework for comprehending the significant accomplishments of the participants during the two-plus years of the MESL project. The detailed reports on particular topics presented in this publication expand on the project milestones to clarify understanding of evolving project priorities and changing perceptions of a particular set of issues.

During the spring of 1995, the group began identifying the images that museums would supply to the universities. Since everyone was eager to ensure that university faculty would adopt the MESL images, mechanisms were devised to involve faculty members directly in the content selection process. Lists of available images were circulated and marked. Faculty who knew the holdings of the participating museums requested specific items. Simultaneously, the Documentation Working Group defined the data structure for the records from the museums' collections management systems. In late spring, the museums began data export and image production (if digital images did not already exist).

During the summer of 1995, data and images were delivered to the University of Michigan, which had agreed to serve as central distribution point for the project. Data was transferred from the transport medium to CDs, which were duplicated and shipped to each university. By late summer, distribution to the individual universities was under way, and the local project teams began mounting images and data on their local systems and designing their delivery environments. In the fall of 1995, less than eight months after the initial meeting, the first course using MESL images and data was taught at the University of Maryland. By mid-fall, the first distribution was complete, with 4,959 images and accompanying data records distributed to each university.

In early 1996, the project's Web site was launched, which facilitated both internal interchange and communication with a larger audience. Content selection for the second distribution began, with much of the selection process carried on electronically rather than through circulation of paper lists. The second distribution of 4,360 images took place in the summer of 1996. Local project teams at the universities continued to refine their delivery systems and work with faculty who used MESL content in their courses.

Once the technical challenges of data creation and export, distribution, and mounting had been met, participants were able to focus their collective attention on the evaluation process. Although evaluation had been discussed since the project began, implementation of evaluation plans had been limited, as resources were focused on the technical agenda and on providing outreach and support. Detailed planning for evaluation took place in the fall of 1996. By early 1997, project teams at all sites were completing detailed reports on their technical and operational processes, and university teams were administering the various survey instruments the project evaluators had developed. The final participants' meeting was held in May 1997. Over the summer and fall of 1997, data analysis and final reporting proceeded, culminating in this publication.

"This project is a textbook example of how much can be accomplished in a short time when committed people put their minds to something and dive right in. Any errors we made in our initial planning would probably have been made worse by more planning. There is no substitute for the experimental approach in this kind of project."

DON MCCLELLAND
FOWLER MUSEUM OF CULTURAL HISTORY
Technical Report

Like many large-scale collaborative projects, the MESL project was evolutionary. While it began with strong leadership by the Management Committee (necessary for the rapid ramp-up required), its character came to be defined by its participants through group process, depending on their available resources and their institutional priorities. Some original goals were abandoned, scaled back, or refocused to reflect the participants' changing perspectives. At times, process and product became inextricably entwined.

The findings of the MESL project, reported in the papers that follow, are a rich and complex reflection of this ambitious undertaking. The goal of this report is to present those findings in such a way that different audiences with different interests can focus on the issues they find most compelling. It is organized around the major issue areas outlined above, reflecting the consensus that emerged in each area.

▶ Notes

1. The idea for the Museum Educational Site Licensing Project emerged at two meetings held in March 1994. The first, sponsored by the Getty Information Institute (then the Getty Art History Information Program), was held at Marina del Rey, California, to announce the launching of the Imaging Initiative. The second, held later that month in New York, was convened by MUSE Educational Media, where a study group had been developing model licensing agreements for digital media on CD-ROMs. The detailed planning for the MESL project took place in a series of meetings and discussions over the summer of 1994 involving David Bearman, Howard Besser, Eleanor Fink, Geoffrey Samuels, and Jennifer Trant.

2. The *Call for Participation to Museums and Galleries* is available on the MESL Web site at *http://www.gii.getty.edu/mesl/about/docs/call.museums.html.* The *Call to Higher Education Institutions* is available at *http://www.gii.getty.edu/mesl/about/docs/call.education.html.*

3. At that time, the members of the Management Committee, their positions, and institutional affiliations were: Jennifer Trant, Consultant and Manager of the Imaging Initiative, Getty Information Institute; Geoffrey Samuels, Director, MUSE Museum Multimedia Study Group; Maxwell Anderson, Director, Carlos Museum and Chair, Information Technology Committee, Association of Art Museum Directors; David Bearman, President, Archives and Museum Informatics; Howard Besser, Associate Professor, Information and Library Studies, University of Michigan; Clifford Lynch, Director, Library Automation, Office of the President, University of California. With the exception of David Bearman, all have since moved to new positions.

4. The Library of Congress was not among the initial group selected; in late February 1995, following the first participants' meeting, it asked to join the group.

5. The Goals and Objectives of the MESL project as articulated at its outset are included in this document as Appendix A, p. 165.

6. The project received administrative support from the Getty Information Institute, which funded the approximately two FTE project staff positions and supported the group by funding the Participants' Meetings. The Information Institute also hosted the project Web site and listservs.

7. As a group, the participants discussed Esther Dyson's article "Intellectual Value," *Hot Wired* 3 no. 7 (July 1995) (*http://www.hotwired.com/wired/3.07/features/dyson.html*). Much of the discussion of the value stream issues took place at the December 1996 Participants' Meeting.

8. The grant proposal was prepared by Jennifer Trant, David Bearman, and Howard Besser. The grant was made to the School of Information Management and Systems at University of California–Berkeley, with Howard Besser serving as Principal Investigator.

9. A Web-based version of the Mellon final report will be linked to the Web-based version of this report. A preliminary economic analysis is included in Part VI of this report, pp. 134–156.

10. Each working group had a Web page accessible from the top level of the MESL Web site, at *http://www.gii.getty.edu/mesl.* From these pages, members of each working group could write mail to the group and review the working group mail archive, task list, and current activities.

11. From February 1995 until June 1996, Jennifer Trant served as Project Director. In September 1995, she was joined by Patricia McClung, who served as Project Manager. Trant was succeeded in September 1996 by Christie Stephenson, who had been the University of Virginia Project Coordinator. Michele D'Amico served as Project Assistant from May 1995 until August 1997.

Project Background—Framing the Issues

CHRISTIE STEPHENSON

The Museum Educational Site Licensing Project (MESL) was conceived in an environment of tremendous excitement about the potential for network access to digital cultural heritage information and uncertainty about issues of control of content and intellectual property rights. A number of the museum participants had been approached by vendors such as Corbis[1] about licensing their images; museum administrators were seeking guidance on how to respond to these and other opportunities. Some of the university participants had been developing digital image archives for curriculum support and had struggled firsthand with intellectual property issues as they attempted to meet the needs of their clientele. The MESL project was viewed as one vehicle for exploring these issues.[2] The hopes of both the museum and educational communities were attached to the project, and expectations for solutions to all kinds of issues—technical, legal, and administrative—ran high.

In articulating the goals of the project, the participants agreed that in working together they would attempt to "propose a framework for a broadly based system for the distribution of museum images and information on an ongoing basis to the academic community."[3] Among the tasks set out under this goal were:

- Define appropriate educational uses of museum images.
- Develop model site licensing agreements that govern the educational use of museum images and information on university and college campuses.
- Explore administrative and technical mechanisms for the ongoing delivery of museum information to academic campuses.

This document reviews the course of the participants' collective attempts to meet the goals and objectives they had set for themselves in this area and serves to introduce a critical piece of the project's findings, "Establishing the Terms and Conditions for Educational Institutional Licensing of Museum Images," which is presented in the two following articles. It is included as an historical record of the development of this MESL product and an explanation of how it evolved (and diverged) from the original goal "to develop model site licensing agreements."

▶ The MESL Cooperative Agreement

When the MESL participants first met in February 1995, they recognized the need to have a set of ground rules under which their experiment would operate. They agreed that the MESL project would be conducted under the umbrella of a cooperative agreement, which broadly outlined the rights and responsibilities of the participants, both content providers (museums) and content users (universities). The earliest articulation of a common understanding between the parties came at the first meeting, with the following agreements about appropriate uses of the museum images and information:

1. There would be no commercial uses (sale).
2. Fully permissible uses would include any academic use, defined as classroom, individual, or research use by faculty, students, staff, and others who are in a community of users regardless of location.
3. Any uses falling between the prohibited and permitted would be subject to notification by the university to the source. Such uses would be disallowed without a sidebar agreement with the suppliers, but the museums generally encouraged such uses to be identified and felt they would normally allow the sidebars to be developed.
4. There is an absolute two-year limit under this experiment, but it is hoped that the arrangements will be extended under a new agreement in the future.[4]

"We've learned a lot about the Web in the last couple of years that has helped relieve our fears. At the first MESL meeting I felt we had to control all of these images because some terrible things might happen that we couldn't even imagine. Now we have much more confidence that no terrible things are going to happen really, and further that it's in our best interest to get information out to as many people as we can reach."

ANDREA NOTMAN
HARVARD UNIVERSITY ART MUSEUMS
Participants' Meeting

In the months following, a cooperative agreement was crafted by Mary Levering of the U.S. Copyright Office, with significant input from Christine Steiner, General Counsel for the J. Paul Getty Trust, and Jennifer Trant, MESL Project Director. A draft agreement was presented at the second Participants' Meeting in June 1995, discussed, and amended.[5] The participants agreed to shepherd the agreement through their respective institutions by September 1, 1995, so that the agreement would be in place when use of the MESL data began. Over the summer, the agreement was reviewed by legal counsel at all participating institutions and further negotiations took place. Significant amendment focused on the indemnification language in the agreement.[6] By the fall of 1995, the cooperative agreement had been executed by all fourteen institutions and the project sponsors. An amendment sent out in late September harmonized the language in the indemnification clause.

While not a license per se, the framework of the cooperative agreement provided the participants with a "safe harbor" for exploring many of the issues involved in articulating the terms and conditions of future educational licensing arrangements. The cooperative agreement outlined the goals of the MESL collaboration, the responsibilities of the museums, of the academic institutions, and of all parties to the agreement, and attempted to permit broadest possible use of the data while protecting the museums' investment in the creation of content. The agreement stipulated that the content could be used for "educational purposes, including faculty research, teaching, or student projects." The participants also agreed that MESL images and text would not be "used for non-educational or commercial purposes, or redistributed for any purpose beyond the participating institutions without prior written permission of the contributing institution" (see Appendix B, "Cooperative Agreement").

▶ Project Experiences : Refining the Understanding of Users and Uses

Throughout the project, but particularly in the first eighteen months, the participants frequently discussed whether or not particular uses were permissible under the terms of the cooperative agreement. They also discussed the ways in which they defined their user communities and were thus able to control access. From time to time, potential uses were proposed that were deemed to fall outside the terms of the cooperative agreement. Similarly, some universities proposed extending access to new groups of users, such as donors or alumni, that were also ruled outside the existing agreement. Each of the discussions surrounding these proposals helped to further articulate the boundaries of the mutual agreement and the values that drove decision making on both sides.

Users

Much of the discussion about the definition of user community took place under the purview of the Security and Monitoring Working Group, chaired by David Millman of Columbia University. At the first meeting, university participants outlined the ways in which they controlled access to other licensed data mounted on campus servers. The record states:

> The museum representatives reacted very positively to what they heard from the universities. They were reassured by the experience that universities showed with the administration of existing license agreements, and by the acknowledgment that much education was needed on campus in order to teach students, faculty, and staff what was appropriate use of licensed information.[7]

Subsequent discussions centered on a request from the University of Michigan to expand access to authorized alumni and others as part of a set of new services they were offering. This use was not agreed to; however, the discussions reflected the changing environment in higher education today, as universities seek to extend the reach of access to their resources beyond their campus networks and to provide access to new groups of users, sometimes charging for such services. Such discussions led the participants to a richer understanding of the networked environment, causing them to expand their definition of "site," but to limit their definition of authorized users to faculty, students, and staff.

After the establishment of the project Web site in January 1996, the Security and Monitoring Working Group mounted a Web page where each university's definition of user community and access control methods was posted. Most of the account holders on campus networks were routinely characterized as faculty, students, and staff, but several of the universities reported a small number of accounts held by other users (alumni, donors, etc.). While this limited "leakage" was acceptable in a demonstration project, it may prove to be a sticking point in the future, when actual licenses are executed. Many potential licensees may not have the technological infrastructure or the resources to install complex authentication schemes to certify that only authorized users have access to the licensed content.

"The MESL project made us focus on copyright issues as an institution more than we had in the past. Before the project began, digital copyright issues seemed difficult and threatening, but as the staff learned more about how digital technology could be used, we began to think more about its benefits. Some issues, such as unauthorized use of images, became less of a concern as we saw how the images were being used and the kind of resolution that was being used for this project."

Marty Stein
The Museum of Fine Arts, Houston
Technical Report

Uses

In the months following the initial MESL Participants' Meeting, a number of specific instances of questionable uses were discussed on the project's listserv, such as inclusion of a MESL image in an alumni publication and a photograph of a faculty member in her office with a MESL image visible on the computer screen.

At the December 1995 Participants' Meeting, those in attendance attempted to codify decisions made to date on permitted uses and those that might require sidebar agreements between the specific parties. The following guidelines were adopted:

1. MESL images, shown in the context of local delivery systems, can be used in publications discussing the project and/or the issues it raises.

2. Full reproduction of a MESL image for publication requires a separate agreement between the user and the contributing institution. Such an agreement will be granted routinely for academic use.

3. MESL images may be used for promotion of the project, within a participating institution.[8]

Other issues that emerged during the course of the project included the extent to which "redistribution" of MESL images and data at a single site was allowable. For instance, in an early effort to make MESL images available, Cornell produced CDs that were available for use in its library. This and other kinds of local redistribution, such as mirroring or copying a subset of images to another server to improve response time, were acknowledged to be necessary to enhance access, but it was understood that this kind of redistribution had to be monitored and controlled to the extent possible. Distribution of images beyond the defined site was deemed unacceptable.

Still another major issue was that of image manipulation, including cropping, overdrawing, montage, and other digital transformations. The discussion of this issue, which continued throughout the course of the project, centered on the tension between the museums' desire to facilitate all educational uses of the images and their mission to preserve the integrity of objects in their care. We came to understand this tension and agreed that it was appropriate that manipulated images always make clear reference to their source and that care should be taken to respect the moral rights of the creator.[9]

"In the end, I think the museum community learned a great deal about the perils and pitfalls of licensing our information, although not as much about the solutions, options, and possibilities as one would have hoped."

STEVE DIETZ
NMAA
Technical Report

▶ Conditions of Use Statements

Another element of the complex of understandings that governed the collective undertaking was the Conditions of Use statement presented as part of each university's MESL implementation. These conditions of use statements were intended to provide users with guidelines for appropriate use of the MESL content.[10] They addressed issues such as copying, mounting subsets of the content on other servers, and redistribution, as well as providing a general statement that the intellectual property rights of the content belonged to the contributing institution, not to the university.

Because of the absence of individual authentication schemes and technically enforced restrictions on copying or downloading the data at most of the university sites, user behavior was governed only by this statement and instruction received in direct classroom applications. In at least one documented case, this resulted in another kind of "leakage"—students in one course, who were using MESL images to illustrate their papers, were copying images to their home directories without understanding that controls were needed to limit access by outside users. As soon as the problem was identified, steps were taken to correct it. This incident revealed the tension between the desire to facilitate use of the content and the potential for inadvertent redistribution.

▶ Moving toward Consensus

Beginning at the May 1996 Participants' Meeting, the MESL participants began to turn their attention to developing a set of terms and conditions for future licensing agreements. Melissa Smith Levine, Legal Advisor for the Library of Congress's National Digital Library Program, and Mary Levering, Associate Register for National Copyright Programs, U.S. Copyright Office, drafted a set of questions, "Questions Related to Draft Model Clearinghouse/Educational Site Licensing Agreement(s) for MESL Project." At that meeting, the participants began to realize the difficulty inherent in developing model license agreements without specifying the administrative structure that would define the parties to the agreement. They turned their focus instead to a discussion that reflected group consensus to date on the issues of content selection, users, and uses.[11]

At the December 1996 meeting, additional discussion of these issues took place. In the interim, discussion of licensing issues in the university community had become increasingly sophisticated, as more and more electronic resources were being offered through licensing. A focused discussion among MESL universities reviewed the variety of licenses negotiated on their campuses. In the large group discussion, the following issues emerged as critical to the process of future site license negotiation: access, pricing, perpetual license and data archiving, security and indemnification, and consortial licensing.[12]

Following that meeting, a small working group was convened in Washington, D.C., to further refine the collective thinking. Mary Levering and Melissa Levine prepared a matrix that examined each element in a possible educational licensing agreement. They reviewed all of the project documentation and, for each element, summarized in one cell the points on which consensus had been reached. Areas of disagreement or tension between the museum and university positions were noted in separate columns below. From this starting point, the working group discussed each element and tried to further harmonize the museum and university concerns, moving elements from the columns below to the consensus box. The working group spent two day-long meetings in this process in the late winter and early spring of 1997.[13] In early April, a third meeting was held to review the document with MESL museum representatives to ensure adequate input. At the final Participants' Meeting in May 1997, the entire group reviewed the document clause by clause, fine-tuned its language, and adopted it as a summation of the project's experience. This document is presented in the following two articles.

"Initially, I was quite skeptical and viewed the project as a mechanism for pushing a vision of an 'ASCAP for museum images.' Now, however, I view the project much more positively and see it as an important initial step in dealing with copyright issues involving digital images."

Sherwood Dowling
NMAA
Technical Report

▸ Emerging Administrative Structures for Distributing Museum Images and Information

At the May 1996 Participants' Meeting, some conflict emerged between the longer-term strategic concerns of some members of the Management Committee and the more immediate and practical concerns of the participants. It manifested itself in the discussion of the "Questions Related to Draft Model Clearinghouse/Educational Site Licensing Agreement(s) for MESL Project," where the participants were unwilling to commit to a single licensing framework that assumed their endorsement of a rights holders collective as the only model for administering content in the future. Although there was widespread acknowledgment of the potential value of a rights holders collective, the participants felt they wanted a deeper understanding of the alternatives. On the final day of that meeting, the group agreed that they would like to see a background paper commissioned, which would "profile options for rights administration, intellectual property management, and management/distribution of digital information." Subsequently, the Getty Information Institute commissioned such a paper, which is scheduled for publication in 1998. This commissioned study is being conducted independently of MESL, although to some extent it is informed by the needs and experiences of the project participants.

As the project team turned its attention inward in its final year to undertake the formidable tasks of evaluation and documentation, several initiatives were launched that reflected the strategic concerns growing in the museum community. These include the Art Museum Image Consortium (AMICO), the Museum Digital Licensing Collective (MDLC), and The Research Libraries Group's REACH project.[14] While some of these initiatives include members of the MESL project among their organizers, the MESL group itself did not have an official affiliation, nor did it endorse any single approach. The MESL participants anticipated that there would likely be a number of initiatives building on the project's findings in several different areas.

The following two documents can be seen as an integral part of the project's goal to "propose a framework for a broadly based system for the distribution of museum images and information on an ongoing basis to the academic community." These documents are not the articulation of a particular administrative or business model, but instead an exploration of common values and tensions that any subsequent licensing entity will need to address. They provide a broad framework of shared values and interests that can guide future license negotiations, as well as highlight the particular areas the group identified where potential challenges may arise.

▶ Notes

1. In 1994, Corbis was known under the name of its predecessor corporation, Continuum Productions.

2. Another simultaneous initiative was the Working Group on Digital Images of the Conference on Fair Use (CONFU). Several MESL participants—Mary Levering, Melissa Levine, Kathe Albrecht, and Jennifer Trant—also participated in those discussions and reported to the MESL group from time to time. Ultimately, the recommendations of the CONFU working group were not widely endorsed by the communities participating in those discussions.

3. Appendix A, "Goals and Objectives," p. 165, and at *http://www.gii.getty.edu/mesl/about/goals.html.*

4. MESL Participants' Meeting Minutes, February 1995, Day 3, Report of Security and Monitoring Breakout Group. In fact, the agreement was later extended for a third year to permit continued use of the MESL data at the participating universities.

5. MESL Participants' Meeting Minutes, June 1995, Day 2, Meeting of Project Coordinators and Project Managers (*http://www.gii.getty.edu/mesl/about/docs/mtgs/9506day2.html*).

6. The state universities participating in the project were limited by law as to the extent of indemnification to which they could agree. The adopted language read "To the extent permitted by applicable state and federal law, each institution ("Indemnitor") agrees to hold the other participating institutions harmless from claims or liability arising from the ("Indemnitor's") activities in the project."

7. MESL Participants' Meeting Minutes, February 1995, Day 2, Image Distribution, Security and User Monitoring (*http://www.gii.getty.edu/mesl/about/docs/mtgs/9502day2.html*).

8. MESL Participants' Meeting Minutes, December 1995, Day 2, Report of the Monitoring and Security Working Group (*http://www.gii.getty.edu/mesl/about/docs/mtgs/9512day2.html*).

9. As a result of their review of this report and of a series of Web pages documenting the MESL teaching experience, the National Museum of American Art further explored the issue of image manipulation. In a series of internal discussions, it articulated the following institutional statement on manipulation:

> The MESL project gave NMAA staff an opportunity to see some of the ways that images were used by students, prompting a discussion among staff about image manipulation and its appropriateness. We feel that it is important to balance the needs of the universities against the responsibility that we have to the artists and artworks that form our collection. Accordingly, NMAA developed a policy that permits image manipulation for student assignments, but restricts subsequent publication of these manipulations.
>
> Within the context of the MESL project, to ensure a full and fair reporting of the MESL experience from both the museum and university perspectives, we are permitting publication of manipulated images as a special one-time exception to this policy which is stated below.
>
> *NMAA Policy on Manipulation of Images*
>
> *NMAA agrees with the terms of the MESL license that permit digital manipulation of museum artworks for educational, curricular purposes. As classroom assignments involving MESL images*

have demonstrated, manipulation of artworks can be a valid part of the learning experience that permits students to gain new insights about composition, aesthetics, and artistic intent.

NMAA further asserts that, although manipulation of artworks can serve valid educational purposes, subsequent publication by electronic or other means misrepresents an artist's original intent and the integrity of the artwork. NMAA therefore declines to give permission for publication of manipulated images. This policy applies to all artworks from NMAA regardless of whether the artwork is contemporary or from an earlier time period.

By applying this policy consistently, NMAA feels that it can best represent the artists whose artworks from part of our collections while still allowing use of our images in class assignments.

10. A sample Conditions of Use statement, from the University of Virginia's MESL site, includes the following language:

Users of the images and texts accessible through the Museum Educational Site Licensing Project at the University of Virginia agree to the following conditions of use:

- *These images and texts are for educational use only by students and faculty and may not be used for any non-educational or commercial purpose. Approved educational uses include faculty research, teaching, and student projects.*
- *These images and texts may not be redistributed in any form for any purpose beyond the University of Virginia without the prior written permission of the contributing institution.*
- *The images and text provided by the contributing institutions through this project remain the intellectual property of the contributing institutions, not the University of Virginia.*
- *Users are not permitted to download images and texts provided through this project in order to mount them on their own servers for public use or for use by a set of subscribers. Mirror sites may be set up on other UVA servers to facilitate classroom or other use only by arrangement with members of the Project Team. It is not in the best interests of our users to mount subsets of these holdings on other UVA servers, as the data is being continuously updated.*
- *Users of these images and texts may be contacted by the Project Team to gather information on use for evaluation purposes.*

If you have questions about uses of these images not covered in this document, please contact the UVA MESL Project Coordinator.

Each of the universities adapted this model statement to its specific situation.

11. MESL Participants' Meeting Minutes, May 1996 (*http://www.gii.getty.edu/mesl/about/docs/mtgs/9605_append.html*).

12. MESL Participants' Meeting Minutes, December 1996, Day 2 (*http://www.gii.getty.edu/mesl/about/docs/mtgs/9612day2.html*).

13. Participants were aided in the process by the concurrent discussions on the LIBLICENSE-L list, moderated by Ann Okerson of Yale University. This list was set up following the ARL/CNI Workshop on licensing held in December 1996 to continue those discussions, and several members of the working group listened in to further understand issues such as archiving and perpetual license which were of interest to the MESL participants as well. The list is archived at *http://www.library.yale.edu/~llicense/ListArchives/*.

14. The Art Museum Image Consortium (AMICO) was founded in 1997 by the Association of Art Museum Directors (AAMD). The members of this not-for-profit organization "will build a shared library of digital documentation of their collections for licensing and distribution to the educational community." A small group of universities will serve as a testbed for the project in the 1998/1999 academic year. AMICO's Web site can be found at *http:/www.amico.net/*.

The Museum Digital Licensing Collective, Inc. (MDLC) is a non-profit corporation "formed to manage the storage, distribution, and licensing of digitized materials to educational institutions, libraries, museums, commercial companies, and the public; provide financial assistance for the digitization of original materials in museums and collecting institutions; and develop and distribute related technical and computer services." The MDLC is affiliated with the American Association of Museums. MDLC is in the early organizational phases. Its Web site can be found at *http://www.museumlicensing.org/*.

The REACH Project (Record Export for Art and Cultural Heritage) is an effort undertaken by The Research Libraries Group (RLG) to create a testbed database of museum object records. The goal is to export existing machine-readable data from heterogeneous museum collections management systems and to analyze the research value of the resulting database when researchers use a single interface to search the database in conjunction with RLG's other resources. REACH documentation can be found at *http://www.rlg.org/reach.html*.

Establishing the Terms and Conditions for Educational Institutional Licensing of Museum Images: A Summary of Issues and Priorities

MARY LEVERING

▶ Background

The framework for institutional licensing that follows this summary delineates the many issues, concerns, and priorities related to licensing terms and conditions identified by participants representing museums and institutions of higher education during the Museum Educational Site Licensing Project (MESL), sponsored by the Getty Information Institute in collaboration with MUSE Educational Media from 1994 to 1997.

One of the MESL project's original goals was to develop common terms and conditions for a "model site license" for the educational use of museum digital images and associated documentation. During the course of the project, however, the MESL participants realized that specific terms and conditions for a model site license would probably not be one of the outcomes of the project, owing to the many variables involved and the need to develop coordinating structures for administration, organization, and delivery of content and pricing of rights.

Although defining specific license terms and conditions seems impractical at this point, the experience of the MESL participants has made it easier to articulate museums' and universities' priorities and concerns as providers and users of content, respectively. Often, because of a common interest in educational uses, both communities shared the same concerns. The participants agreed that a significant benefit would be gained from a clear and helpful written summary of issues and priorities identified during the project, which would also articulate areas of common agreement among cooperating MESL institutions.

Furthermore, some issues of initial concern to each group later proved not to be of significance in actual practice; in other instances, issues that had not been identified at the beginning arose during the course of the project. This summary reflects the results of these real-life experiences.

▶ Summary of Issues and Priorities

Purposes

The purposes of this summary and the following framework document are as follows:

- To articulate the shared values of museums and educational institutions. Most museums have an educational component as part of their mission, and both groups agree that they have a real commonality of interest in providing high-quality museum images for educational purposes.

- To summarize the issues and priorities identified during the project, in order to make it easier for museum image providers and educational users to draft and negotiate institutional licenses for digital images provided by museums.

Shared Assumptions

MUSEUMS AS CULTURAL INSTITUTIONS A basic assumption underlying all discussions is the permanence of museums as cultural institutions and their ongoing commitment to the preservation and documentation of material culture, represented by the objects they hold in trust.

SHARED CULTURAL VALUES AND EDUCATIONAL GOALS All MESL participants also agreed that any license agreements developed should reflect the shared cultural values and educational goals of both communities and should therefore enable broader uses by authorized users for educational purposes within qualifying institutions.

Both groups acknowledged that such institutional license agreements should cover a range of educational uses, including, but also going beyond, uses usually considered within the doctrine of "fair use." They agreed that subsequent agreements should not seek to limit "fair use" of images and data, and in fact, that license terms should permit additional educational uses beyond fair use.

Both groups also agreed that each community has much to offer the other in supporting shared values and goals. Museums can provide collections of high-quality digitized images of, and related documentation for, works in their collections. In return, educational institutions may sometimes be able to provide additional scholarly information on specific works in museum collections.

RIGHTS IN MUSEUM IMAGES There are many different layers of rights in museum images. MESL participants agreed that museums themselves are probably in a better position than educational institutions to research these layers of underlying rights, to determine the status and extent of all the rights in images they digitize, and to clear the rights necessary for educational access and use. Universities, on the other hand, are in a better position to manage access and use policies relating to management of the rights in the digital images and documentation provided.

POLICIES OF EDUCATIONAL INSTITUTIONS REGARDING ACCESS TO MUSEUM IMAGES MESL participants also confirmed that museums will need to rely on educational institutions to provide a framework to help educate users and encourage them to comply with the terms of license agreements, as much as (or perhaps even more than) they will be relying on technological solutions to security concerns. Educational institutions may need to think of defining copyright infringement as a violation of academic codes of conduct just as plagiarism is defined now.

Such a general cultural change may be fostered by the kinds of notices and alerts described in the following framework document, as well as a more broadly targeted "copyright orientation" that may need to become a standard part of university and Internet training in the future. Such alerts may be either provided by educational institutions or prepackaged with image data sets. Examples of such alerts may include a formal "sign-on" to alert students to the conditions of use. While license agreements may not require these kinds of copyright orientation/education programs, they do help to encourage a climate that permits flexible institutional licenses, allowing a wide variety of innovative educational uses.

Nature of the License

SITE LICENSE One of the initial goals of the MESL project was to develop a model site license agreement, because the participants believed that site licenses enabled the broad access and uses that educational institutions need in order to fulfill their educational missions.

INSTITUTIONAL LICENSE Based on experience from the MESL project, however, participants agreed that the original concept of "site license" is less practical and unnecessarily limiting. They replaced this with the concept of "institutional license for authorized users and authorized uses," which is not limited to specific geographic sites—consistent with the way universities now provide educational services. The discussions in this document therefore presuppose a simple institutional license for a body of works to which certain rights are attached; this would be made available to a specific institution for a defined period of time for a wide variety of educational uses.

NONEXCLUSIVE LICENSE Both groups agreed that any agreements reached together should be based on the concept of "nonexclusive, nontransferrable licenses" for "nonprofit educational purposes."

OTHER OPTIONS Both groups agreed that, for both museums and universities, institutional licenses for an unlimited number of uses with a fixed fee for a predetermined period of time are probably the most useful option at this time. However, they also recognized that this is not the only option for service delivery in the future:

- Museums are willing to consider at some time in the future the options of usage-based fees or pay per use when these become more viable as electronic commerce matures.
- As an alternative to institutional licenses for unlimited uses, some educational institutions want the option to pay per use or per access, or employ some other fee schedule based on actual usage (assuming they do not want/need to use *all* images in a compilation), especially for little-used or highly specialized groups of images.

Interrelationships Among the Variables for Delivery Options and Pricing Structures

License agreements represent a complex interrelationship among the following factors:

- Types of authorized users
- Categories of licensed uses
- Content provided
- Service delivery options and related transaction costs
- Pricing structure

Each license agreement embodies a number of choices for both providers and users. The types of uses and users licensed have implications for fees charged, as well as other potential restrictions. Proposed pricing structures would also need to reflect the costs of various delivery options.

Many factors influence the pricing of intellectual property such as museum images and related documentation, including the following:

- Cost of clearing and managing rights for proposed uses
- Value of the uses permitted
- Number of transactions and cost per transaction
- Overhead costs of administering service coordination and delivery
- Number of users

EXAMPLES A *"single-item" license* based on use of only a few or a limited number of individually selected images and text would very likely have higher fees per work and per use, for some kinds of uses, particularly considering that at this time the transaction costs would be considerably higher. A *"single use" license* would very likely have restrictions about making derivative products such as CD-ROMs, because to do so would violate the terms of a single use license. A *"pay-per-use" license* would have stricter monitoring and reporting requirements and would prohibit use of the images outside a monitored environment, restricting or eliminating use of other delivery models and the creation of derivative works.

STATISTICAL BASES FOR PRICING STRUCTURES Pricing models for licenses are often based on aggregate figures such as institutional enrollments, annual budgets, and similar measurements. It is advisable that universities cite a recognized external objective source when supplying such measurements rather than relying on informal (and perhaps less accurate) estimates of their own.

FUTURE DELIVERY OPTIONS Both groups agree that fee structures and delivery models for digital data in general are in a state of flux and that emerging markets will help define future pricing models, fee structures, and delivery options. Both groups acknowledge the need to work together in exploring and defining future models. In addition, certain terms of access, use, distribution, related fees, reporting, and so forth are inextricably tied to certain distribution models. This document does not endorse any particular business model; rather, it focuses on the general terms and conditions under which museum materials could be made available and used by educational institutions.

Efficiency of Collective Administration

Both groups agree that it is not feasible for individual museums or universities to assume the extensive administrative burden of negotiating and administering many individual one-to-one license agreements for educational purposes.[1] For ease and efficiency of administration, both groups would prefer to deal through a well-organized, efficiently operated central organization that distributes digital images and documentation supplied by museums for use by nonprofit educational institutions.

Some of the benefits of collective administration include the following:

- Systematic coordination of the efforts of many participating institutions, including both museums and educational institutions
- The ability to create an integrated resource by implementing shared standards (including both technical and data standards)

- Capacity to service large volumes of requests
- Ease of access to large data sets with predictable and consistent technical specifications and searching capability
- Predictable and consistent terms and conditions of use and pricing structures
- Consistent requirements for reporting and security
- Economies of scale
- Efficiencies of centralized administration

Educational institutions prefer to have flexibility in content selection and pricing structures, but these needs require an infrastructure to support them. Administration of such an infrastructure would affect costs and would require distribution mechanisms that enable specific item- and group-level ordering.

Both groups agree that the costs of central administration should be kept as low as possible, while recognizing that collective administration will probably permit economies of scale. Procedures (such as reasonable and equitable fee structures and income redistribution) will need to be developed in recognition of the diversity of educational institutional users and uses as well as the differing size and composition of museums.

Finally, MESL participants acknowledge that any museum educational license agreement is actually just the start of an ongoing relationship in which the parties should maintain communications and may need to make adjustments later based on mutual agreement to accommodate unusual circumstances.

Note

1. In this regard it may be interesting to note that there are actually many more museums (estimated at more than 8,000) in the United States than the average number of serial titles to which most university libraries subscribe. Therefore administering one-to-one license agreements, even with only the major museums, might require a university to have a whole department or administrative infrastructure just to support its museum image license agreements.

Establishing the Terms and Conditions for Educational Institutional Licensing of Museum Images: A Framework for Museums and Universities

MARY LEVERING AND MELISSA SMITH LEVINE

In the final months of the project, the MESL participants sought to find a method to focus and refine the discussions they had been having about the terms and conditions for educational licensing of museum images. The following framework document served that purpose. It was refined through an iterative process by the Terms and Conditions Working Group, in a series of meetings that took place in early 1997. The document was reviewed by all the participants present at the May 1997 Participants' Meeting, revised and accepted by the entire group.

The framework that follows lists most of the common terms and conditions that a license agreement between museums and educational institutions would include. Under each clause or issue is summarized the many areas of general consensus among representatives from museum and educational institutions that emerged during the MESL project. In addition, certain emphases important to each group are described in the two lower columns on each page (labeled "Licensor/Museum" and "Licensee/University," respectively). All representatives agreed that the concerns articulated in the two columns are not mutually exclusive, but are primarily explanatory or illustrative, reflecting slightly different emphases on the part of the museums or universities represented.

The document follows the outline below and closes with a list of definitions of terms used throughout.

1. Purpose and Goals
2. Parties to the Agreement
3. Nature of the License
4. Content Selection and Provision
5. Scope of License/Users and Access Permitted by the License
6. Scope of License/Uses Permitted by the License
7. Technical Requirements: Data Exchange
8. Technical Requirements; Security
9. Notices to be Displayed
10. Fees
11. Term of License
12. Warranties and Indemnities
13. Reporting
14. Rights Administration
15. Preservation and Data Archiving
16. Breach/Termination
17. General Provisions

▶ Institutional License Issues/Clauses

1. Purpose and Goals

Both museums and universities:

- want to provide digital access to a wide variety of high-quality museum image collections and associated data through a variety of means, including stand-alone systems, "campus networks," and "intranets," that nonprofit educational institutions maintain to promote computer-based learning.
- seek to foster research, education, and scholarly uses of museum images to help fulfill the educational missions of both types of institutions.
- want to encourage a full range of traditional and nontraditional uses of museum images for educational purposes.
- agree that this license would be a nonexclusive agreement for educational purposes.
- agree that it is important to maintain the integrity of the high-quality images and related basic identification information in the primary data set.

▶ Licensor/Museum

- Museums want to control images and information about their artwork and collections, including quality of the images and basic identification information.

▶ Licensee/University

- Universities prefer to have the least restrictive terms museums will allow in order to provide users with broad access and enable a full range of traditional and nontraditional educational uses within a broadly defined university community.

2. Parties to the Agreement

- For ease of administration, both groups would prefer to deal through a well-run central organization/collective administrative body (museum to collective . . . collective to university . . . university to collective).
- Both groups agree that neither has the capability or staff time required to execute many separate license agreements with many individual institutions; thus a well-run central organization/collective arrangement is preferable.

▶ Licensor/Museum

- Museums want to work with a wide variety of "educational" organizations in the broad sense, e.g., schools (K–12), libraries, other museums, and colleges and universities.

▶ Licensee/University

- Universities want a license agreement tailored to the specific needs of institutions of higher education, e.g., colleges and universities.
- Universities want the option to license material either by individual institution or through educational consortia such as state or regional organizations.

3. Nature of the License

- Both groups agree that this license would be a nonexclusive, nontransferable agreement to reproduce, perform, display, and create derivative works of licensed images and related documentation under specific conditions to authorized users for educational purposes within the limits specified in the agreement.

4. Content Selection and Provision

Both museums and universities:

- agree that a critical mass of images, representing breadth and depth of subject matter (including standard, well-known, widely available images as well as lesser-known, unpublished, or previously unavailable images) is essential for meeting educational needs.
- agree that specific groupings or compilations are needed as licensing options for particular educational purposes.
- agree that the content licensed comprises compilations of images and text (including basic identification information about each image offered): in effect, a multimedia "library" of museum digital images and related documentation.
- agree with the value and benefit for both museums and universities in sharing additional research information/data about the images provided, but also acknowledge that such sharing may be subject to resource availability, intellectual property concerns, and other institutional restrictions.
- acknowledge that there is an ongoing scholarly interest in previously available images and data, as well as the continuity of their citation over time, so that previously available images and text should continue to be available in some archival fashion, even if augmented later or removed from future distributions; practical mechanisms to fulfill this will need to be developed in concert.

▶ Licensor/Museum

- Museums have certain needs/criteria for selecting groups of images to be digitized (e.g., preservation, special projects, ease of rights clearance) that may differ from university priorities.
- Museums may be willing to provide additional data, e.g., authoritative curatorial notes and other descriptive data related to images if this is feasible, depending on resources available and other constraints.

▶ Licensee/University

- Universities need access to a whole range of images (e.g., images that are relevant to existing curricula, ongoing and new research, and development of new curricula) and therefore want input into the selection of images to be digitized and made available by museums.
- Universities want as much descriptive data about each image as possible.
- Universities want option(s) to:
  - subscribe to the whole image database for a defined period of time with updates provided, or
  - subscribe only to one or a few specific images in some collections, as well as enjoy potential access to a whole body of images.

5. Scope of License/Users and Access Permitted by the License

Both museums and universities:

- agree that each university needs to define the "Licensed Institution" (e.g., campus-wide, enrolled students regardless of where located, all authorized users, users who have been issued library or Internet accounts, etc.).
- agree that universities can provide access to a standard community of "authorized users" to include educators and students defined broadly as follows:
  - *educators* include faculty, teachers, instructors, curators, librarians, archivists, scholars, or staff who engage in or support instructional, research, or scholarly activities for educational purposes as their assigned responsibilities at educational institutions
  - *students* include full-time and part-time participants enrolled at the Licensed Institution.
- agree with the need to provide access to "authorized users" regardless of location, in a way that is reasonably flexible and consistent with the way in which individual university campus networks are structuring access to their campus networks and intranets, and museums are willing to accept this.
- agree that each licensed university should define, as part of its license:
  - which specific site(s) connected with the university network are considered part of the "campus network" under the license, and
  - which groups of users have access to the university intranet.
- agree that "minimum access" should include access in classrooms, libraries, and media centers and elsewhere to "authorized users," e.g., dormitories, educators' and students' homes or study/research sites, distance learning sites administered by the university, etc.

► Licensor/Museum

- Museums agree that the standard community of university "authorized users" includes educators and students as defined above, and may be willing to include the following as well:
  - authorized university staff members,
  - on-site users in university libraries and media centers,
  - other on-site users (e.g., campus kiosks).
- Museums may be willing to provide access to other groups such as alumni or donors, but this would probably require separate licenses and fees.

► Licensee/University

- Universities want the standard community of authorized users to include educators and students as defined above and may also want it to include the following:
  - authorized university staff members,
  - on-site users in university libraries and media centers,
  - other on-site users (e.g., campus kiosks).
- Universities may be interested in providing access to alumni or donors off-site and understand that this use would probably require separate licenses and fees.

6. Scope of License/Uses Permitted by the License

Both museums and universities:

- acknowledge that the license covers a whole range of educational uses while extending (and including) those usually considered within "fair use" concepts; agree that there is no intention to limit "fair uses" of images and data; and acknowledge that license terms should enable additional educational uses beyond fair use.
- agree that educators may display images for "educational uses," both in teaching and for after-class review or directed study. Examples of "educational uses" (e.g., copying, printing, downloading, display, and distribution) that are permitted by "authorized users" include the following:
  - printouts for classroom handouts, student reports, study notes,
  - reproduction in slides for classroom or lecture use,
  - reproduction in printed notices or handbills for class use (but not for other uses such as promotional posters or commercial purposes without separate permission),
  - downloading to hard drive/diskette for later study during the term of the course,
  - retransmission to university distance learning sites or programs,
  - Web sites created for specific classes, limited to authorized users under the license, and
  - public presentations by educators to their scholarly communities.
- agree that educational adaptations of images and related text (under "fair use" principles) are permissible as long as (1) the integrity of the original distribution set is maintained, (2) all adaptations are for educational purposes only, and (3) all such adaptations are appropriately cited.
- agree that derivative works made by a Licensed Institution for the purpose of providing access to the images and text are also governed by the terms of the license and must remain under the control of the Licensed Institution, such as slides for classroom presentations or fixed media (e.g., CDs, videotapes) for freestanding presentations.
- agree that the license does not cover commercial, fundraising, or other noneducational campus activities (e.g., film series, promotional posters for campus lectures); users must request permissions and negotiate such uses separately.
- agree that students should be able to copy and use images in academic course assignments and retain these in their academic portfolios (e.g., for graduate school and employment applications) or use them for educational exhibits and displays.

Licensor/Museum

- Museums want copying restricted except as permitted under "applicable law."
- Museums want to prevent or minimize redistribution, retransmission, or copying beyond the license terms and Licensed Institution without permission.
- Museums are concerned about the integrity of the basic set of images and data.
- Museums are concerned that adaptive uses for educational purposes by educators and students not violate the moral rights of creators.

Licensee/University

- Universities want to be able to mount thumbnail versions of images as identification aids on public Web sites as part of their catalog of images.

7. Technical Requirements: Data Exchange

Both museums and universities:

- agree that access to images of a specific quality should be provided for various uses, i.e., *thumbnail images* for cataloging or identification purposes, *high-quality images* (and large files) for classroom use.
- agree that thumbnail images are acceptable for identification purposes, e.g., cataloging or searching, but not for actual academic uses.
- agree to the benefits of adopting standard data interchange formats for textual and image data.

Licensor/Museum

- Museums want agreement on certain specific standard formats for export and distribution, so they do not have to change or adapt these for individual needs (including compression, resolution, etc.), i.e., they want to deliver a "standard product."

Licensee/University

- Universities want to receive data in standard formats, but also want flexibility in adapting the standard image and text distribution formats for local delivery in specific instances.
- Universities want the following delivery options:
  - access licensed image databases from museum collectives' servers, or
  - mount the image databases on university servers (making necessary backups as needed), or
  - both.
- Universities want textual data associated with works to conform to widely accepted metadata standards employed by other information products delivered through their campus networks.

8. Technical Requirements: Security

Both museums and universities:

- agree that access should be restricted to authorized users for authorized uses.
- agree that images and text should be responsibly secured using reasonable technical capabilities that are practical and feasible to implement through existing university campus systems.

► Licensor/Museum

- Museums want access controlled to minimize further retransmissions or copying that exceeds the terms of the license.

► Licensee/University

- Universities recognize that there are a variety of technological solutions for security, and they need flexibility in meeting general security requirements under a license. Restrictions imposed on licensed users should be practical and flexible enough for universities to be able to provide authorized access through existing campus systems.

9. Notices to be Displayed

Both museums and universities:

- agree that the license terms and conditions of use should be readily available to users at all times; this notice should inform users of the uses permitted or not permitted under the license and provide the name of a university contact to whom to address licensing questions.
- agree that museums may create a basic rights statement to accompany each compilation or image as appropriate, identifying any donor restrictions or other basic limitations; universities are willing to retain connections between images, rights statements, and basic museum identifications. A *rights statement* is defined as a general description prepared by the museum, describing the rights and limitations on use of a particular image, and may include a *copyright notice,* i.e., statutory definition— "©, owner, year."
- agree to exempt the notice requirement in clearly defined and limited circumstances, such as exams, where its use would conflict with the educational purpose of the exercise.

10. Fees

Both museums and universities:

- agree that a fixed fee for unlimited access and uses during the license term is generally preferable at this time for selected compilations of images, e.g., "bulk licensing of corpora."
- agree that a number of pricing models may be developed that reflect users/uses/distribution costs/administrative costs.

Licensor/Museum

- Museums want to be compensated in relation to their contributions and want the fee structure to reflect their investment costs (at a minimum, cost recovery), and a little more, if possible and appropriate.
- Museums want permissions and fees negotiated separately for uses beyond educational uses, e.g., reproducing and publishing images in university publications.

Licensee/University

- Universities want access to large bodies of works on a fixed-fee basis, which makes costs predictable.
- Universities want the fee structure to be based on noncommercial, nonprofit, educational uses, with fees as low as reasonably possible.
- Universities want the fee structure to reflect a lower rate per year over the period of a multi-year license, especially for static compilations.
- Universities indicate that fees based on "simultaneous users" may make some sense in theory, but may not work in practice because it is too hard to control.
- Universities want variable fee structures for varying products, e.g.,
  - a fee structure based on some reasonable formula which is easy to administer,
  - a subscription to the whole image database or portions of a database for a defined period of time,
  - a fee (if required) to retain all or some of the database beyond the license term (but with no subsequent updates),
  - a subscription to value-added services or products such as image manipulation software, art history texts in digital form, supplementary enrichment materials, reference works, and annotated bibliographies.

11. Term of License

- Both museums and universities agree with the need for fixed-term licenses for ease of administration and predictability.

Licensor/Museum

- Museums want the license to require return or destruction of backups of databases and all derivative products, such as slides or CD-ROMs for classroom display, after license periods expire.

Licensee/University

- Universities prefer license terms by year (for budget purposes).
- Universities might accept multi-year agreements under certain circumstances, e.g.,
  - lower rate per year over the period of the multi-year license, or
  - museum agreement to add a specified number of additional images per year or provide other added value.
- Universities may be willing to return backups of databases after license periods expire, provided there is a convenient mechanism to assure access to identified items in support of a particular curriculum.
- Universities may need some flexibility in unusual circumstances, especially under multi-year licenses, to have continued access for a limited, specified time period to a portion of the data set to meet specific curriculum needs, after termination of the license.

12. Warranties and Indemnities

Both museums and universities:

- agree that museums will clear the rights necessary for all the materials and uses provided under the license.
- agree that it is highly desirable for museums to warrant/promise to universities to the fullest extent possible that they either own or have obtained all necessary rights for the authorized educational uses permitted by the license.

► Licensor/Museum

- Museums may want universities to warrant/promise that they will indemnify museums for any losses or penalties to museums due to breach of the license by the university, i.e., gross negligence in permitting commercial access or use.

► Licensee/University

- Universities want to limit their liabilities as much as possible and want full indemnity by museums for breach of warranty.
- Universities may want museums to warrant/promise that they will indemnify the university for any losses or penalties to universities owing to breach of the license by the museum.

13. Reporting

Both museums and universities:

- agree with the need for universities to maintain and report basic, aggregate usage statistics.
- acknowledge that individuals' usage records are generally considered confidential library records; however, aggregate statistical records can be reported.
- agree that universities should provide timely incident reports identifying any known violations of the license, together with a summary of the steps taken by the educational institution in response.

► Licensor/Museum

- Museums would like to have periodic statistical reports from universities on usage, as well as information or qualitative feedback on how their images are being used in the educational process.
- Museums would like feedback from universities on categories of images needed in the future to help them set future priorities for which images to digitize.

► Licensee/University

- Universities may be willing to provide some feedback on usage patterns, preferred materials, etc. (within the requirements to maintain the confidentiality of records of specific usage by individuals) to help museums set future priorities.
- Universities want to have a voice in content selection and are willing to provide input to museums on content needed in the future.

14. Rights Administration

Both museums and universities:

- agree that it is necessary and important for all users to honor the rights of content owners with respect to the images provided.
- agree that it is important for museums to provide rights information with images and image collections (see Notices to be Displayed, p. 28), and for universities to retain the rights information associated with the images and accompanying data.
- acknowledge that some museums may provide only public domain or rights-free images.
- agree that universities should inform their users of the need to use these materials in a responsible way.

► Licensor/Museum

- Museums may want some form of copyright/rights education provided to users upon initial access to the data set to get the attention of users (especially students) and raise awareness of the requirements to use these materials in a responsible way.
- Museums may want to require universities to provide some form of copyright education as a condition for the license.

► Licensee/University

- Universities will make reasonable efforts to provide some copyright and other rights education to authorized users, especially if this is provided as part of the standard introduction to the data set.
- Universities want mechanisms in place for easy, convenient licensing of uses that are beyond the terms of the license; they would also like to have information from museums on whom to contact for additional rights clearance or permission (for potential uses beyond the license agreement).

15. Preservation and Data Archiving

- Both groups agree that it is necessary and important to define the responsibilities for image and data archiving, refreshing digital images and documentation as needed, and providing other safeguards regarding quality and future availability.

► Licensor/Museum

- Museums acknowledge their responsibility to maintain the visual and textual documentation of their collections and make them available over the longer term, but they may not have the technical means of providing this information efficiently for all digital versions of images and text.

► Licensee/University

- Universities expect that a system will be in place that fulfills responsibilities for archiving images, refreshing images as needed, and providing other safeguards regarding quality and future availability.
- Universities want an option to retain all or some of the images in their university digital archive beyond the license term.

16. Breach/Termination

Both museums and universities:

- agree that infractions/breaches by individuals using licensed materials should be addressed first by the Licensed Institution within its institutional honor code system for internal adjudication, and then reported (see Reporting, p. 31).
- agree that the license agreement could be terminated "for cause" in the case of a serious "breach," that is, failure of either party to fulfill responsibilities under the agreement after (1) receipt of formal notice of breach and (2) failure of breaching party to cure the breach within an agreed-upon time.
- agree that any formal notice of breach should be given in writing and allow a reasonable time for the breaching party to "cure" the breach before termination of the license agreement for cause.

► Licensor/Museum

- Museums want to be able to terminate the agreement "for cause," i.e., for breach of the terms of the license.

► Licensee/University

- Universities want any "termination for breach of the terms of the license" to be carefully worded to prevent a campus-wide turn-off for minor infractions or, for example, a single breaching event by a student.

17. General Provisions

Other terms and conditions that are likely to be addressed in a museum/educational institution license agreement may include (but are not limited to) the following:

Notices and Authorized Representatives: The parties need to agree to send all formal notices to Authorized Representatives, either by certified mail or another method that confirms receipt. The agreement also needs to specify names, titles, and organizations, with contact information (mailing addresses, telephone, fax, e-mail addresses) for the Authorized Representatives and key contacts, including both the licensor's and licensee's contacts for contractual matters and for day-to-day administrative matters.

Promotional Use of Names/Institutional Logos: Use of names, trademarks, and logos, including use for endorsement, promotion, press releases, reports, and advertising purposes, needs to be clarified in the agreement. Museums and nonprofit educational institutions have a particular interest in ensuring that their names are not used in a manner that might diminish their stature or integrity. Parties may agree in advance to certain acceptable uses, contexts, and text; then as long as the other party uses the name or logo within the agreed-upon parameters, additional permission is not required. For other uses or contexts, prior written permission would need to be requested.

Force Majeure: The agreement should specify when performance by either party would be excused because it was prevented or delayed by a "greater force," such as government restrictions, war or warlike activity, insurrection or civil disorder, labor disputes, or any other natural disasters or causes that are beyond the control of either party and are not foreseeable at the time the agreement was made.

Dispute Resolution: The agreement should specify how disputes are to be resolved short of litigation, including (but not limited to) campus judicial processes, nonbinding mediation, and binding arbitration.

Choice of Law: The agreement should identify the jurisdiction and the laws that are to be applied to the enforcement of the agreement when necessary. Some institutions may be subject to mandatory choice of law provisions either by law or by institutional policy.

No Waiver of Breach: The agreement should specify whether or not the waiver by one party of a breach or default of any provision by the other party constitutes a waiver of any succeeding breach of the same or another provision. This item refers to the intentional or voluntary relinquishing of rights or privileges under an agreement or the failure to complain or take action when the other party fails to perform in some instance.

Limitations on Liability: The agreement may need to specify the limitations on liability, including limitations on monetary damages, if any, resulting from failure to perform any part of the agreement.

Entire Agreement (Modifications, Amendments, Assignments): The agreement needs to include a statement that the agreement should not be modified, amended, or assigned except in a written document signed by the Authorized Representatives of the participating institutions.

Severance of Terms or Separability: The agreement may need to specify that if one or more terms or provisions of the agreement are held to be invalid, void, or unenforceable, "the balance of the agreement remains in force."

▶ Definitions

Authorized representatives are the individuals named in a license agreement who are identified to send or receive any formal or official notifications to the other party regarding contractual matters under the agreement and who has the power to legally bind the party they represent.

Authorized users include a standard community of university users, including educators and students as defined broadly below.

Campus networks are defined as a specific geographic site or sites connected by the university's network.

Copyright notice, according to U.S. copyright law, consists of three elements: (1) the symbol © (the letter C in a circle), or the word "Copyright," or the abbreviation "Copr."; (2) the year of first publication of the work; and (3) the name of the owner of copyright in the work, or an abbreviation by which the name can be recognized, or a generally known alternative designation of the owner. Whenever a work protected under copyright law is published in the U.S. or elsewhere by authority of the copyright owner, a notice of copyright may be placed on publicly distributed copies from which the work can be visually perceived, either directly or with the aid of a machine or device.

Educators include faculty, teachers, instructors, curators, librarians, archivists, scholars, or staff who engage in or support instructional, research, or scholarly activities for educational purposes as their assigned responsibilities at educational institutions.

Intranets are defined as restricted university networks, accessible only to authorized users of the licensed educational institution (but not restricted to specific geographic sites or physical locations).

License agreement is a written contract which sets forth the terms and conditions under which a **licensor** (the one who owns or controls the rights covered by the license and who grants the license) grants a **license** (permission to do something which, without permission, the licensee would otherwise have no right to do) to a **licensee** (one who receives permission under the license).

Licensed institution may be defined differently for each educational institution, e.g., campus-wide, enrolled students regardless of where located, all authorized users.

Minimum access includes access in classrooms, libraries and media centers, and elsewhere to "authorized users," e.g. dormitories, educators' and students' homes or study/research sites, distance learning sites administered by the university, and others.

Rights statement is defined as a general description prepared by the museum, describing the rights and limitations on use of a particular image, and may include a *copyright notice,* i.e., statutory definition— " ©, owner, year."

Students include full-time and part-time participants enrolled at the Licensed Institution.

Introduction

The content supplied through the MESL project occupied the primary position in the chain of challenges addressed by the participants. Without content, there could be no technical investigation. Without the "right" content, there would be little or no adoption by educational users. Without use, there would be no framework for testing the parameters of future licensing agreements.

In her article, Andrea Notman reviews the project strategies for approaching the content selection process and gives an overview of the content provided. In addition, she reflects on a number of the broader issues raised by the MESL participants regarding content selection and provision. As with several other pieces in this report, her article closes with a series of questions which are as yet unanswered. They reflect the fundamental tension between museums' need to adhere to institutional priorities in pursing the creation of digital content and their desire to meet the needs of educational users.

For many of the traditional users of images—especially teachers and students of art history—the availability of a significant portion of the images they are accustomed to having access to will be a critical component in their decision to make the transition to using digital images in their teaching and research. As we move forward, attempts to match demand with available content will pose a formidable challenge.

Content Selection in the Museum Educational Site Licensing Project

ANDREA NOTMAN

Context

Choosing images for the MESL database represented one of the biggest challenges in the project. In order for the MESL experiment to yield useful data about the impact of digital image availability on teaching and learning in universities, two important things needed to happen: Faculty had to be recruited to use the images in their courses, and images—and their related textual information—had to be readily available in a form that faculty and students could use.

"Necessity is the mother of invention" would be an apt title for the story of content selection for the MESL project. (A close second might be "If at first you don't succeed, try, try again.") From the outset, there were some significant challenges. The project time frame was ambitious, and the number of images was quite limited (4,959 images were selected and mounted on university networks in the first year, supplemented by an additional 4,360 in the second). Faculty recruitment in the universities had to occur simultaneously with image identification and processing in the museums. At the same time, there were innumerable technical issues with which to contend, and limited resources.

The MESL project did not produce a scaleable model for image database content selection; however, there were significant—and promising—accomplishments within this part of the experiment. In addition, there is much to be learned from the trial and error efforts that were employed, as well as cautions to those who follow about what types of constraints may be insurmountable.

The Process

What follows is an account of the process that the MESL participants undertook and general descriptions of the content that each institution supplied to the database.

In February 1995, the seven museums and seven educational institutions selected to participate in the MESL project met in Washington, D.C., to discuss and implement the project. Given the two-year time frame of the collaboration, all realized that in order to accomplish the project goals, an aggressive schedule must be agreed to and implemented immediately. By responding to the Call for Participation, museums had agreed to supply at least 500 images in each of the two years of the project. At this preliminary meeting, the seven museums and seven universities were charged with the initial task of determining the content for the first year of the MESL project. To a certain extent, the overall success of the project was at stake. Without pertinent content in usable form with which to teach (or create) a course or unit, the educational community would not be interested in participating in an experiment to explore new methods of teaching with digital materials.

Immediately, the museums faced two key questions: What images could they share, and how did those intersect with the images universities might want? Meanwhile, the universities grappled with complementary questions: How could they identify faculty willing to teach with MESL images, and what images would they find useful? These questions provoked inquiries and challenges on both sides of the project and were addressed in creative ways in both years of the content selection process.

As it turned out, museum offerings to the MESL database were determined in large part by institutional situations at the time MESL was launched. By design, the MESL project included a full range of experience and technical sophistication among its museum participants. While many museums already had collections of digital images, others had none. Some had no digital imaging experience or equipment, while others were quite comfortable with the technology. One thing they all had in common was a wealth of photographic resources from which to create digital content. Nevertheless, several were unable to create any new digital materials for the project because of conflicting institutional priorities.

A tight schedule put a great deal of pressure on the content selection process. A discussion was held during the February 1995 meeting of MESL participants where they attempted to identify potential content for distribution in the first year. The MESL Management Committee[1] and the participants charted an elaborate matrix detailing what museums might have to share and identifying areas of strength from both chronological and geographical perspectives. Universities tried to match this potential content to course schedules for fall 1995—which was no mean task. In order to attempt a distribution of images and data for teaching in the fall of 1995, a timetable was established. This preliminary outline of tasks and deadlines highlighted several key areas that required immediate attention. The MESL Management Committee proposed that by February 28 (only three weeks after the meeting), museums provide the university community with summary descriptions of images that could be shared. Conversely, universities were to provide museums with course descriptions for fall and spring semesters, listing types of images that might be required. The MESL Management Committee offered to serve as the collator and distributor of these hard copy materials to facilitate and manage this preliminary exchange of potential content.

During early March 1995, museums and universities communicated back and forth on what content would satisfy the course requirements over the next academic year. Long lists of image descriptions were sent from the museums via the project managers to the universities, who, in turn, redistributed the information packets to faculty. Further exchange ensued directly between universities and museums in order to define and specify those images that would complement the curricula. By the end of March, museums were expected to finalize their content lists.

Once this initial hurdle was passed, each museum was charged with preparing approximately 500 images (with descriptive data) and delivering them to the University of Michigan, which had agreed to serve as the central distribution point. Michigan's job was to "normalize" the structured data and package everything for delivery to individual universities.[2] Michigan required delivery of images and data by mid-June 1995 in order to prepare and distribute the information to the universities for the fall semester.

Once the images were distributed, universities faced the challenge of designing and implementing delivery systems on their campuses that enabled immediate use of these new materials. Although all of the museums managed to deliver their content to Michigan—and Michigan massaged it and passed it on to the university sites—the timing was a serious problem. The images arrived at most universities just as the fall semester was getting under way. The summer window for figuring out how to load and present this material on the campus network systems was past, and faculty had long since made plans for their fall course content. A few universities managed to load the MESL database in time for fall courses, but others were unable to recover from the delays.

Selecting Content in the First Year

The museums addressed their content selection responsibilities in a variety of ways, depending on pre-existing factors and institutional priorities. General descriptions of the content that each institution provided during the first year of the MESL project are provided below.

FOWLER MUSEUM OF CULTURAL HISTORY

When the project began, the Fowler Museum of Cultural History already had approximately 25,000 digitized images of its collections. The museum was committed to helping faculty find rich and comprehensive material, in hopes that an educator could build and teach a course around a subset of its collection. This approach required direct communication between the Fowler staff and the university participants interested in using its extensive collections of ethnographic materials. Based on faculty requests, the Fowler shared images and text related to a recent exhibition of Peruvian ceramics, for which a catalog had been produced. Based on an initial collaboration between one of the museum curators and faculty interested in African materials, the Fowler also shared materials from its Yoruba and Akan cultures. As it turned out, approximately half of the materials made available were based on Fowler priorities, and the rest were based on requests articulated by the educational community.

GEORGE EASTMAN HOUSE

The George Eastman House (GEH) entered the project with very little experience in building a digital collection and no existing digital images to share. The institution's enthusiasm for participating in the project sparked a major institutional effort to identify a body of material that could easily be digitized within the time constraints. Its 540 images were produced first on slides and then captured on Kodak PhotoCD. After much discussion, the preferred methodology was to provide depth rather than breadth, by featuring its holdings of three photographers: Francis Bruguière, William Henry Emerson, and H. P. Robinson. Bowing to the constraints of tight time frames for selection, preparation, and delivery, selections were made without input from the universities (a strategy the GEH project coordinator dubbed "the path of least resistance").

HARVARD UNIVERSITY ART MUSEUMS

The Harvard University Art Museums (HUAM) also had little experience in building a digital archive, although they had experimented internally with digital capture methods. The ability to join the MESL project accelerated this process. HUAM's selection process began with an assessment of the available body of existing color photography, including both color slides and 8 x 10 color transparencies. This information was made available to the MESL universities in the form of extensive printouts of object-level data; university project coordinators and professors were asked to return copies to the HUAM indicating the images desired. The HUAM project coordinator analyzed the university requests and decided to share images that were requested by more than two universities, with special attention being given to fulfilling particular requests by professors that would affect a particular teaching unit. The museum shared over 500 images, particularly in the area of nineteenth-century European paintings and drawings. While the universities had an opportunity to select images, the selection was confined to the most popular and frequently published parts of HUAM's collection.

LIBRARY OF CONGRESS

The Library of Congress had extensive digital collections available to share at the onset of the project, in large part because of the ambitious American Memory project[3] which was already available on the Web. During the first year of the MESL project, the Library of Congress shared approximately 1,400 photographs by Carl Van Vechten, which represented nearly the entire holdings of this single photographer's work at the Library. These images, dating from between 1932 and 1964, documented individuals in the arts and included many prominent African-American entertainers, as well as a small assortment of American landscapes. Owing to restrictions on the 1966 gift of these materials to the Library, these images were unavailable to the general public until 1986; others continue to be protected by copyright. The Library of Congress selected its materials for the MESL project in an internal process with no feedback from the university community.

THE MUSEUM OF FINE ARTS, HOUSTON

When the project started, The Museum of Fine Arts, Houston had rich resources but no experience with digital imaging. Nevertheless, staff enthusiastically tackled the MESL project and delivered 745 images for the database. These images represented works from collection areas spanning 6,000 years of art history, including classical antiquities, European, pre-Columbian, Native American, eighteenth- and nineteenth-century American, African, Oceanic, and Asian art. Owing to the strict timing of the first round, The Museum of Fine Arts, Houston selected images that represented the richness and breadth of its collections, driven more by its own priorities and needs than those of the educational community. Relatively little communication occurred between educators and the museum during the first round of selection decisions.

NATIONAL GALLERY OF ART

The National Gallery of Art (NGA) had approximately 1,200 digital images available at the beginning of the MESL project, which reflected its current cataloging projects undertaken to meet publication schedules. Its first-round selection included over 700 objects of European and American paintings, sculpture, and decorative arts, chosen from among those digital images. NGA was able to respond to requests from a professor at the University of Maryland for American paintings, and also to requests from a Cornell faculty member for specific images related to the Renaissance. All other selections were dictated primarily by NGA's own internal priorities.

NATIONAL MUSEUM OF AMERICAN ART

When the project began, the National Museum of American Art (NMAA) had an existing body of approximately 1,000 digital images reflecting the breadth of the institution's holdings. NMAA made lists of these digital images available to the university community as candidates for sharing in the MESL project. From these, the museum selected 541. These images consisted of a subset of American art from the colonial period to the present and represented multiple stylistic periods.

Selecting Content in the Second Year

By the beginning of the second round of the selection process for the MESL project, digital materials were becoming more commonplace in the museums, and technological changes were also beginning to affect the content selection process. Several museums that were not connected to the Internet in the first year had installed electronic mail service at their institutions, thereby meeting an initial requirement of project participation. Electronic mail had quickly become the communication vehicle for the MESL project, allowing working groups, project coordinators, and Management Committee members to work efficiently on issues despite geographical distances and infrequent (semiannual) group meetings. Several new museum Web sites allowed professors and educators to view potential content offerings. A year of experience and technological advances in virtually all of the MESL institutions prompted new strategies for content selection in the second year.

Despite the fact that the museums delivered content the first year, and the majority of the universities mounted the data on their servers, it was clear that a better approach to content selection was required in order to engage professors and the university community in the MESL experiment. Concerns expressed by the universities about the limited nature of the content in the first round indicated that the universities required a more direct method of communication with the museums for suggesting and specifying content. At the third MESL meeting held in early December 1995, alternative solutions to this process were proposed.

WEB-BASED SELECTION EXPERIMENT

To support the second-round selection process, Christie Stephenson and Thornton Staples, from the University of Virginia, developed an electronic request form on a Web site at Virginia during early 1996. The electronic form, which was available for use by all participants with Web access in February 1996, allowed an individual to send a request for specific images to one or more of the MESL museums (see Figure 1).

The intention was that by completing a simple form, an individual could easily address the MESL museum community and identify the artist or subject desired. The form included a place for comments and allowed for further clarification of the requests. Both requests to specific museums and museums' responses to those requests were exchanged among project coordinators and immediately posted to the Web site. Project participants were then able to view these discussions about the collections and particular images desired by the universities (see Figure 2 on page 44).

While requests did not guarantee inclusion, the Web form was intended to facilitate communication between universities and museums. The plan was that the form would be in use through February 1996, with museums determining and declaring their material for the second round by mid-March 1996. Images and data were to be delivered to the University of Michigan by early May 1996 for data normalization and subsequent distribution to the universities.

What was intended as a simple form and methodology turned out to be quite confusing to a subset of the university faculty. Some of the professors, who had been encouraged by MESL project coordinators to make content requests, had little prior experience with electronic communication. They found the forms difficult to use and didn't always understand the concepts behind them.

Unfortunately, new versions of Web browsers released during the development and testing of the request form created unanticipated problems that ultimately delayed the implementation of this online selection process. This delay condensed the time frame for content selection and adversely affected the number of requests made in this manner. Consequently, more traditional means—namely mail and telephone—were also used to supplement the selection process. While most participants still believe the Web-based selection option has promise, more work needs to be done to ensure its success in future implementations.

Although all of the museums received requests from universities, many either were not answered or could not be accommodated for a variety of reasons. Nevertheless, the museums filled significantly more individual requests from the university community during the second year. General descriptions of the content that each institution provided during the second year of the MESL project are shown in Figures 1 and 2.

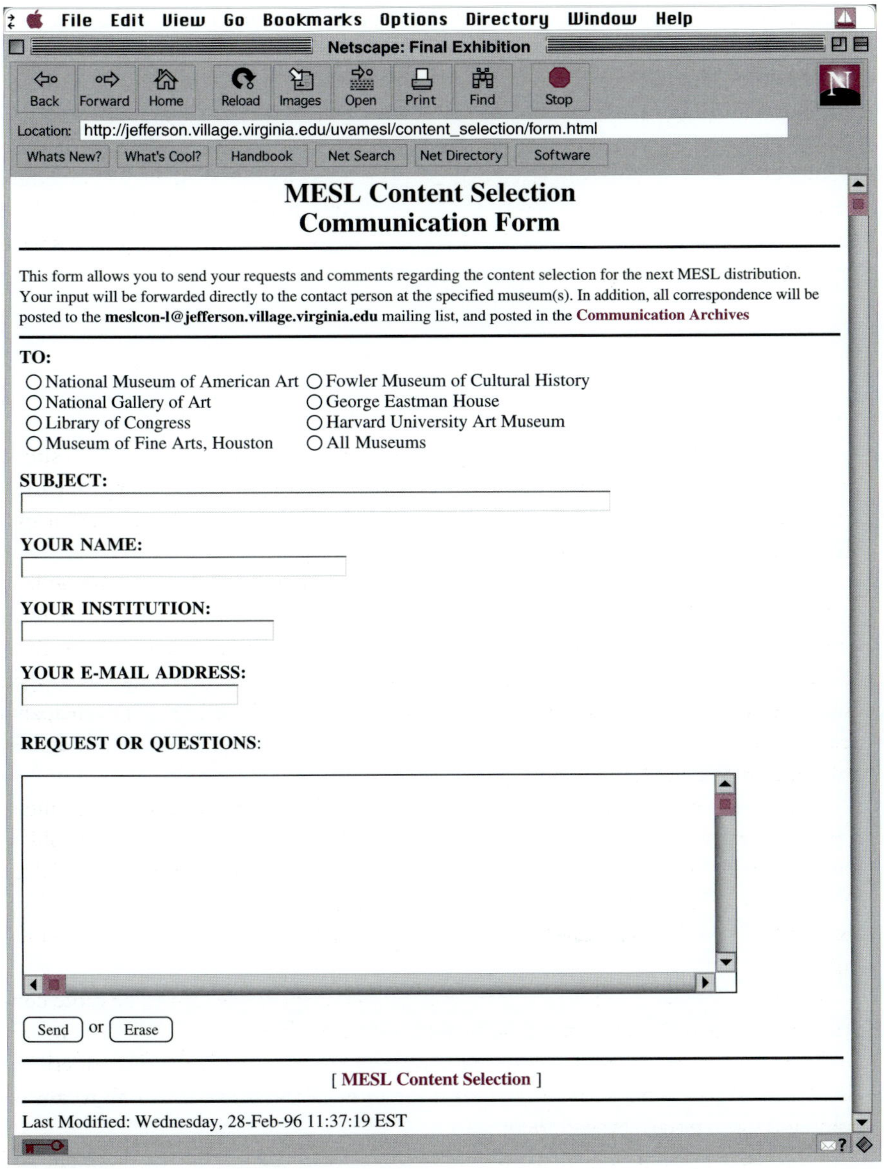

▶ **FIGURE 1** Content Selection Web Form

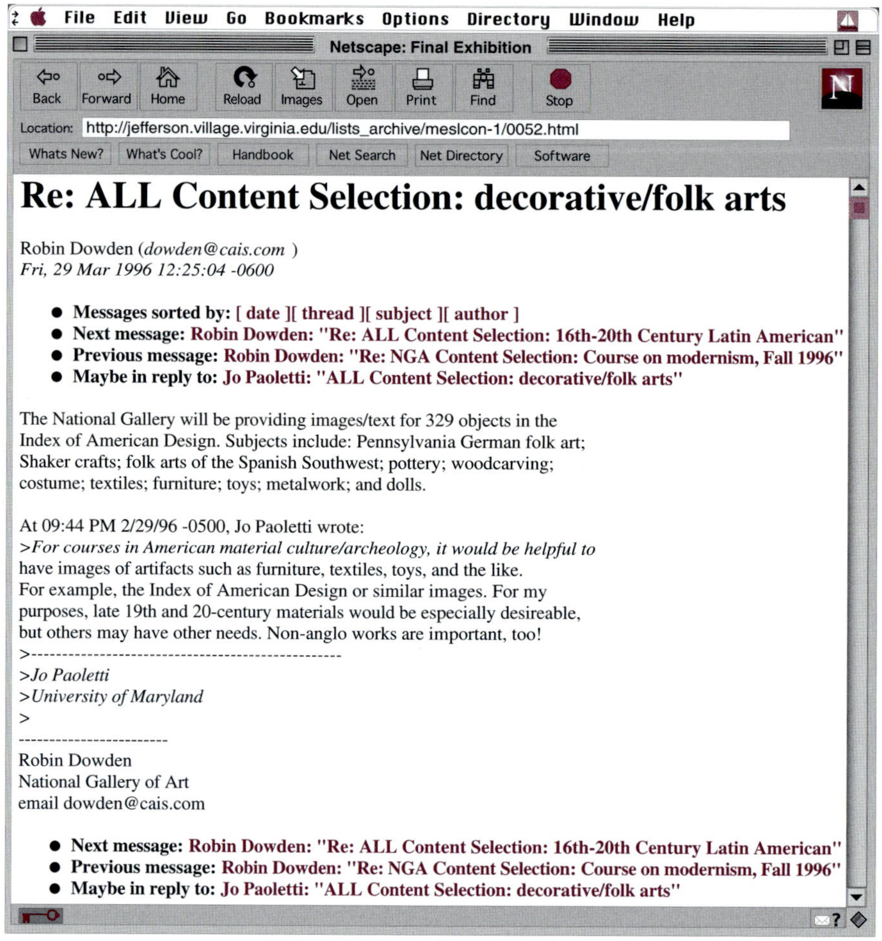

Re: ALL Content Selection: decorative/folk arts

Robin Dowden (*dowden@cais.com*)
Fri, 29 Mar 1996 12:25:04 -0600

- **Messages sorted by:** [date][thread][subject][author]
- **Next message:** Robin Dowden: "Re: ALL Content Selection: 16th-20th Century Latin American"
- **Previous message:** Robin Dowden: "Re: NGA Content Selection: Course on modernism, Fall 1996"
- **Maybe in reply to:** Jo Paoletti: "ALL Content Selection: decorative/folk arts"

The National Gallery will be providing images/text for 329 objects in the Index of American Design. Subjects include: Pennsylvania German folk art; Shaker crafts; folk arts of the Spanish Southwest; pottery; woodcarving; costume; textiles; furniture; toys; metalwork; and dolls.

At 09:44 PM 2/29/96 -0500, Jo Paoletti wrote:
>*For courses in American material culture/archeology, it would be helpful to*
have images of artifacts such as furniture, textiles, toys, and the like.
For example, the Index of American Design or similar images. For my purposes, late 19th and 20-century materials would be especially desireable, but others may have other needs. Non-anglo works are important, too!
>--
>*Jo Paoletti*
>*University of Maryland*
>

Robin Dowden
National Gallery of Art
email dowden@cais.com

- **Next message:** Robin Dowden: "Re: ALL Content Selection: 16th-20th Century Latin American"
- **Previous message:** Robin Dowden: "Re: NGA Content Selection: Course on modernism, Fall 1996"
- **Maybe in reply to:** Jo Paoletti: "ALL Content Selection: decorative/folk arts"

▶ **FIGURE 2** Hypertext Mail Archive Showing Dialogue between MESL Participants

FOWLER MUSEUM OF CULTURAL HISTORY

The Fowler Museum of Cultural History supplemented its initial round with images of approximately 700 objects, including additional African material and an extensive collection of Indonesian and Malaysian textiles. The inclusion of the African material resulted directly from discussion between the Fowler and a university professor who had requested Fowler material in the first round. During the selection process, the Fowler made thumbnail and full-screen versions of its entire imaged collections (approximately 37,000 items) available via the Web to facilitate faculty decision making. In fact, the rich content available from the Fowler was instrumental in the professor's redesigning and restructuring his course—exactly the type of activity the MESL experiment hoped to stimulate.

GEORGE EASTMAN HOUSE

The second-year selection from George Eastman House (GEH) provided approximately 500 photographs from three unique collections of photographs: the works of Lewis Hine, Eugene Atget, and Alvin Langdon Coburn. Previously the images had been virtually inaccessible—even at GEH—because of unusual storage formats. Including them in digital format as part of the MESL database made them accessible to educational communities for the first time.

HARVARD UNIVERSITY ART MUSEUMS

The HUAM's content for the second round of selections reflected current projects at the museum. Noteworthy and previously uncataloged material from the John Singer Sargent archive was provided (digitized for use in a museum Web site), as well as selected images from the Ben Shahn collection of photographs. Additional images from a centennial catalog of the museum's collection were included to meet the content requirement. Conveniently, the inclusion of Sargent material matched perfectly with requests from faculty at the University of Maryland. Communication via the content selection Web form resulted in selection of additional materials requested specifically by professors; however, internal museum priorities drove the content selection to a greater degree than in the first year. In all, the museum shared just over 500 images in the second round.

LIBRARY OF CONGRESS

In the second year, the Library of Congress chose 759 items from a significant collection of eighteenth- and nineteenth-century American political prints. The collection included a wide range of prints from a time when printmaking was used as a tool for promoting political ideas and causes. This collection lent itself to interdisciplinary study, more so than the more traditional art history images; however, there was no interaction with faculty during the selection process.

THE MUSEUM OF FINE ARTS, HOUSTON

The Museum of Fine Arts, Houston, answering a call for American material, provided content from its Bayou Bend Collection of American Decorative Arts. However, despite the content selection Web form, the museum reported little direct exchange between itself and the universities in the second-round selection process. Its selection process mirrored the same strategy used in the first selection round, reflecting the general breadth of its collection.

NATIONAL GALLERY OF ART

The National Gallery of Art followed similar guidelines for the second-round content selection, relying on the priorities of the gallery's publication schedule. The majority of its content consisted of American and European paintings. However, direct requests to the NGA via the content selection Web form resulted in the inclusion of images from the *Index of American Design*, a federal Works Progress Administration (WPA) project. Additional requests for contemporary photography and images from the twentieth century were not included owing to issues of copyright, a common dilemma that all content providers faced in both content selection periods. The project coordinator at the NGA also commented that in a specific case, the gallery was asked whether images existed that would have been censored or considered questionable by a government agency or a political (or social) entity capable of censoring materials. This request highlighted the fact that a museum's perspective on its collection might be very different from that of a social historian and underscored the benefit of such a collaboration between museums and universities.

NATIONAL MUSEUM OF AMERICAN ART

The NMAA, which shared just under 500 images in the second round of selections, was very responsive to requests from the university community. Its descriptions of the content provided reflected themes and classifications specifically requested by faculty. However, it also received impossible requests for works by artists who were not represented in its collections. The content selection Web form turned out to be quite useful in promoting a dialogue between NMAA curators and faculty at several universities.

"The long-term success of MESL will be determined by our ability to develop ways to capture and deliver information in a timely and efficient manner. We should bear in mind the constraints posed by the academic calendar to ensure that faculty have access to the images and information far enough in advance to incorporate them into their courses. The content side of MESL needs much more work in future implementations. We need to figure out how to incorporate images into information delivery systems."

ANGELA GIRAL
COLUMBIA UNIVERSITY
Participants' Meeting

▸ Conclusion

In summarizing the experience of the MESL content selection process and reviewing the selection methodologies employed during the project, there are a number of key issues that are important to emphasize and reflect upon. In the first place, very few museums currently have large bodies of digital materials. Many of those who do are attempting to identify ways they can use these resources, both as further documentation of their collections and as potential resources to share. Secondly, technological changes under way in all cultural institutions necessitate that more resources be committed to documenting collections digitally. However, the benefits must first be clearly understood and supported by every institution's administration. Otherwise, database and collection management initiatives are likely to be short-lived—as many case histories in the museum community can attest.

As a third issue, museum cataloging and the adoption of standards for cataloging collections affect content selection as well as use. The manner in which a museum catalogs its collection reflects the particular perspective and value an institution places on its holdings. A museum may catalog a particular work of art from a specific art historical context, attaching pertinent keywords describing both content and theme. However, a researcher or educator may see its value from an entirely different—and perhaps unacknowledged—perspective. These new perspectives can add richness to the descriptive data if museums can find ways to capitalize on them. And if they don't, the risk is that educators and researchers who need access to imagebases of art and cultural resources may not find what they need.

An additional issue raised by the delivery of the MESL content at the university level dealt with the challenge of how to advertise or publicize the availability of materials. Most institutions found it difficult to inform or educate its users about the content available for use. As the MESL project moved from the first year into the second year, some universities modified their interface by inserting a browsing—or intuitive layer—between the user and the content. Increasing a user's awareness of the available content is a challenge that should never be underestimated.

Lastly, faculty want to be reassured that content they select for a course will be available in the future, especially because of the tremendous investment of time and effort that is required to incorporate new media into the curriculum.

The MESL experiment stimulated many new questions:

- How can we can apply what we learned from the content selection process to the creation of broader-based digital holdings?
- Who should drive the content selection process?
- Have we arrived at a point within our content provider and user communities where a simple, powerful tool such as the content selection Web form could be used to identify larger bodies of material, approximating the "critical mass" necessary to satisfy users?

- Can content providers and users work efficiently together to successfully articulate and fulfill requests?
- Do content providers have a sufficient body of material available to share for educational use that will satisfy the diverse and wide-ranging needs in the academic community—without violating their intellectual property responsibilities?
- How can content providers balance their institutional needs and priorities for digitization with user requests for digitized content?

In future implementations, "post-MESL," it will be necessary to strive for a balance in the selection process that addresses the requirements and obligations of both content providers and the user community. Inevitably, there will be significant financial and related institutional commitment issues to be resolved in order to provide large-scale digital resources.

► Notes

1. At the time, Jennifer Trant was serving as Project Director, supported by other members of the MESL Management Committee: Howard Besser, Clifford Lynch, Geoff Samuels, Maxwell Anderson, and David Bearman.
2. A fuller explanation of the role that the University of Michigan played as the central distribution point appears later in this report in the article "The MESL Distribution Process" by Christie Stephenson and Clifford Lynch, pp. 62–69.
3. For information on the American Memory project, visit the Web site *http://lcweb2.loc.gov/ammem*.

Introduction

The following four articles survey the major technical areas addressed in the MESL project: data provision, image creation, distribution, and delivery to end users. As in every other portion of the project's agenda, some of the processes employed were unique to MESL's nature as a time-bounded demonstration project, and others were more general in nature. In either case, the experiences of the MESL participants in confronting the technical agenda helped focus attention on the issues and challenges that remain to be resolved in order to build a scaleable model for the delivery of museum information to educational users.[1]

In her article on the MESL data dictionary and data export process, Robin Dowden discusses the process employed to repurpose existing collection management information in order to build databases that can be searched effectively by users outside the museum. She reviews some of the stumbling blocks that were encountered and overcome; she also articulates some issues that surfaced but were not fully resolved.

In reviewing the technical issues surrounding the digital images themselves, Christie Stephenson makes a case for stronger guidelines governing image creation, in order to provide a more consistent and predictable end product. She also raises continuing questions concerning our understanding of image quality requirements.

Clifford Lynch and Christie Stephenson document the MESL distribution process—a process which taught us unexpected lessons about the data as well as the more predictable ones about moving digital files from one location to another. This article closes with some speculation about next-generation models for distributing images and information about cultural heritage objects.

In the final article, Howard Besser reviews the plethora of technical issues raised by the process of mounting images and data on local servers. His article also highlights the issues surrounding the design of interfaces and systems to effectively deliver the images and data to end users.

▶ Note

1. The project teams from each MESL institution produced a detailed technical report on the details of implementation at their site in January 1997. Those reports provided background information for each of the reports that follow.

The MESL Data Dictionary and the Data Export Process

ROBIN DOWDEN

This article discusses the textual data distributed in the MESL project, focusing on the definition and use of a data dictionary as a vehicle for exchange. It documents the variety of problems that participants encountered in mapping and exporting their data to the dictionary and makes suggestions for further data analysis that could prove valuable if the MESL model is extended.

▶ Assumptions

A key goal of the MESL initiative was to enable university communities to make broad use of a large number of images and associated text. In order to provide those images and text records within the two-year framework of the project, the participating museums had to draw on information sources already in place, namely, their collections management systems. For the most part, these systems contained structured data that was compatible with the database applications currently under development at the universities to provide public access to these and other images.

▶ Defining a Framework for the Exchange of Textual Data

Each of the content providers had its own type and structure for textual data. As shown in Table 1, content providers were using a wide variety of software to record the textual information that would be distributed as part of the MESL project.

▶ TABLE 1 MESL Museums' Collection Management Systems

Institution	Collection Management System
Fowler Museum of Cultural History	■ Packaged application software ARGUS (Questor Systems, Inc.)
George Eastman House	■ Custom application developed internally using Software AG's ADABAS and Natural DBMS
Harvard University Art Museums	■ Custom application developed internally using a 4th Dimension database; migrated to EmbARK (Digital Collections, Inc.) during the MESL project
Library of Congress	■ Standard application software Minaret (MARC format)
The Museum of Fine Arts, Houston	■ Packaged application software Quixis (Willoughby Associates, Ltd.)
National Gallery of Art	■ Custom application developed internally using Nomad and DB2/VM (SQL database) software
National Museum of American Art	■ Custom application developed internally using Inquire software

The content and structure of the textual data set was established by the Documentation Working Group. At its initial meeting in February 1995, the entire MESL team decided that, to expedite data transfer, documentation would be supplied more or less as it was found in museum databases, although attempts would be made to normalize its structure. This decision was predicated primarily on the need for rapid delivery of the data within the project time line, but also on the acknowledgment that resources for recataloging objects would always be scarce.

Museum participants agreed to provide four levels associated with an object:

1. *Credit or Identifier Data.* The minimum data, probably the museum name and accession number, that must appear when an image was displayed.
2. *Label Data.* Defined by the individual museum, this included elements such as title, creator, date, object type, and collection (if necessary), which the museum normally included on a label and which suppliers felt needed to be available in every application.
3. *Fielded Data.* The most common or important fields in art and culture museums, estimated at from 20 to 40 in number, that would provide access points to the images.
4. *Supporting Documents.* A combination of structured and unstructured documents available in electronic form. These documents might include additional textual data such as exhibition, publication, and ownership histories extracted from structured databases, or free text and prose drawn from exhibition catalogs and wall labels. Supporting documents might also include documents in formats such as sound or moving images. Although not required to do so, museums were encouraged to supply supporting documents, which were viewed as a rich source of documentation, particularly for use in university research and graduate programs.

Reflecting museums' concerns about proper identification of their images, early discussions focused on minimal identifier and label data that was required to appear in every display or be readily available in every application.

By April 1, 1995, David Bearman and Robin Dowden, cochairs of the Documentation Working Group, drafted the first MESL data dictionary. The data elements were defined by the MESL content providers, each of whom had the opportunity to respond to a series of drafts ensuring that their data could be mapped into the structure as fully as possible. The first data dictionary included 28 fields and simple definitions; the number of fields expanded to 32 by the time of the first distribution in July 1995 (see Appendix C).[1] The fields were grouped into major categories, including object identification, object description, credit information, image file names, unstructured text file names, image capture information, and version identification.

The MESL documentation framework stipulated that each object be represented by at least one image and a structured data record. Multiple images and unstructured documents could also represent the object, but were not required. All cataloging would be object level (not collection level).

It was agreed that if a museum had no structured data mappable to a specific field, the field would be present but empty in its records. All fields were of unlimited length, although some, such as names and dates, were recognized as obviously limited in reality. In some cases the dictionary provided format recommendations. For example, it was suggested that the terms describing material or medium should be those found in the *Art & Architecture Thesaurus* (AAT) and be expressed in lowercase. However, since the use of existing data was a basic premise of the project, such recommendations were not binding.

During the delivery cycle, each museum was responsible for exporting its existing information into a delimited ASCII file in which the field delimiter, the internal delimiter for repeating values within a field, and the end-of-record delimiter would be defined and declared by the museum. Structured data was to be distributed without field labels, in the order described in the data dictionary. With each distribution, content providers were asked to supply maps of their files to the data dictionary, including the total number of records, in order to verify the success of an upload.

University participants were expected to mount the structured data and images in a DBMS, searchable from the campus network, and to provide access to the accompanying structured or unstructured documents either as text components of those records or as linked additional records.

"Prior to MESL, the National Museum of American Art had taken some strategic directions to prepare and move rapidly into the digital age. MESL reinforced these decisions . . . MESL underscored the absolute necessity of better management and integration of images, texts, and databases if we are to be responsive to future projects that call upon these assets."

RACHEL ALLEN
NMAA
Technical Report

▶ Problems and Resolutions

The MESL project's makeshift data interchange methods allowed for a quick transfer of data from content providers to universities. However, when the first data set was mounted, universities reported difficulties in two general areas: structural integrity problems and inconsistent field values.

Structural problems in the data sets included records for which there were no associated images, noncompliance with the data dictionary in terms of field definitions and positions, missing data in fields where required values were assumed, the use of different character sets to render data, and the selection of a wide variety of field and record delimiters that were not always unique to their declared use within a file. One institution, whose works were not attributable to individual artists, omitted creator names and object titles. In another case, the creator/maker was also omitted, but not by design. Not detected by the content provider, this oversight was variously interpreted by the universities as either a failure in the local import procedures or a purposeful omission.

On the other hand, inconsistent field values highlighted the absence of standards for the description of museum collections. Artists' names, object types, place names and regional designations, materials, and mediums all appeared in a number of variant forms. For example, the Spanish painter Goya was referred to in the two of the museums' data sets by his full name *Goya y Lucientes, Francisco José de*, whereas a third museum used the familiar form *Goya, Francisco de.*

John Weise from the University of Michigan reported that the "biggest barrier to putting museum data to use was the inconsistency in the structure of the data. The occasional record with a missing field and the misplaced/misused delimiter were the most common troublespots." Michigan, the central distribution point for the MESL data, created a number of tools for checking the integrity of the data structures and made them available to the museums. Nevertheless, the Documentation and Distribution Working Group concluded that more stringent guidelines and tools alone would not correct the basic data deficiencies and inconsistencies. As aptly stated in an e-mail from John Weise, "[F]or museums to benefit in the long run, they need to work within their systems to discover methods of quality control that address the identified problems."

Before the second distribution of MESL data, many of the data integrity problems were addressed by revising the data dictionary to include expanded field definitions, entry rules, and the declaration of required fields. At the December 1995 meeting, many museums admitted problems in mapping their data to fit the MESL-defined data categories. The group felt that better documentation, including real examples of correct usage from the first distribution, would do a great deal to clarify the structure. (This expanded data dictionary is included in this publication as Appendix C.) The participants also decided to adopt the ISO Latin 1 character set and a standard set of field and record delimiters for future distributions.[2] In addition, the University of Michigan, which had acted as the central distributor during the first phase of data gathering and distribution, agreed to assume authenticating responsibilities. It was suggested that the model of a central authenticator—i.e., a body responsible for verifying the structural integrity of the data file—was a better fit with reality and would scale better in any future solution. It also provided a reimbursement framework for the distribution function; ultimately providers would pay authenticators for whatever intervention was required.

Beyond difficulties with the structure of the data set, universities also noted problems with the consistency of data values. Unfortunately, a full investigation of this issue was beyond the scope of the MESL project. A typical university perspective was that of Beth Sandore from the University of Illinois, who requested clarification of the term "anonymous" in the creator/maker field: "It would help to have consistent usage of this term across institutions. Also, it would help for retrieval purposes if museums could indicate in the subject or another field the genre/period of art, so that we could retrieve on, for example, 'anonymous' and '19th century American.'" Indeed, three of the seven museums never furnished style/period data, and the field was used only occasionally by one other.

Similarly, subject access, which was often mentioned as the most desirable index for university implementers, was omitted by one institution, and terminology was otherwise applied inconsistently across institutions. For example, views of American farms can be found in the MESL data by searching on some combination of the following terms:

Agriculture
Farm
Farmers and Farming
Landscape–farm
Landscape–Kentucky–Cumberland Gap
Plantations and planters
Topographical, United States
United States% (where % is a wildcard)

"It's interesting to look back at when we first started and the project was all technology driven . . . In the future it would be interesting to divorce technology a bit. It's out here, we know it's available, we know it works, you can do whatever you want with it. So now what do we want to do with it."

"This project obliged the museums to do what libraries normally do, which is concoct a database with pictures and words such that they can be searched in some way. It may not be interpretive in the same way as an online exhibition, but we believe that a research database is extremely educational . . . "

Carl Fleischauer
Library of Congress
Participants' Meeting

▶ Conclusions

The fields selected for the MESL data dictionary were based on our understanding of the most important and common fields used to describe art and cultural heritage collections. Although all content providers had the opportunity to participate in defining the dictionary, in reality the dictionary reflected neither a close examination of the participants' databases nor particular knowledge of end-user applications.

The majority of the MESL content providers found mapping existing collections data to the project's data dictionary time consuming and complex. In the project's evaluation reports, each museum reported that some type of special programming was required to prepare the MESL textual data. Those institutions capable of writing special export routines had the least amount of difficulty and the greatest rate of success in converting their data. For others, forced to work with existing report generators, the process was time consuming and often entailed importing records into word processing programs, then extensively reworking the data with a variety of macros and search-and-replace operations.

Examination of Appendix D, "Chart of MESL Field Usage," suggests that content providers had databases much less complex than the MESL data structure. To properly populate the dictionary, institutions reported the need to repeat and/or parse single data values into multiple MESL fields and alternately concatenate multiple values for a single MESL field. Having no data to fill a field was the only reported reason for leaving fields blank.

From the outset, the MESL participants recognized the value of external authority files, both as a means of normalizing data on the collection level and as a method of term expansion in university retrieval systems. Nevertheless, only three of the seven museums reported using external authorities to govern data values, and all three implementations appear to be ad hoc relationships to standards rather than methodical governing of data values. The Getty Information Institute provided the MESL participants with copies of the *Union List of Artist Names* (ULAN) and the AAT, but the reality of getting systems up and running quickly prevented integrating such tools in the query interfaces (it could be noted that the ULAN could have solved the Goya problem mentioned above).

The two-year MESL project has concluded without a quantifiable means of measuring the value of MESL data elements. Nonetheless, we observe that repurposing collections management data into public access data underlines the essential differences between the two. For example, subject access, which seems to be of great importance to universities, is an unequal (low) priority in museum collections management systems. On the other hand, acquisition method was included because it was a common element in the museum systems, but its value to a university is unclear.

In the technical report for the Fowler Museum of Cultural History, Don McClelland posited that a simple, nonrigid structure for the exchange of information would make the transfer of data from a variety of provider institutions easier and would yield more accurate results. Except for the fixed-content fields identifying the data agreement number, holding institution, and version identifier, he suggested that the following test might be applied in specifying fields:

> (1) Is the field likely to be searched? (2) Would searches be substantially more efficient (fewer misses and false hits) if the information were in a separate field rather than a combined or free-text field? (3) Are fields independent, i.e., can all information from most source databases be mapped unambiguously into the target database? (4) Is the field necessary to the overall construction of the database and the linking of its components (e.g., "Accession Number" and "Accompanying Image" and "Accompanying Document" fields)?

In a similar vein, Carl Fleischhauer, reporting on behalf of the Library of Congress, stated:

> The transformation process required detailed knowledge of the specific collection's data characteristics. The Library finds that such detailed data mapping would not be affordable with multiple diverse collections. MESL's goal of helping users by presenting data from diverse sources in a uniform appearance is admirable but, for the Library, the cost of data conversion was high, even when learning curve aspects are discounted. If this type of activity is to continue in the future, the organizers should consider protocols like Z39.50 that "map" data displays on the fly. There is also little incentive for a library with MARC format records to convert data that is already distributed through numerous library networks.

While the preceding arguments are worth considering, the fact is that nothing in the MESL experience supports either the highly granular or the simpler representation of collections data. As previously noted, specificity of the data dictionary was in part a result of not knowing university application requirements, which could only begin to be understood at the close of the experiment. What we can conclude is that future projects will continue to depend upon existing data, and that the development of relatively flexible and simple systems for mapping data into interchange formats will be a requirement if these endeavors are to be successful.

▶ Notes

1. The Data Dictionary included as Appendix C is the expanded version, revised prior to the second MESL distribution cycle. The list of fields remained the same across both distributions, but expanded definitions and examples were added.

2. The decisions of the group were posted to the Working Group's Current Activities Web page at *http://mesl.itd.umich.edu:800/~docdistr/distrguide_0396.html*, making them readily accessible to the project teams. In addition, the University of Michigan created an elaborate table in which to report status and problems for the second MESL distribution (*http://mesl.itd.umich.edu:800/~docdistr/d2status.html*).

Digital Image Production Issues

CHRISTIE STEPHENSON

While MESL was a project about shared access to and delivery of digital images, the project's findings with respect to the images themselves reflect the uncertainty of operating in an environment of rapid technological change, as well as the lack of one-size-fits-all solutions. However, we are able to describe our decisions and practice, make some broad recommendations, and note issues for future discussion and research.

MESL museum participants operated within loose guidelines for image production, as they had with text data. One of the fundamental tenets of the experiment was that museums might create digital images for a variety of internal purposes (publications, CD-ROM), not specifically for networked delivery. We wanted to learn whether or not these diverse types of images could be repurposed for networked delivery. Would the images delivered be of high enough quality to meet the needs of teaching and research, classroom projection, and a scholar's close study via monitor? Would they overburden the network infrastructure, making delivery so time consuming as to discourage use? Would the museums learn enough from this experiment to ensure that future imaging projects could be designed to meet both their internal needs and requirements for a robust delivery environment for educational applications?

▶ Image Production by the Museums

At the initial MESL meeting in February 1995, there was considerable discussion about appropriate formats and sizes for images to be distributed in the project.[1] These discussions exposed a lack of common vocabulary between the museum and university communities, a lack of standardization within either community, and a lack of specific knowledge about user needs. The group finally agreed that where images were being created specifically for the MESL project, museums would supply either the largest lossless JPEG/JFIF images they felt comfortable releasing, or PhotoCD files.

In reality, the images distributed to the universities deviated significantly from these guidelines. Most of the images supplied were 24-bit color continuous tone images, but some grayscale images and a few 8-bit GIF line drawings were supplied. Only one institution supplied images in PhotoCD format. Others supplied TIFF and JPEG/JFIF files, but the JPEG compression ratios varied widely (none were lossless). Some of the image files were derived from PhotoCD files, removing them further from the original source image and relying on a lossy compression format as an intermediate. Likewise, the size of the images varied widely. The characteristics of images supplied in the project are summarized in Table 1.

One of the reasons for the large variance in format and file size was that several institutions (e.g., NMAA, Library of Congress) had already digitized and compressed images and were simply supplying existing digital files. Others, such as the National Gallery of Art, had already created very large TIFF files and produced resized and compressed JPEG derivatives for MESL. Frequently the image capture and storage parameters had been determined by the needs of another project, such as producing an exhibition catalog or conducting an internal documentation project.

TABLE 1 Characteristics of Digital Images Distributed in the First MESL Distribution (Largest and Smallest Compressed Image Files)

Museum	File Format	Largest File	Smallest File
Fowler Museum of Cultural History	JPEG/JFIF, GIF	D1: 1472 × 999 1.43MB compressed 4.12MB uncompressed D2: 1506 × 954 1.85MB compressed 4.11MB uncompressed	D1: 1035 × 314 20K compressed 315K uncompressed D2: 187 × 470 39K compressed 258K uncompressed
George Eastman House	D1: PhotoCD D2: JPEG/JFIF	D1: 16 Base 3072 × 2048 D2: 642 × 492 429K compressed 926K uncompressed	D1: Base/16 192 × 128 D2: 183 × 353 78K compressed 190K uncompressed
Harvard University Art Museums	JPEG/JFIF	D1: 1024 × 672 819K compressed 1.97MB uncompressed D2: 988 × 768 819K compressed 2.17MB uncompressed	D1: 605 × 483 31K compressed 857K uncompressed D2: 681 × 707 98K compressed 1.38MB uncompressed
Library of Congress (all images grayscale)	JPEG/JFIF	D1: 540 × 420 39K compressed 222K uncompressed D2: 1956 × 2828 2MB compressed 5.28MB uncompressed	D1: 552 × 420 32K compressed 227K uncompressed D2: 1246 × 2565 215K compressed 3.05MB uncompressed
The Museum of Fine Arts, Houston	JPEG/JFIF	D1: 1284 × 1876 2.27MB compressed 6.89MB uncompressed D2: 1269 × 1629 1.71MB compressed 5.92MB uncompressed	D1: 608 × 1802 332K compressed 3.13MB uncompressed D2: 1081 × 1621 215K compressed 5.01MB uncompressed
National Gallery of Art (supplied three sizes of derivative images)	JPEG/JFIF	D1: 1024 × 742 546K compressed 2.17MB uncompressed D2: 952 × 767 702K compressed 2.09MB uncompressed	D1: 333 × 768 59K compressed 750K uncompressed D2: 375 × 768 78K compressed 844K uncompressed

(continued on page 58)

▶ **TABLE 1** *continued*

Museum	File Format	Largest File	Smallest File
NATIONAL MUSEUM OF AMERICAN ART	TIFF	D1: 1056 × 930 2.8MB uncompressed D2: 1050 × 857 2.58MB uncompressed	D1: 286 × 892 800K uncompressed D2: 172 × 857 432K uncompressed

For those undertaking digitizing specifically for the MESL project, the project guidelines seemed to be of little help in determining actual practice, as the learning curve was relatively high in the early months of the project. Internal staff were mastering new skill sets, and outside contractors were unable to meet project specifications.

At the outset of the project, it was apparent that not all imaging concepts and requirements were defined consistently by all participants. For example, a discussion at the first meeting revealed that there was considerable difference in interpretation of the term *high resolution.* For the universities, this meant high resolution on the screen, typically around 3MB. For the museums, high resolution meant large enough to produce a high-quality four-color print, sometimes 60MB or larger.[2]

Another example of a widespread terminology problem in digital imaging practice is reflected in how participants described their image capture process. Capture methods were to be recorded in a specified field in the data record. The list in Table 2, extracted verbatim from that field's contents, reveals an interesting variety of capture methods and demonstrates dramatically the lack of standard terminology in describing those methods.

Participants' responses to the request to record image capture method in this field reflect the relative experience of each of the participants, and highlight the need for common definitions and standards.

In their technical reports, museum participants provided more extensive information on their capture methods and noted details about their source images. In addition to employing a wide variety of capture methods, museums used a wide range of source images, ranging from direct digital capture, through scanning 8 × 10 and 4 × 5 transparencies, to digitizing from rolls of 35 mm film to PhotoCD. Presumably, the variety of source images reflects the variety of project participants' collection documentation practices. The variety of source images coupled with the broad range of capture devices employed makes it very difficult to generalize about the quality of images supplied by the project.

▶ **TABLE 2** **Capture Methods Recorded by Museums in MESL Data Records (Field 29)**

Museum	Capture Methods
GEORGE EASTMAN HOUSE	None recorded.
FOWLER MUSEUM OF CULTURAL HISTORY	■ 35 mm slide scanned onto Kodak PhotoCD (resolution 4 Base). ■ Scanned from catalog using HP IIcx flatbed scanner. ■ Scanned from drawing using HP IIcx flatbed scanner. ■ Digital photograph using Kodak DCS420 digital camera. ■ 4 × 5 transparency duplicated as 35 mm slide which was scanned onto PhotoCD. ■ Digitized image from Sony three-chip video camera.

▶ **TABLE 2** *continued*

Museum	Capture Methods
Harvard University Art Museums	■ Scanned using a Sharp JX-600 from 8 × 10 transparency. Reduced to fit within 1024 × 768. Minimal color correction. ■ Scanned using PhotoCD from 35 mm. Reduced to fit within 1024 × 768. ■ Scanned using a Pixelcraft 8000 at 300dpi from the original. Reduced to fit within 1024 × 768, minimal color correction. ■ Scanned using a Pixelcraft 8000 at 600dpi from the original. Reduced to fit within 1024 × 768, minimal color correction. ■ Scanned using a Pixelcraft 8000 at 500dpi from an 8 × 10 transparency. Reduced to fit within 1024 × 768, minimal color correction. ■ Scanned using a Pixelcraft 8000 from 8 × 10 transparency. Reduced to fit within 1024 × 768. Minimal color correction. ■ Scanned using a Polaroid Sprintscan at 2700dpi from 35 mm. Reduced to fit within 1024 × 768, minimal color correction.
The Museum of Fine Arts, Houston	■ From 35 mm slides scanned onto Kodak writable CD. ■ Scanned at 1350dpi from 35 mm slide with JPEG compression onto Kodak writable CD.
Library of Congress	■ Scanned from film intermediate, uncorrected (see also file lvvimage.txt). ■ Scanned from film copy negatives or copy color transparencies (see also file appimag.txt).[3]
National Gallery of Art	24 bit color: corrected.
National Museum of American Art	PCD->UR->TIF. Photo CD—The NMAA Way.[4]

▶ Image Delivery by the Universities

Most of the participating universities used the World Wide Web as a delivery platform for MESL images. To accommodate various presentation environments, they needed to derive several sizes of images. However, since most of the images delivered to the universities had been previously compressed with some amount of loss, those responsible for local deployment were concerned about the effects of further resizing and recompressing the images.[5]

Anecdotal reports from the universities recorded a broad range of observations about image quality. Reports came both from users and from technical teams who did local image processing to produce derivatives for Web delivery.[6] A number of problems were noted, particularly with the quality of the PhotoCD images and with variations in image brightness from museum to museum and distribution to distribution.[7]

Some university users appeared to be very satisfied with image quality overall, while others felt it was not as good as what they were used to with slides or even with other digital images. We were unable to do a complete testing of image quality for classroom projection, because in most of the universities high-tech classrooms were simply not available. In most cases, the MESL images were deployed in the form of Web pages developed for individual courses and viewed on monitors outside of class rather than projected in class.

▸ Findings and Recommendations

What did we learn about imaging practice in the course of the MESL project? Our experiences with terminology reinforced the awareness that we need to be precise in expressing practice and procedure in an area as complex as this one. Standard ways of expressing notions of resolution and compression/quality relationships need to be established and reinforced. The community has long been recommending the development of standard ways of recording metadata about image capture and image processing.[8] Our experience, reflected in the range of capture methods recorded in the MESL data, certainly underscores this need.

"I think the project is, and was, worthwhile, but for slightly different reasons than we expected. From my point of view, the opportunity to think through various issues with like-minded people was stimulating and rewarding. The real-world experience of trying to implement the plans was a concrete reminder and painful eye-opener of both the necessity and current inadequacy of standardized procedures and common standards for image processing, distributed information sharing, and robust information retrieval."

STEVE DIETZ
NMAA
Technical Report

As long as derivative images are being produced at various points along the delivery chain, the original images delivered to a central distributor or a delivery point should probably be lossless compressed or uncompressed TIFF files, which will place quality/compression decisions in the hands of those charged with local delivery. In the future, this issue may become less critical, as software will probably emerge that can zoom or resize on demand or by using knowledge of the characteristics of the user's display device. But for now, there are too many opportunities for uncontrolled loss of quality along the delivery chain.

Because there have been few studies of image quality needs (Ester 1990, 1994)[9], it is difficult to make strong recommendations in this area. For now, most designers of delivery systems select standard image sizes for their derivatives based primarily on dimensions of display devices or screen "real estate" within standard Web browsers, trying to strive for some balance between dimensions, quality, and file size/compression. Also, there is little we can say conclusively about the relationship between image production specifications and user satisfaction. While there are anecdotal reports of both satisfaction and dissatisfaction with image quality, so many variables are involved that it is impossible to draw conclusions or make clear recommendations. A sophisticated study that could isolate the variables—including source image, image size, post-processing, and the requirements of the end user—might prove useful. But it is likely that, in the foreseeable future, image creation parameters will frequently be determined on a specific project basis, based on internal priorities, available resources, the nature of the originals and film intermediates, and the like.

It is unclear whether articulating any absolute guidelines for producing digital images is possible. What *is* possible is the articulation of a sound project planning framework and guidelines developed for particular types of originals and surrogates, digitized for specific uses and users. Although institutions new to digital imaging are still clamoring for absolute standards, those with more experience can say that, at best, guidelines must be driven by project priorities and the nature of the source images. Each institution must be guided by its own needs and make the best informed decisions, while recognizing that it is aiming at a moving target. The experience of the MESL project did not contradict this operating premise, nor did it further elucidate absolute requirements for image quality on the part of educational users.

▸ Notes

1. This section is based in part on the author's previous work with Howard Besser, "The Museum Educational Site Licensing Project: Technical Issues in the Distribution of Museum Images and Textual Data to Universities," in James Hemsley (ed.) *EVA '96 Electronic Imaging and the Visual Arts,* Hampshire, UK: Vasari Ltd., 1996: 5-1–5-15.

2. MESL Participants' Meeting Minutes, February 8, 1995, Day 2 *(http://www.ahip.getty.edu/mesl/about/docs/mtgs/9512day2.html).*

3. These two files were distributed with each of the Library of Congress data sets and include detailed information on the source images and scanning specifications.

4. The NMAA's digitizing process, "Image Preparation the NMAA Way" is described on its Web site at *http://nmaa-ryder.si.edu/deptdir/pubsub/thenmaaway.html.*

5. University decisions on image deployment are treated more fully in Howard Besser's article, "MESL Implementation at the Universities," pp. 70–84.

6. For a fuller treatment of image quality as reported by the universities, see Howard Besser's article, "MESL Implementation at the Universities," pp. 70–84.

7. Calibration technologies and standards for computer displays vary significantly from platform to platform, and each display station may be affected by user adjustments to the display and ambient light. If an image appears too light or too dark on a particular display, it does not necessarily indicate suboptimal image quality, but most likely that the image was calibrated for an output device other than that being used.

8. See, for example, Howard Besser's article, "Image Standards Needed" prepared for the Napa CIMI Meeting at *http://sunsite.berkeley.edu/imaging/Databases/Standards/napa.html* and Jennifer Trant's article "Framing the Picture: Standards for Imaging Systems" at *http://www.archimuse.com/papers/jt.ichim/ichim.1.intro.html.* This kind of information has come to be referred to as "administrative metadata."

9. Michael Ester, "Image Quality and Viewer Perception," *Leonardo* 23, no. 1 (1990): 51. Michael Ester, "Digital Images in the Context of Visual Collections and Scholarship," *Visual Resources* 10, no. 1 (1994): 11.

The MESL Distribution Process

CHRISTIE STEPHENSON AND CLIFFORD LYNCH

The distribution of images and associated textual data in the MESL project took place using methods dictated by the project's experimental and short-term nature.[1] Yet many of the lessons learned in the MESL distribution process can inform future projects. The MESL distribution experience also raised some complex issues that could not be fully addressed owing to the short-term nature of the project. This article describes the iterative process of MESL distribution, the issues it raised, and the lessons learned. It also speculates on possible models for future distribution and some of the issues that the MESL experience suggests might need to be addressed.[2]

▶ Early Decisions

At the initial MESL participants' meeting, Clifford Lynch addressed the group on a variety of possible distribution methods that could be adopted to move the project data from the museums to the universities. The minutes state:

> Lynch noted that essentially there are two possible distribution models: either each of the 6 content providers can distribute to each of the 13 recipient institutions or we have a central distribution coordinated by one entity, which would require a volunteer. This would also centralize some data normalization and quality validation efforts. Lynch also identified two models for how distribution takes place: push or pull. Providers either distribute data or the users collect it. Noting that moving gigabytes by network is a production headache, Lynch proposed that it would be better to move things in small chunks more often and/or distribute on fixed media by Federal Express.[3]

Lynch also noted two other points: The approach taken in the MESL project needed to solve a short-term problem, and thus did not need to be scaleable or sustainable in the long term; the most important thing was to come up with a model that shipped material out to the recipients as quickly and easily as possible. Also, the nature of the MESL experiment was that every recipient would get access to all the material; selection was part of the negotiation between content providers and content users as to what materials would be made available, rather than having users select from an existing corpus of digitized content. This participatory process would likely be infeasible in a very-large-scale production image distribution framework.

At that meeting, the breakout group discussing distribution issues reluctantly recommended the all-to-all method to divide the cost of distribution across all participants. However, a small group of individuals convened over lunch to press for a more centralized solution. Project management agreed to seek support from the Getty Information Institute for a single institution to serve as a central distributor for the project. The University of Michigan offered to provide this service at cost.[4]

As with other aspects of MESL collective decision making, expediency was a factor in the distribution decisions. Less than six months were to pass between the first meeting and the beginning of the first semester, when faculty were expecting to be able to teach with MESL images.

▶ The First MESL Distribution

According to the project schedule, the first distribution of MESL data was to take place by July 31, 1995. Michigan did not merge the data sets of the contributing museums—they were received in batches (structured text, images, unstructured text) from each museum and redistributed in the same batches, by institution. Three batches of text and image data were delivered to the universities in early August, three more in late August, and the final batch in September. The delays were largely attributable to difficulties the museums had in producing the data according to project specifications, as well as the fact that Michigan had to invent the procedures and tools to enable distribution as it went along.

In the first distribution, the role of the University of Michigan "Distribution Central" unit was to receive the data, then copy and redistribute it. Because the data was simultaneously being processed to be served on Michigan's own campus network, some basic checking was performed that made it possible to identify and resolve some problems before distribution to the other campuses. Data was received using a variety of methods and physical formats and redistributed entirely on writable CDs that included the images, structured data, and unstructured data.[5] The first distribution can, therefore, be characterized as employing the "push" method of data distribution. Twelve CDs—roughly 6 GB of content—were delivered to each of the MESL participants. A total of 442 hours of staff time at Michigan was devoted to the first distribution.

The following table summarizes the types of problems identified in the first MESL data distribution.[6] In addition, there were character set inconsistencies across the data sets provided by the various museums.

▶ TABLE 1 Problems Identified in First MESL Data Distribution

	Type of Problem	Number of Occurrences
Structured Data	Extra field	492
	Missing field	3
	Delimiter in content	26
	Missing delimiter	3
Image Files	Misreferenced image file	122
	Missing image file	22
	Misnamed image file	1

Michigan's report on the first distribution provided the participants with important insights into the data-checking process:

1. Problems with data structure halt the checking process. Data can only be parsed until the point at which the first structural problem is encountered. It is difficult to proceed until the problem is resolved. This is characteristic of first-generation data validation tools that are developed with little experience in the specifics of data format problems.

2. Troubleshooting the source and extent of a data structure problem can be complicated and time consuming.

Numerous anomalies in the data were also discovered and reported by the universities when they parsed the data for local mounting. Managing all of the many problems reported presented difficulties for each of the implementing sites, which were trying to do fixes on the data while also trying to refine delivery systems and support adoption of the content by end users.

▸ Planning for the Second Distribution

The problems encountered in the first data distribution resulted in the adoption of certain accords by the MESL participants before the second distribution. These accords centered on the structured text records, since these were the source of the majority of problems in the first distribution (though it is also worth noting that the text records were validated more extensively than the image files). At the suggestion of the Distribution Working Group, structured data distributed in the second round used a standard set of delimiters to indicate repeating fields, end of field, and end of record. The participants also decided to adopt the standard ISO Latin 1 character set to avoid the character-set problems encountered in the first distribution. The full record of instructions to content providers for the second distribution was made available on the project Web site at *http://mesl.itd.umich.edu:800/~docdistr/distrguide_0396.html.*

▸ The Second MESL Distribution

The target date for distribution of the second round of MESL data was June 15, 1996. The second full distribution actually began on June 26, 1996, with data from four of the content providers made available to the universities via file transfer protocol (FTP), with the remainder available by August 8, 1996 ("pull" method of data distribution). The first batch of CDs was shipped on July 5, 1996. Additional CDs of images were shipped August 28, 1996. This meant once again that university project teams were processing images under pressure at the beginning of the fall semester. There was a complete redistribution of data from the George Eastman House in November 1996. The last problem report from the second distribution, with an appropriate fix, was communicated on April 27, 1997.

The combination of pull and push distribution techniques used in the second distribution seemed most effective. Text files could be retrieved from the Michigan FTP server when a deploying university was ready to process them locally, ensuring that it was getting the latest version of the text data. Push distribution of images via CDs continued to be effective owing to the size and number of files. However, the pull method was useful to redistribute single images that were found to be corrupted in the initial mass distribution.

In the second distribution, the Michigan group employed more sophisticated data validation tools that included checking both the integrity of the structured data records and compliance with the group accords about delimiters and character sets. In addition, they developed a Web page (*http://mesl.itd.umich.edu:800/~docdistr/d2status.html*) that reported on the availability of data and presented a chronological list of problems and resultant fixes. This made tracking of errors much less difficult for the universities than it had been in the first distribution, where all errors were reported by e-mail. The Web site provided a single reference source for checking on the status of various problems.

Despite the additional effort, a certain number of problems slipped through the cracks. A few corrupted images were discovered by the deploying institutions, as Michigan did not open and examine all images, but simply copied image data onto the distribution CDs. In addition, there was a problem with the data from the George Eastman House, where inappropriate data had been exported into the subject field. Since this was a data content issue, not a data structure issue, the Michigan structural check had not caught the problem.[7]

The cost of the second distribution was much less than the first, with salary costs dropping by approximately 50 percent and other costs dropping significantly as well. These savings were realized in spite of the fact that twice as much metadata was checked and delivered, character set checking was added to the process, and one museum redistributed all 1995 images in addition to new 1996 images.[8] Staff time at Michigan for the second distribution totaled 258 hours, as opposed to 442 for the first. The decline was attributed to the following:

1. Processes were already established.
2. Both export and validation software programs were maturing rapidly.
3. Museums were experienced and better able to handle data preparation.
4. Hardware was in place (FTP server, disk space).
5. People knew what to expect.
6. CD-ROM preparation, duplication, and shipping took much less time (familiar routines, and no PhotoCDs were produced).[9]

The evolution in Michigan's processing procedures and tools between the first and second distributions is striking; unfortunately, the limited duration of the MESL project meant that we would be unable to reach a steady state, where we could observe the costs of a production data validation and redistribution process that was dealing only with relatively "routine" problems.

The following table summarizes the types of problems identified in the second MESL data distribution. Problems were recorded and counted differently for each distribution, making comparison difficult, but the number of problems was significantly reduced in the second distribution.[10]

▶ **TABLE 2 Problems Identified in Second MESL Data Distribution**

Type of Problem	Number of Occurrences
Content	5
Delimiter	19
Case of associated file names	1
Accession number error	1
Missing or misnamed text files	2
Character set	3
Missing or misnamed image files	10
Corrupt image files	3
FTP	3
Readme file incomplete or missing	2

▶ Lessons Learned, Issues Raised

Some of the problems raised in the MESL data distribution were addressed during the course of the project itself. These included the adoption of standard delimiters and a standard character set. The project experience also indicated that the process of data export is more difficult for some museums than for others and that all the museums would benefit from simple tools that would allow them to view and examine their exported data before shipment to the distributor. At the December 1996 meeting, John Weise suggested that the museums might consider developing export routines to move data into simple, widely available desktop database programs such as Microsoft Access or Claris FilemakerPro. This would allow the content providers to have a simple window into their data to do further examination and checking. Solutions such as this would facilitate processing, allow the museums to have a better understanding of the structure and content of the data they are exporting, and ultimately lower costs for both export and distribution.

Project experience also indicated that the process of data export and distribution took longer than expected. Although there was some improvement between round one and round two, it was still difficult for the universities to mount the data locally in time for fall semester delivery to end users.

One difficult issue raised by the MESL experience is that of how to handle updates and changes to data, including changes to structured records, additions to unstructured texts, and availability of replacement images. In general, it was easier for the deployers to replace an entire data set than to try to make changes to individual records as problems were identified. Replacing entire data sets allowed them to use established processing routines and scripts rather than develop new ones—hence the decision to completely redistribute the first round of structured data as part of the second MESL distribution.

Finally, we confirmed that it is not feasible to deliver large numbers of very big files via FTP. It is slow, unreliable, and can result in file corruption. This was true even for university participants who enjoyed comparatively good network connectivity and local infrastructure.

▶ Speculation about Future Distribution Models

The approach taken in the MESL project was pragmatic—it was intended to minimize collective effort among the content providers and users within a short-term framework and a limited number of participants. This approach took into account the historical lack of standards and standardized local systems in the museum community, the lack of tools and infrastructure, and the varying capabilities of the participating institutions.

As we consider the future beyond the MESL project, it is possible to make a number of observations based on the MESL experience. First, it is important to recognize that the technical and operational issues involved in content distribution can be separated from the current debate about how to manage rights and licensing for cultural heritage content. No matter what solution eventually emerges for licensing and related business issues, there will still be a need for content providers to deliver material to content users. The economics and technical issues in distribution need to be considered separately from the licensing arrangements; any number of licensing organizations could reasonably subcontract delivery to one or more appropriate distribution services.

Second, it is important to recognize that, in the longer term, not every consumer organization is going to want to or have the right to receive everything that the content provider community can supply. Rather, it is likely that consumer organizations will want to acquire materials selectively. This means that the consumer organizations will want to view the corpus of available materials as a database, select materials from this database (in conjunction with the negotiation of license agreements), then access only those selected materials.

The third issue is scaleability. There will be many content providers and many consumers. Distribution services will need to be structured to work in this environment. And, as the MESL experience has already suggested, there is a real economic value to knowing that data has been validated and that it is in a standardized format. Business models that recognize the value of these services will have to be developed.

The limitations of the current Internet were a very real consideration in planning content distribution for the MESL project. It is hard to guess when it will be feasible to move tens of gigabytes of content quickly and reliably. Internet 2 may change this equation in the next eighteen months, at least for some institutions—but it is important to recognize that few museums will have direct connectivity to Internet 2 (though a central redistribution service might well obtain such connectivity). Until this problem is solved, a major component of distribution will involve the manual shipping, receiving, and processing of media. It is also worth noting that as the number of consumer institutions grows, pragmatic issues, such as scheduling file transfers so as not to overwhelm the distribution points when new content is available, will need to be addressed.

Finally, the MESL data distributions attempted to be closely tied to the rhythm of the academic calendar. This is not going to make sense in the long run; rather, we need to think in terms of ongoing contributions to the corpus by content providers and ongoing delivery to the content consumers. Certainly, activities on the consumer side will still reflect the timings implicit in the academic calendar, but it is unreasonable to expect that activities on the content provider side will be driven by this schedule. The MESL data distributions also minimized the amount of synchronization needed between providers and consumers as new content or corrections to already distributed content became available. As the distribution system scales up, effective synchronization and schedule coordination will become an increasing problem.

It is clear that more attention needs to be paid to standards for data interchange and to tools that support these standards. Local museum collections management systems will need to support export standards. We will need tools deployed throughout the community—which will be used by content providers, content consumers, and intermediaries—to validate and help with problem diagnosis for data streams. Unless there is some central redistribution agency that has a vested interest in making these tools available to the whole community, it is not clear from where the incentives to produce and distribute them will come.

We believe that the MESL experience demonstrates the real value of data redistribution points, as opposed to having each consumer receive a direct feed from each content provider. There is a clear economic value in this. It is interesting to note that similar models have served the bibliographic community well in the distribution and use of bibliographic records, for example. However, it is also interesting to note that in the scholarly publishing community, the model has now shifted to publisher-managed sites rather than local mounting of electronic versions of scholarly journals. In large measure, this reflects problems with standards and the ability of local systems at consumer institutions to process large numbers of data streams from publishers. We need to consider the possibility that the marketplace for museum information will ultimately restructure along the same lines, with consumer institutions accessing museum Web sites (or Web sites maintained under contract to the museums) remotely, thus avoiding many of the standards issues involved with directly importing content into the consumer organizations. Assessing the likelihood of this change, given that cultural heritage images and related metadata are used in very different ways in the context of instruction and research from scholarly journals, will be an important consideration in understanding the possible futures.

"Library of Congress joined this project in order to learn more about copyright and related legal issues. Influenced by MESL, staff have learned a lot about site licensing and will continue to do so, building on MESL. There was another area that a follow-on project might develop further: how the data was compiled and distributed. We found it awkward to fit our cataloging into the MESL project's format, and the compilation was probably more labor-intensive than it should have been."

CARL FLEISCHAUER
LIBRARY OF CONGRESS
Participants' Meeting

Looking ahead, one of the key questions is whether there will be one—or perhaps a small number—of validation and distribution services, or whether we will evolve into a model in which consumer sites either contract to receive data feeds from content providers, or simply to have access to materials mounted directly by the content providers. The ability to connect suppliers and consumers directly is predicated on a very rigorous implementation of standards, which experience shows is best accomplished when a limited number of vendors dominate the marketplace. Achieving this level of interoperability among a large number of locally developed transmitting and receiving systems is almost impossible—it simply does not scale well. Similarly, it seems unlikely that most content providers will be prepared to deal with the operational problems of direct mounting of content for end users at the licensing institutions in the near future; certainly, within the MESL context, this seemed to be a major barrier. The cash flows that are allowing the scientific, technical, and medical publishers to move into this role do not seem to be present in the museum community. All of this suggests that redistribution services will continue to play a key role in the dissemination of museum content, at least for the next few years.

In summary, for the next few years, and perhaps longer, there will be a compelling marketplace need for at least one or more organizations to fill a role similar to that which the University of Michigan played in the MESL project, almost independent of how the marketplace for licensing materials evolves. These centralized distribution agencies will have some important differences from Michigan's operating role; for example, they will probably distribute specific subsets of the available corpus upon demand to consumer institutions (subject to the negotiation of appropriate licensing agreements, of course) rather than distributing everything to everybody. The redistribution organizations will need to be more flexible about receiving updates, as opposed to complete replacements, from content providers, although complete replacement may continue to be a viable interface to content providers for the near future. As a consequence, the redistribution organization will become much more involved in notifying consumers when new materials become available and synchronizing activities between providers and consumers. They will take on some characteristics of a brand name—for example, "data validated and supplied by . . . " will have a real value and a real marketplace significance. They will become arbiters of adherence to standards; the MESL experience has already illustrated the tangible market value of such a function. And, for the near future, it is likely that distribution will continue to be based on a mixture of file transfer and physical shipment of media.

▸ Notes

1. Within the MESL project, distribution was narrowly defined to include only the process of data transfer from the content providers (the museums) to the content deployers (the universities). It did not include delivery of data to end users.

2. This report relies heavily on the distribution reports prepared by John Weise and his team at the University of Michigan. The authors would like to acknowledge their contribution.

3. MESL Participants' Meeting Minutes, February 7–9, 1995, Day 2 (*http://www.ahip.getty.edu/mesl/about/docs/mtgs/9502day2.html*).

4. "The principal barrier, it seems, had been whether this effort could be paid for by the project, not whether it was a better idea." MESL Participants' Meeting Minutes, February 7–9, 1995, Day 3 (*http://www.ahip.getty.edu/mesl/about/docs/mtgs/9502day3.html*)

5. Michigan experienced some problems with several of the tape formats used to transmit data in the first distribution, and was forced to locate both hardware and software to read them.

6. Extracted from detailed report on Distribution 1 prepared by the University of Michigan, April 1996.

7. This problem was reported in October 1996 by the University of Illinois, and a fix (redistribution of all GEH data) was posted on November 1, 1996.

8. All first distribution structured data was redistributed in the second distribution, ensuring that it conformed to the new rules governing delimiters and character sets.

9. MESL Participants' Meeting Minutes, December 9–11, 1996, Day 1 (*http://www.ahip.getty.edu/mesl/about/docs/mtgs/9612day1.html*)

10. Extracted from detailed report on distribution prepared by the University of Michigan, November/December 1996.

MESL Implementation at the Universities

HOWARD BESSER

All seven MESL universities mounted the identical set of approximately 10,000 images and accompanying text records on their campus servers—each in their own way. These implementations varied widely, with each university making different choices as to the search options, the indexed fields, the display choices, and the overall look-and-feel of the access systems. Methods for defining and implementing access control, authentication, and the choice of text fields that displayed with an image differed not just from one university to another, but even within some universities over time.

This article reviews the steps the universities took to process and mount the MESL images and data and examines the different deployment systems utilized, primarily from the viewpoint of a user's interactive experience. It also speculates on the reasons the implementations differed from one another, including the lack of standard practices and procedures, the varying goals and models of the implementers, and the effects of particular software decisions. Lastly, the article presents the issues surrounding access control, as well as the role of technological change in areas like authentication.

▸ University Deployment : Early Decisions

From the beginning, the MESL Management Committee encouraged the universities to pursue independent solutions when they deployed the MESL images and data. Many of the universities had joined the MESL project hoping to experiment with ways to integrate image delivery with their existing text-based information delivery systems. This fact, coupled with the short lead time, precluded the development of a single deployment solution across all sites.[1]

The seven independently developed deployment systems that emerged allowed us to compare them and begin to investigate the effects local implementation decisions had on search results.

▸ Receiving the Data

During each of the two main MESL content distributions, the Michigan central distribution site received batches of images and text from the museums and forwarded these on to each university. This section briefly describes the variety of different processes and issues each university faced in preparing this data to load into its local information delivery system.

Processing of Text

In most cases, the universities took the flat delimited text files they received and used a variety of application tools (e.g., Perl scripts, Microsoft Excel, Claris FilemakerPro, Microsoft

Access) to parse (or separate) the data, create HTML pages for each record, and load the data into a database for user retrieval. The exception was the University of Virginia, which used Perl scripts to create records from the MESL data in pseudo-SGML format, and then ran real-time database queries against this stored data (using Open Text) and generated HTML pages from it on the fly.

During the first distribution, the universities had significant problems parsing and loading the text data. Among the reasons cited were:

1. Some records did not have all the prescribed fields present.
2. Some fields were not properly delimited.
3. Museums did not all use the same set of delimiters.
4. Some records had line feeds embedded in them.
5. Museums used different character sets for their text records.

Many of these problems disappeared in the second distribution, as the MESL participants agreed on more extensive specifications and standardized practices with respect to delimiters and character sets.

The MESL experience made it clear that the specifications for data export must be extremely precise. This pilot study involving a heterogeneous pool of institutions revealed numerous divergent practices of the participating institutions that were not taken into consideration in establishing the initial specifications. Over the course of the project, MESL participants developed a set of standard specifications intended to be precise enough to assure consistent data structure. However, future projects will have to tackle the even more difficult problems associated with normalizing data values to improve retrieval (see the article by Robin Dowden titled "The MESL Data Dictionary and the Data Export Process," page 50).

"The problems we faced with MESL were overwhelmingly technical: how to clean up the data; how to manipulate and store image collections; how to make the data and images available via the Web; and how to structure the data and images to be of greatest use to faculty and students."

CORNELL UNIVERSITY
Technical Report

Image Processing

Most university sites based their user interface and general design decisions on the particular image sizes and/or other visual qualities. Some sites already had an investment in a particular size of image, based on experience and development in previous projects. During the MESL project, instructors expressed concerns about image size, such as: that the images be big enough for classroom projection; that they be as big as possible, yet fit on the "average" screen without scrolling; that they fit within a specific application without scrolling, etc.

None of the implementations had software in place to support the generation of smaller derivative images on the fly.[2] Therefore, when the images were received from the central distribution site, each university generated several sizes of derivative images (thumbnail, large image, and often intermediate ones) as a part of designing their deployment systems. Applications like Debabelizer and ImageMagick made this process relatively simple to accomplish (completely unattended) in batch mode.

However, many of the MESL images had been previously compressed by the museums in such a way (using lossy compression) that it was necessary to uncompress the files, reduce or resize the images, and then recompress the files so they could be deployed in a particular information environment supported by the university. As suggested elsewhere (Besser and Stephenson 1996), in future distribution schemes, content suppliers could provide uncompressed images to a central distribution site, where both image derivation and lossy compression could be performed. As a result, the duplication of effort by the entire set of deploying institutions could be eliminated, as well as the problems of multiple lossy compressions. For this strategy to be effective, all of the deploying sites would need to agree upon common specifications for image sizes, bit depth, and compression ratios.

Table 1 illustrates how image sizes varied widely among the different deployment sites, even among well-recognized "sizes" such as thumbnails.[3] Though most sites deployed compressed images, an accurate comparison of compression ratios or quality is inhibited by the lack of a standard scale for measuring these.[4]

▶ **TABLE 1 Image Sizes and Formats Delivered at Each Site**

	Screen Size			
University	**Thumbnail**	**Medium**	**Large**	**Other**
American University	small: 50 × 50 JPEG/JFIF large: 200 pixels high JPEG/JFIF	400 pixels high JPEG/JFIF	offline TIFF	
Columbia University	100 × 70 GIF 89	350 × 250 JPEG	700 × 500 JPEG	1200 × 900 JPEG
Cornell University	120 pixels max dimension JPEG/JFIF	390 pixels max dimension JPEG/JFIF	As supplied; PhotoCD images converted to JPEG or TIFF	
University of Illinois	125 pixels high JPEG/JFIF	400 pixels high JPEG/JFIF	Compressed but not resized JPEG/JFIF	
University of Maryland	150 pixels max dimension BMP/GIF	700 pixels max dimension BMP/GIF	As supplied; delivered by FTP on request	
University of Michigan[5]	90 pixels max dimension GIF 89A	640 pixels max dimension JPEG/JFIF	960 pixels max dimension	maximum—the full size image supplied by the museum
University of Virginia	130 pixels high GIF	600 pixels high JPEG/JFIF	offline	

Though the batch post-processing method worked well for creating most derivative images, certain kinds of image types posed problems. For example, all of the universities noted that PhotoCD images were quite difficult to work with. And batch compression did not work well across different content format types, such as line drawings, engravings, and paintings. Future projects might address this problem by separating the images by content types (line drawings would be handled together, as would continuous tone images), and using compression techniques that have been optimized for the different content types.

In general, the universities were pleased with the digital images they received from the museums. Nevertheless, they experienced a number of problems with image quality. According to the Columbia University technical report, "The quality of the digital images varied from museum to museum, but in general we found the resolution to be too low when compared with [digital] images we have been able to obtain commercially." And when the Columbia faculty compared projected slides alongside projected MESL digital images of the same object, they found the quality of the digital image sorely lacking.[6]

Some university disappointment stemmed from the scanning process the museums had used; others reacted to the fact that some images had been scanned from poor-quality intermediates. Other quality issues cited in the university technical reports included: images that were too small for the universities to make effective use of them and images that were dark and muddy, probably because they had either not been color-balanced or had been viewed only on one particular monitor/platform combination. (There are not yet adequate color management tools to assure that images will look good and consistent from one platform and monitor to another.) As "best practices" continue to evolve and be promulgated in the museum community, many of these image quality issues will inevitably disappear.

Museums also differed in their policies and practices regarding such things as the placement of borders around images or the matting of backgrounds (particularly on thumbnails) to create images of a consistent aspect ratio. Such alterations make it difficult to handle images "en masse" and will need to be standardized if a single source is to produce all derivative images in the future.

Other challenges the universities experienced arose in the process of transferring the images from machine to machine and linking them properly to accompanying text. Some image files were corrupted and others were missing, misnamed, or misreferenced. These problems may have been introduced anywhere along the distribution chain, which led from the museums to the central distribution site to various processing points within the universities. Explicit procedures and quality assurance checks could minimize such problems in the future.

▶ Designing the Deployment System and User Interface

Each university independently designed its own system for deploying images and text on its campus. This section discusses some general differences between the various university implementations. It also discusses how the different implementations looked to users and the ways in which search results differed. Owing to their heterogeneity, a precise empirical study of user response to each implementation could not be usefully undertaken. However, observations about the ways in which various design approaches affected the look and performance of the individual deployment systems were still possible.

General Differences between the Implementations

Six out of seven of the universities eventually chose the World Wide Web as the primary access mechanism for their users. Initially the University of Illinois at Urbana–Champaign and Cornell University began with different delivery systems, but moved onto the Web midway through the first year of the project. The University of Maryland provided user access through a local network[7] and enabled more limited secondary access through the Web.[8]

University implementations of the MESL data varied dramatically. The differences resulted primarily from the fact that institutional situations—such as the local information delivery architecture, the encoding and searching systems, as well as the expertise of the staff—had a major influence on the choices that were made at each site. In addition, a few of the project staff at some of the MESL sites had been involved with digital imaging projects and drew on these experiences when making interface design and other related decisions. The degree of institutional support for MESL implementation—manpower, equipment, classroom facilities, and available expertise—constituted another significant variable from one university to another.

Cross-Implementation Comparisons of Initial Presentation and Query Options: The Berkeley Study

There was a wide variety in the way the different university implementations looked to and behaved for the end user. A group of Berkeley students performed the only cross-implementation study, comparing six of the seven MESL implementations. The findings of their informal study are presented below.

Eight students in a UC Berkeley graduate class were given access to the implementations at six university sites for a one-month period.[9] The students had different academic backgrounds, and thus the expectation was that they would search in a variety of ways and also notice different features of the various systems. By design, none had extensive art history training so that their queries would be more like those of naïve users than experienced art historians. They were given the following assignments:

- Compare the user interface and display options on all the MESL sites. Look at how the user is supposed to navigate through the system (including how the information is "chunked," the order in which options are presented to the user, and the placement of buttons). Also examine search options and the layout of search results.
- Compare size and quality of thumbnail (as well as larger) images on all the MESL sites. Note the approximate sizes of images offered and how the sizes differ among implementations.
- Perform three identical searches on each of the MESL sites and note whether or not the same query on the same data set yielded different results.

Results of the student study are reported below.[10] Five of the six implementations studied provided a browse function that allowed the user to scan through large batches of images and records without first performing a query.[11] In most of the systems, the browse applications limited the user to browsing within only a single museum at a time. The study chose not to examine these initial browse applications.

TECHNICAL ENVIRONMENT

All of the Web-based delivery systems provided searching via HTML fill-out forms that generated CGI (Common Gateway Interface) scripted calls to a back-end database or search engine. Back-end databases/search engines included products such as FilemakerPro, Microsoft SQL server, and Glimpse, and locally designed systems such as Full Text Lexicographer (see Table 2).

TABLE 2 Back-end Search Engines Employed at Each Site

University	Database/Search Engine
American University	Flat database files (in-house)
Columbia University	Glimpse
Cornell University	FilemakerPro
University of Illinois	Microsoft SQL Server
University of Maryland	Microsoft Access, customized with Visual Basic (Maryland ISIS) MIniSQL (Web)
University of Michigan	Full Text Lexicographer (locally developed)
University of Virginia	Open Text

Most sites presented the user with several layers of explanatory information before allowing the user to compose a query. This information was designed to interest users in the MESL data, to contextualize the project and clarify its scope, and to explain conditions of use. One member of the Berkeley study group observed that "nesting the search page so deep within the Web hierarchy discourages repeated user queries." It was recommended that future designers should provide one set of paths for initial users and another set for repeat users.

Query screens for most implementations employed HTML fill-out forms with pull-down menu choices to allow searching across all collections, to limit searches to a single collection, or to limit searches to a single user-selected field. Most sites provided forms for both simple and complex (e.g., Boolean) searches, either as separate pages or combined on the same page. Examples of query screens from the Cornell University (Figure 1, below) and the University of Michigan (Figure 2 on page 76) sites are shown. These illustrations show how similar searching options can be presented to users in different ways, depending on the choices made by interface designers.

Most interfaces offered users the option of undertaking either simple or complex searches. Several Berkeley students found this distinction between simple and complex searches confusing. Simple searches generally allowed the user to search for a single word or phrase. In most cases, the "complex" searches permitted the user to use Boolean operators to search for specific values in each of two fields (such as Artist=Cezanne **and** Subject=fruit). The Berkeley students felt that "complex" was a poor word choice for this type of search.

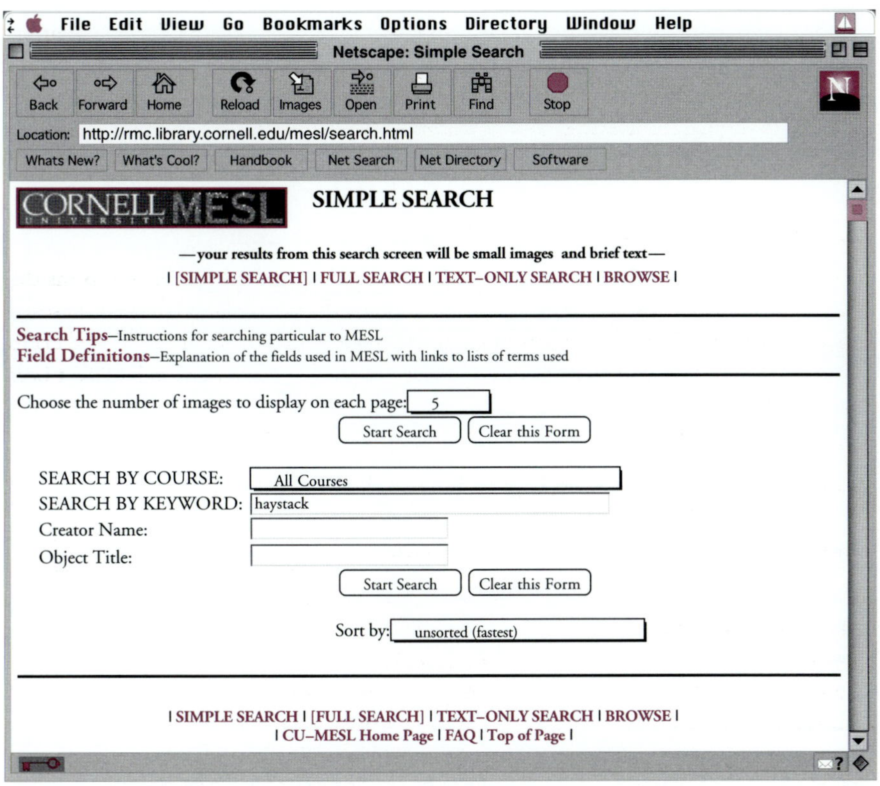

▶ **FIGURE 1** Example of Query Screen—Cornell University MESL Site

Each site chose to index a different subset of the available MESL fields. Some sites chose to provide keyword access while others did not. Some sites provided access by categories of local interest (such as by course using the image). And, in many cases, "searchable fields" on the user's query form were really composed of indexes made by concatenating a variety of related fields in the database rather than by presenting the fields defined by the MESL data dictionary. Different sites combining their indexes in different ways was one of the factors that led the same query to yield radically different search results between sites.

COMPARING SEARCH RESULTS

As part of the study, each Berkeley student created three search strategies which they then performed at each site. Because the list of searchable fields presented to the user differed from site to site, students needed to use their own judgment in an effort to replicate the

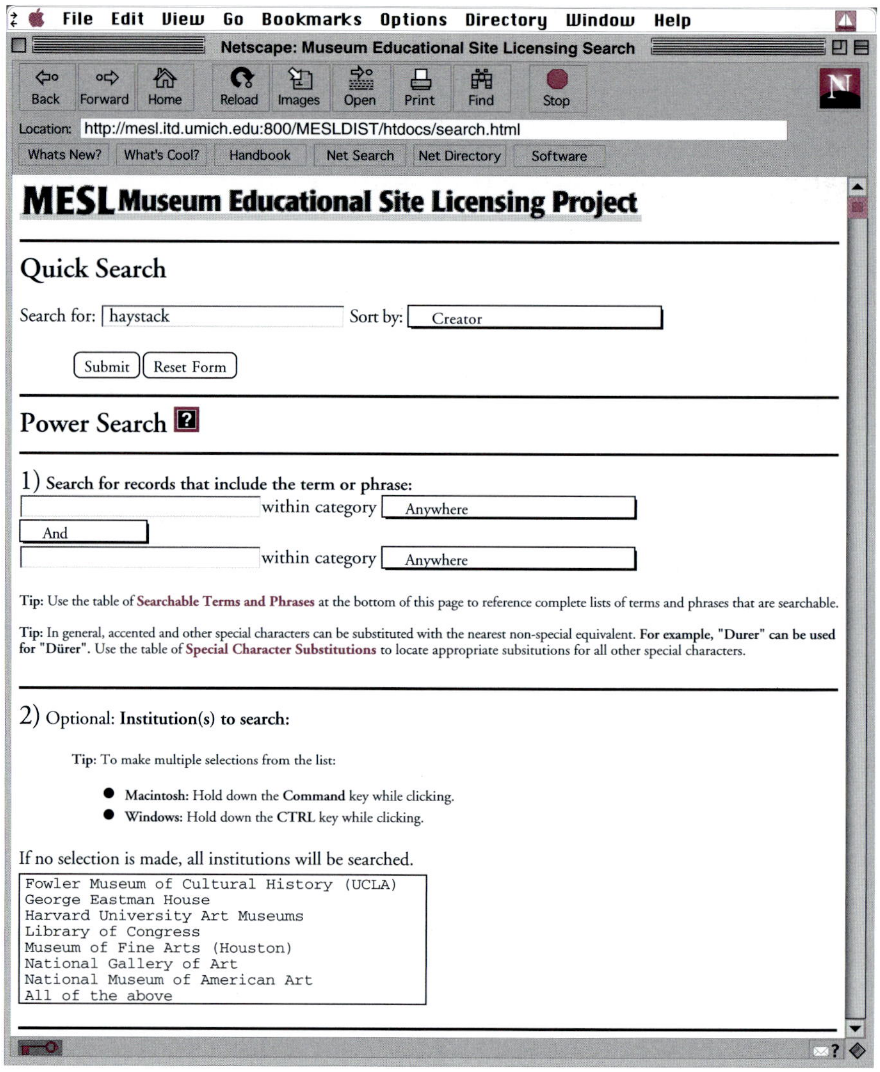

▶ **FIGURE 2** Example of Query Screen—University of Michigan MESL Site

search as closely as possible at each site. Their searches yielded vastly different results from site to site, for example:

- Searching for title="birth" yielded from one to twelve results, with only the University of Virgina and Cornell University yielding the same number of hits (eight).
- A simple search query for "german landscape" yielded no results at the University of Virginia. A compound (or "complex") search produced no results at the American University, University of Michigan, and University of Maryland sites, yet yielded six results at both the University of Virginia and Cornell University sites, and five results at the University of Illinois site.
- Searching for "haystack" retrieved six results at Michigan (see Figure 3 below), five at Cornell and Virginia, three at Maryland, two at Illinois (see Figure 4 on page 78), and American, and one result at Columbia (see Figure 5 on pages 79).

"A number of electronic initiatives have been successfully developed at University of Virginia, in large part because of the availability of the MESL images. At Virginia MESL has become the focal point for a new kind of collaboration. MESL's data dictionary approach is now a model for other 'media-bases.' In addition, thanks to MESL, more digital images are available for teaching and research (with improved access)."

JUDY THOMAS
UNIVERSITY OF VIRGINIA
Participants' Meeting

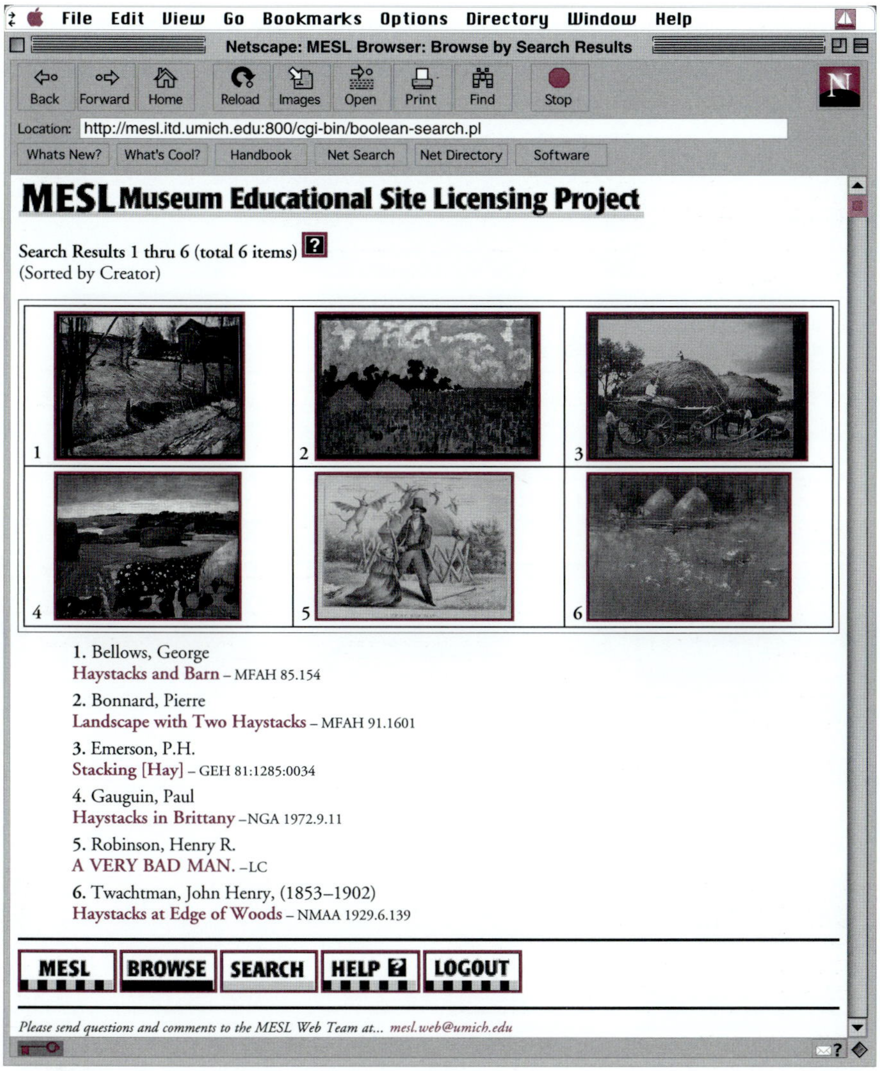

▸ **FIGURE 3** Example of Search Results Returned for "Haystack"—University of Michigan

- Searching for oil portraits of children (using the terms *child, oil,* and sometimes qualified by *portrait*) yielded a wide range of results. All searches at American and Maryland and a "quick" search at Michigan yielded no results. Searches at Illinois yielded two items, neither of which had anything to do with oil paintings of children—rather, they were works created by an artist named "Child" about the Free S**oil** Party. However, a fielded search ("child" within subject and "oil" within medium) at Michigan yielded 31 results, over half of which were oil portraits of children. Fielded searches at Cornell (material-medium=oil and concepts-subject=child) and at Virginia (subject=child and material=oil) both yielded 82 records, over half of which were oil portraits of children.
- The keyword phrase "black and white" yielded no results at Maryland, three results at Illinois, the identical nine results at American and Cornell, and the same 22 results at both Virginia and Michigan.

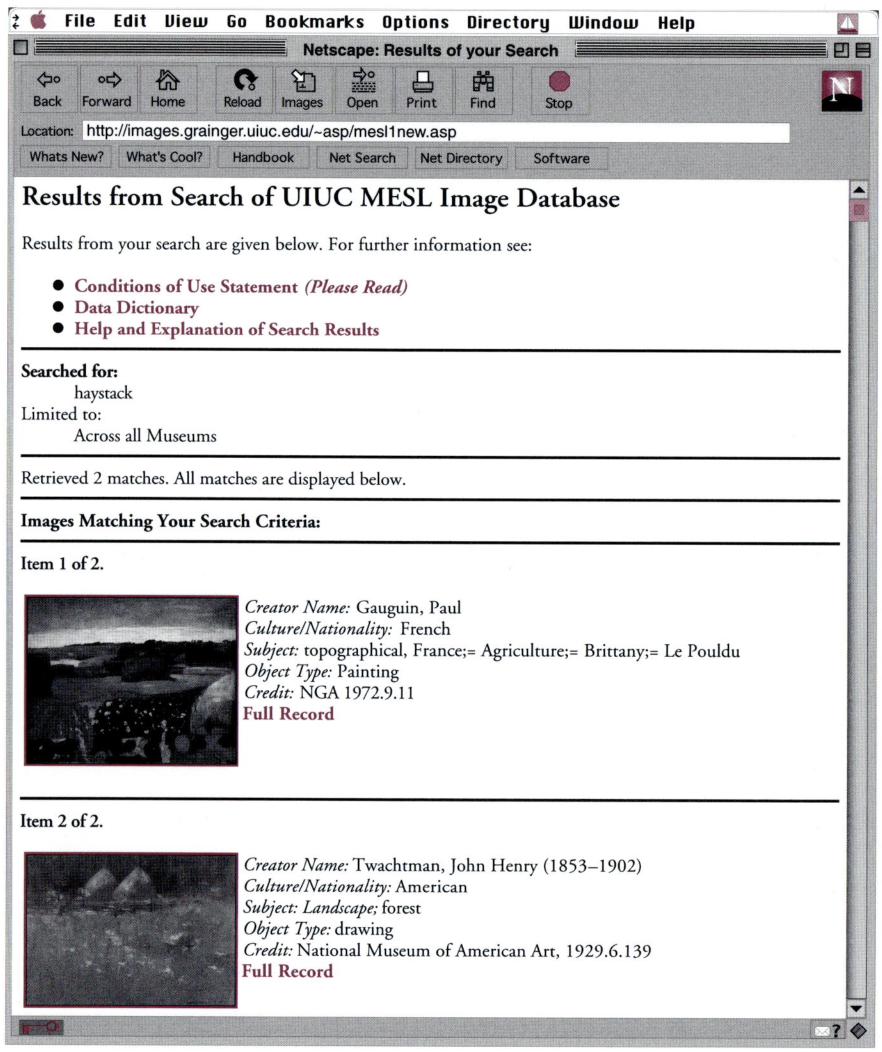

▸ **FIGURE 4** Example of Search Results Returned for "Haystack"—University of Illinois (UIUC)

- A search for French Still Life yielded no results at American and Maryland, 20 results at Illinois, 22 at Cornell (see Figure 6 on page 80), and 23 at Michigan and Virginia. (see Figure 7 on page 81 and Figure 8 on page82).
- A search for Madonna and Child yielded no results at Maryland, 57 at American, 60 at Cornell and Michigan, 61 at Illinois, and 66 at Virginia.
- A search for "Surreal" yielded two results at Cornell, Illinois, Maryland, and Michigan, and four at American and Virginia.

There were a number of reasons for these divergent search results: the fact that some sites combined different sets of the original data fields into unified indexes, the characteristics of different search engines and their differing approaches to indexing, and the effect of whole-word versus character-string searches on various fields (e.g., a character-string search would pull up "soil" in a search for "oil," and a whole-word search would not).

One of the most significant reasons for discrepancies in search results on the same data (at different implementation sites) had to do with choices institutions made when they combined data fields in order to simplify searching for users. The MESL data dictionary contains 32 fields, far too many to present effectively in a typical search interface. Consequently, institutions made local decisions about how to group sets of fields within the MESL database and what to label each of these combined indexes. As a result, at each site users were presented with different indexes to the same underlying content.

The way "keyword" indexes were constructed accounted for many of the discrepancies that occurred when the same search was tried at different sites. Keyword indexes were formed by combining prominent fields like subject, description, and title, by relying completely on the words within the label field, and by other variations on these themes. The

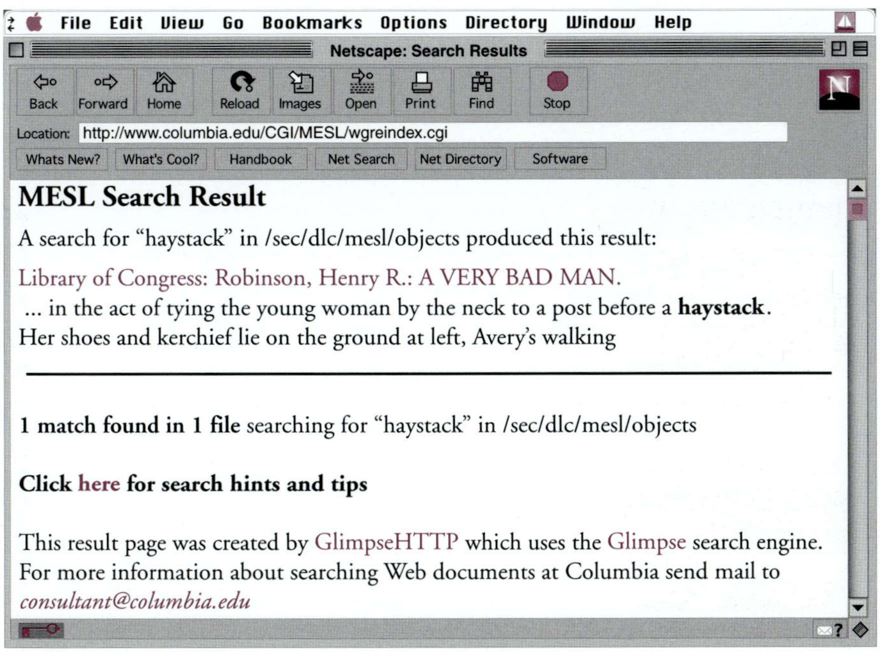

▸ **FIGURE 5** Example of Search Results Returned for "Haystack"—Columbia University

choice of which fields to index for keywords can have a significant impact on search results, such as finding an artist named "Child" when looking for portraits of children. The importance of these choices is compounded by the fact that simple searches, which are often used by less experienced users, tend to rely on the keyword approach.

Another reason the results differed across sites had to do with search engine characteristics—that is, whether all matches must start exactly the same, beginning from the left side of any field; whether the system looks for character strings or whole words; or whether the system matches stems, truncates, or performs other search tricks. The impact of such search characteristics drastically affected search results in this study.

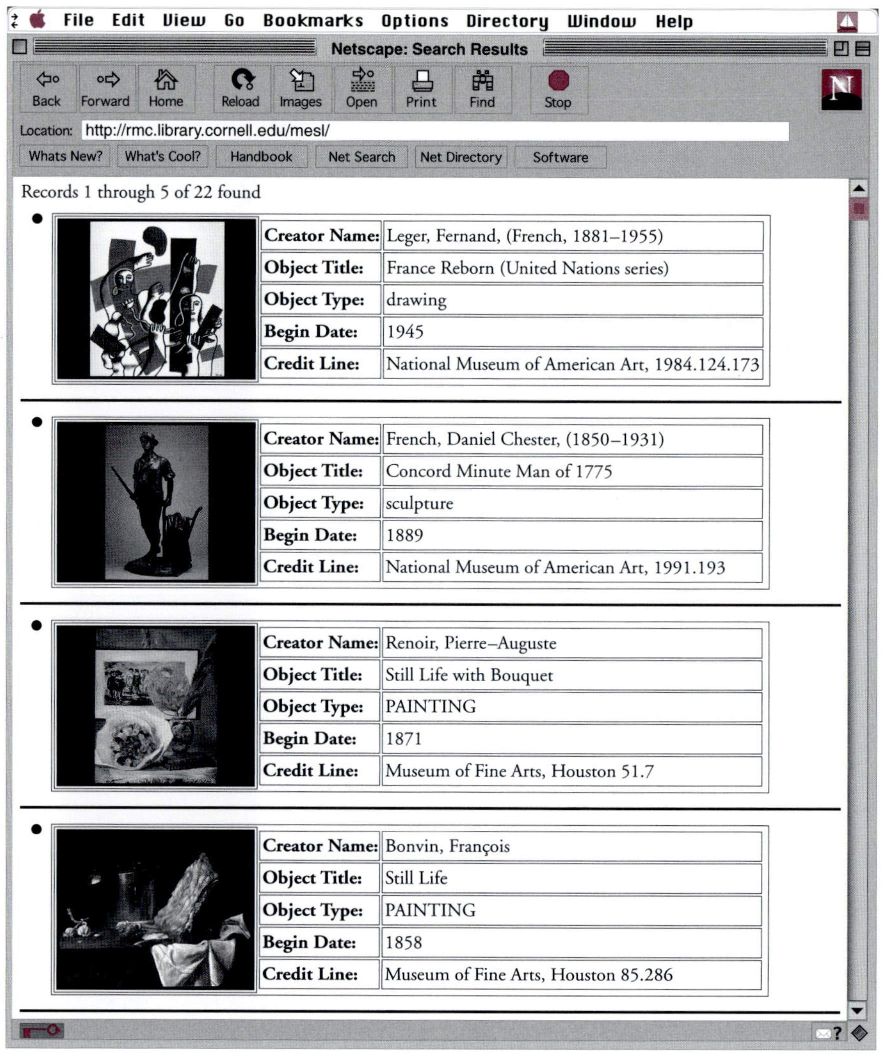

▸ **FIGURE 6** Example of Search Results Returned for "French Still Life"—Cornell University

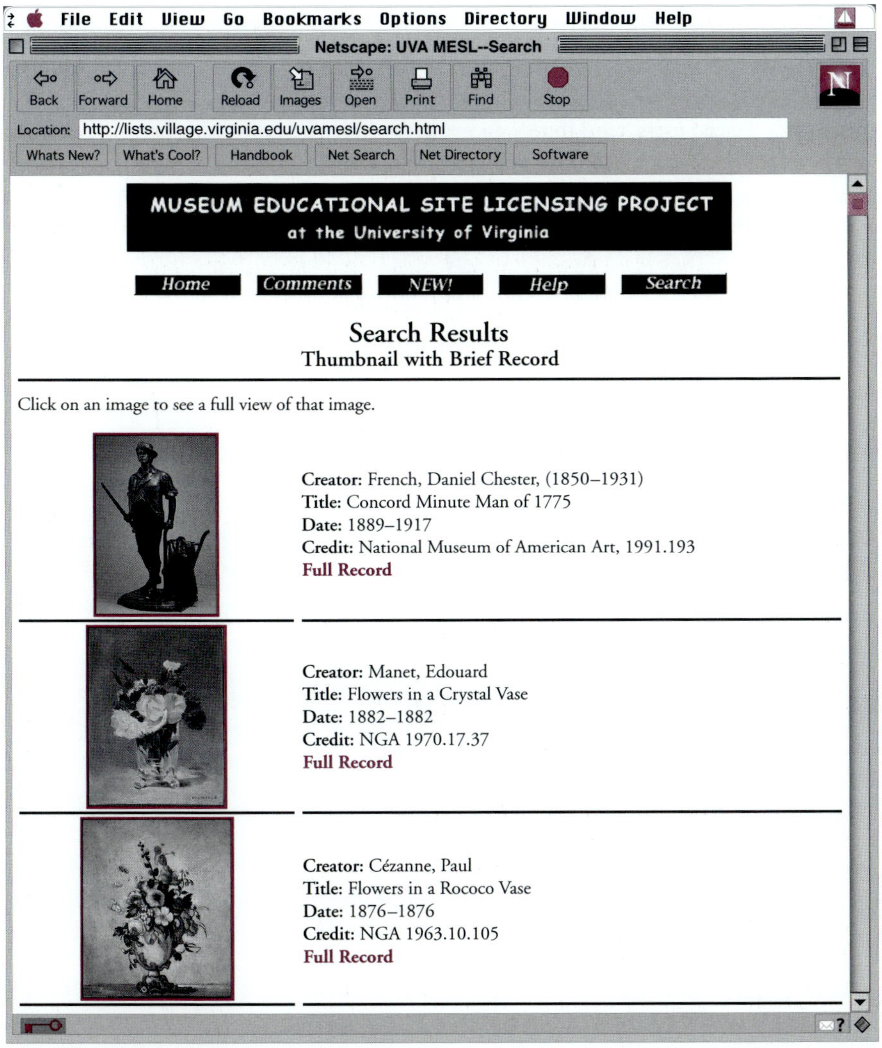

▸ **FIGURE 7** Example of Search Results Returned for "French Still Life"—University of Virginia

▸ Access Control

In addition to testing a variety of search and retrieval choices, the MESL experiment explored issues surrounding the provision of access to and security of the museum data mounted on campus servers. Each implementation used fixed Internet Protocol (IP) addresses as its initial form of access control.[12] This form of security is quick and easy to implement and only requires that a list of valid campus domains or IP addresses be precompiled and then checked whenever a search on the "secure" database is initiated. While this IP access control worked relatively well for this experimental project, it poses serious problems for a true production-level delivery system.

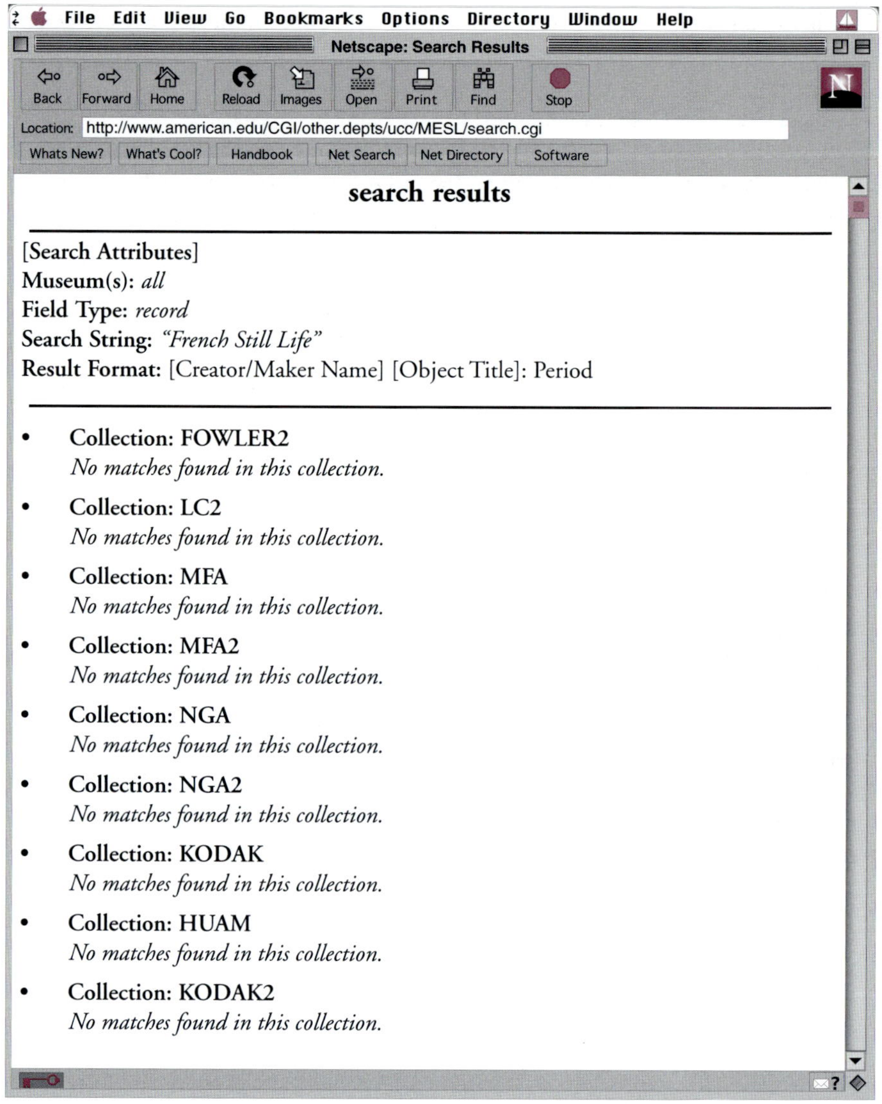

▸ **FIGURE 8** Example of Search Results Returned for "French Still Life"—American University

Groups of IP addresses tend to be too general and may include too many users in some areas and not enough in others. For example, commercial entities leasing campus space, private technology-transfer spin-offs, alumni dial-up access, and other groups that might not be valid members of a "campus community" (as defined within a licensing agreement) are often included within the campus IP domain. In many cases, it is not possible to isolate these invalid users from permissible student, faculty, and staff users. Another problem stems from the fact that many legitimate users (e.g., those from satellite campuses and programs in other cities, students and faculty who dial up through their own Internet service providers, faculty on sabbatical at other campuses, etc.) do not share the main campus domain or do not have fixed IP addresses, and may be blocked from accessing the system. (Even if a campus could create a list incorporating most of these other valid fixed external IP addresses, managing such a fluctuating list would quickly become unwieldy.)

Because most Web security has used IP addressing to control access to an individual directory, this approach can require that different sizes of images and text be stored into directories based on access control rather than upon logical arrangement. For example, a university wanting to control access to all images bigger than thumbnails, but allow any user to see textual descriptions, would have to store thumbnails and text in an uncontrolled-access directory and all other images in a controlled-access directory.

Midway through the MESL project, several of the campuses began to implement experiments with more sophisticated means of access control. In the second year of MESL, the University of Illinois added log-in and password access to supplement IP access as a way of serving those outside its core IP cluster. In 1997, both the University of Michigan and Columbia University implemented systems requiring log-in names and passwords for users of the MESL data and other restricted collections, and authenticated them against already developed databases of valid campus users.

It is clear that simple IP access control will not support the kind of security measures that most image rightsholders expect. More sophisticated methods need to be explored, based upon individual users rather than upon workstation addresses. Most of these methods will require universities to keep track of their users' various affiliations (e.g., to isolate alumni or drop-outs, to identify valid users of material intended only for a particular course, etc.). Because of privacy concerns, universities have the responsibility to maintain and protect authentication systems based upon this level of information about their users, even when distributors are delivering licensed material directly to members of the university community. Some universities have begun experimenting with public key encryption and digital certificates to try to solve the authentication problem while still maintaining user privacy.

▶ Conclusion

The heterogeneous mix of deployment systems in the MESL project has revealed a number of interesting factors that would have been difficult to discover in a more homogeneous environment. While the design of an information retrieval system may at first appear to be trivial, decisions over how to combine indexes to present to the user and how to implement searching strategies are critical in determining the user's experience. By examining the different ways in which an identical data set can be searched and presented to users, implementers should be able to better design future interactive projects.

Centralized delivery models are likely to be increasingly employed as technological impediments (such as reliable high-bandwidth delivery over wide-area networks, secure authentication of users as being part of the authorized university community, and protection of user privacy) begin to ease. These centralized approaches will offer greater consistency of searching and display between sites, but at the expense of local control.

The preliminary results yielded by the Berkeley study suggest that additional research needs to be done to further refine our understanding of the complex interaction between database design, search engines, interface design, and user behavior. Efforts to develop successful systems for image delivery, undertaken in tandem with those to repurpose collections management data for public access to images, present formidable challenges.

Acknowledgments

Portions of this chapter appeared in a paper by Howard Besser titled "Comparing Five Implementations of the Museum Educational Site Licensing Project: 'If the Museum Data's the Same, Why's It Look so Different?'" (*Proceedings of the Fourth International Conference on Hypermedia and Interactivity in Museums* (Paris, France, 3–5 September 1997). Pittsburgh: Archives and Museum Informatics: 317–325).

Thanks are due to the MESL participant institutions for providing permission and access to the images, records, and retrieval implementations, and for compiling data for their technical reports. Financial assistance from the Andrew W. Mellon Foundation helped fund the effort to gather and compile technical data about the university implementations. Christie Stephenson compiled information about image delivery and offered keen observations on many other aspects of the topics covered in this article. She and Patricia McClung provided significant editorial assistance. Students in Howard Besser's spring 1997 SIMS 296A course at UC Berkeley participated in the cross-implementation study.

Notes

1. See the author's previous work with Christie Stephenson, "The Museum Educational Site Licensing Project: Technical Issues in the Distribution of Museum Images and Textual Data to Universities," in James Hensley, ed. *EVA '96 Electronic Imaging and the Visual Arts,* Hampshire, UK: Vasari Ltd., 1996: 5-1–5-15. It is also available on the Web at *http://www.gii.getty.edu/mesl/about/docs/EVA.html.*

2. Applications to generate derivatives on the fly were not available at the time, but in the future these may prove useful.

3. Table 1 compiled by Christie Stephenson.

4. JPEG files were produced with a variety of different batch image-processing programs (HiJaak95, Lview, PhotoShop, ImageMagick, Debabelizer, Graphic Converter, Multimedia Converter, Alchemy) at a variety of quality settings. It is difficult to compare quality settings across software as each has a unique method of representing the quality/compression ratio scale.

5. Michigan also supplied an intermediate "small" size JPEG, with a maximum pixel dimension of 320 pixels. Availability of derivatives in the full range of sizes was dependent on the size of the original.

6. Reported anecdotally by Angela Giral in the Columbia University technical report.

7. See "The Maryland Interactive System for Image Searching: Implementing a System to Facilitate Teaching with Digital Images," *Images Online: Perspectives on the Museum Educational Site Licensing Project,* Patricia McClung and Christie Stephenson, eds. (Los Angeles: The Getty Information Institute, 1998): 35.

8. Examples from the University of Maryland cited herein were gathered from their Web implementation, which was never intended as the primary means of access for Maryland users. Consequently, these examples are not indicative of the access that most Maryland users experienced via their campus network system.

9. The Columbia University site was inaccessible to the students during the study period.

10. This article summarizes the preliminary findings, focusing primarily on the searching process. Future reports from the Berkeley study will examine how search results are presented to users at each of the university sites and will compare record display features, thumbnail sizes, and other interface variables.

11. The University of Virginia did not provide a browse function.

12. IP access control allows a systems manager to create a file containing a list of valid Internet addresses, and to prevent access to all the information in specific directories by any users not coming from one of those listed Internet addresses. The most common IP access control at universities is to limit access to the university's domain name. (For example, by placing just a few lines of code (specifying *cornell.edu*) in a file in a particular directory, Cornell University could prevent access to all files in that directory by anyone at a workstation whose address did not end in *cornell.edu.*)

Introduction

Project evaluation was a major component of the MESL effort and occupied center stage during the second year of the project. The assessments took several forms, including break-out discussion groups, Web surveys, questionnaires, institutional reports, and site visits from project staff. This section reports on what we learned about how MESL images were used during the project and what impact they had on the participating institutions, involved staff members, faculty, and students.

From the outset of the project, one of the goals was to document the impact of the MESL project on museums and universities—and their constituents—as fully as possible. Initial plans called for several "baseline" studies that would gather data on visual collections—particularly their management and use—as well as on institutional infrastructures that support visual collections and access to them. The primary question that the MESL project hoped to resolve was: What impact, if any, did the introduction of digital images have on instruction, visual collections management, networking, budget allocation, and institutional collaboration? Participants and project managers worked together to devise various strategies for collecting and analyzing both quantitative and qualitative data that would answer this question.

Initially, evaluation efforts focused on the development of a complex evaluation document and measurement framework that was dubbed "MESL Metrics." It started as a long questionnaire that would: (1) solicit baseline data on institutional visual collections and the infrastructure that was in place to manage and make them accessible to the public and (2) document the impact of MESL. The framework included five categories of measurement: collections, delivery systems, instructional use, project data, and intellectual property. This far-reaching, ambitious list of desirable data elements was distributed in draft to the participants, who assessed the practicality of gathering the information. Based on this feedback, it was pared down and eventually transformed into an outline that formed the basis for each institution's technical report.

At the May 1996 meeting, the Evaluation Group was reconstituted and organized to conduct (or subcontract) several additional studies.[1] By that time, the University of California at Berkeley had submitted a grant proposal to the Andrew W. Mellon Foundation for a project that would study the economic impact of the MESL project on participating institutions—and compare the relative costs of access to and use of "traditional" analog images (e.g., slides and photographs) with those of digital images. Howard Besser, who would become the principal investigator for the Mellon Study, met with the Evaluation Group to ensure that these parallel efforts would complement each other as much as possible and avoid unnecessary duplication of effort.

As a practical matter, the entire MESL group also had to contend with the fact that implementing the MESL project—that is, delivering digital images and data, mounting the images on campus servers, and providing successful access options (as well as faculty and student training)—was consuming far more resources than they had anticipated. The idea of mounting a labor-intensive study of all aspects of the participating institutions' visual collections and technical infrastructure was one that had to be leavened with large doses of "reasonable expectations."

▸ Evaluation Instruments

Ultimately, the outcome was that the University of California, Berkeley Mellon Study on the economic issues was launched in August of 1996, and the Evaluation Group coordinated several additional efforts, including: pre- and post-project surveys (conducted by the University of Illinois) of faculty and students who used the MESL data in academic courses, and two studies by the Cornell Interactive Media Group: one of general users of the MESL images (conducted via a Web-based questionnaire) and another of the attitudes and reactions to the project by the MESL participants themselves. The participants' study was supplemented by information gathered at facilitated discussions during MESL project meetings.

This part leads off with two articles addressing the effect that the project had on museums and universities. The MESL project constituted a pioneering experiment that engaged them at an unanticipated level of commitment and complexity. There was no way to predict in advance how difficult it would be to implement the original MESL vision; further, there were no models to follow. In addition, project design mandated that each institution would work out its own internal procedures for complying with project requirements: capturing images and data, exporting data, providing campus access, loading and managing data, working with faculty to use the images in courses, etc. In the end, this "every tub on its own bottom" approach produced a wealth of valuable experience. It also drew the participants into a cohesive team, motivated to find more generalized solutions to many of the problems they had struggled with alone.

The remaining two articles represent executive summaries of two of the studies undertaken as part of the MESL evaluation: the faculty and student surveys and a "casual" users survey. These were undertaken to capture as much information as possible about the impact that the MESL project had on the end users of the MESL images and data: faculty and students who used MESL data in conjunction with their courses and casual (or random) campus users of the data.

The article "Findings of the Instructor/Student Survey" summarizes a thorough study, conducted by Beth Sandore and Najmuddin Shaik at the University of Illinois, of faculty and students who used MESL images as part of university courses or related assignments. This study was central to the purpose of the MESL project because, when all is said and done, it is the impact on teaching and learning that will form the basis for decisions on whether or not to invest in a major transition from analog to digital images for educational purposes.

The MESL Casual User Survey is a report from the Interactive Media Group at Cornell. This survey was conducted on the World Wide Web via links from university MESL sites to a central online questionnaire. Various incentives were advertised to encourage MESL users to follow the link and fill out the questionnaire. The survey was intended to capture information from a cross section of MESL data users, particularly those who used the database independent of class assignments. Although the number of respondents was quite low, the feedback on the uses made of the data, the interface designs, and the reactions to having access to MESL data is informative.

▶ Common Themes

Although these articles report on data gathered from many different perspectives and instruments, there were some common themes.

- Implementing the MESL project was not a trivial exercise and required significant retooling of the infrastructure, as well as a high degree of technical and administrative support at both universities and museums.
- More standardization at virtually every link in the data delivery and access chain is needed.

- Improvements in image availability (more images desired), image quality, and delivery mechanisms would be welcomed by all users.
- There was a steep learning curve for many faculty, but this was less true for students.
- Digital images enhanced the classroom experience and were easily incorporated into student work.
- The MESL project was a worthwhile experiment and taught participants a lot about what is required to incorporate digital images into the campus information "mainstream."
- Those involved demonstrated a keen enthusiasm for the potential that MESL foreshadowed.

Note

1. In a year-long process led by Beth Sandore, several working groups developed and implemented the surveys.

MESL Impact: Museum Perspective

PATRICIA McCLUNG

▶ Background

Each museum that participated in the MESL project entered it with different goals in mind, as well as varying levels of expertise and relevant experience. The MESL project had a profound impact on all of the participating museums and, by extension, on many other institutions that were watching the project in the hopes of informing their own decisions and planning with regard to digital imaging and public access to their collections via electronic means. This article summarizes feedback and comments from MESL meeting minutes, papers, and talks by museum participants, as well as various conversations with project coordinators and others. It is an amalgam of impact statements rather than an overall consensus, given that the impact varied depending on an institution's position along the digital imaging continuum when it entered the project and on its original (and subsequent) goals for MESL participation.

▶ MESL Process

All museum participants agreed that the MESL project was enormously challenging, sometimes frustrating, and ultimately rewarding. At times, participants were overwhelmed by the nature of the requisite tasks involved. In just a few months, the museums were expected to choose the images to be used in the MESL project, oversee their capture in digital form, assemble the relevant documentation/cataloging, and make them available in digital form for distribution to the seven university participants. Decisions about image size and compression were left to local debate (e.g., provide the biggest you are willing to share), and there were innumerable quality control issues with regard to both the images and their related text. In retrospect, participants suggested that their frustration levels and anxiety might have been alleviated by more planning time up front, with mechanisms built in for group decision making on such issues as image file size and technical specifications. When it was all said and done, participants acknowledged they were motivated by the mission of the MESL project itself and by their fellow project team members.

▶ Institutional Impact

Museum participants highlighted the overall significance of the MESL project's effect on their institution. At a breakout session for museums held at the last working meeting of the MESL group in May 1997, a lively discussion ensued about how institutional views on sharing had been affected by the project. Most had entered the project thinking that it was either a strictly legal experiment targeting site licensing or a technical project focusing on making digital images more widely available. But in the end, the majority agreed that the

MESL project's educational issues were paramount. Both the technical and the legal challenges were subsumed by the opportunities to extend and transform the educational mission of museums and to support and enhance the teaching and study practices in universities. To this end, new alliances were forged within the museum community, as well as between museum and university participants. Several museums discussed the ways in which relationships between their internal education and information systems departments were strengthened, while others expressed regret that there was not more intra-institutional support for the project. All agreed that the MESL project underscored the necessity for new ways of thinking about institutional goals and practices—and that there was a need for additional breakthrough-thinking in their education departments with regard to the kinds of outreach opportunities that the MESL project enabled. Partially influenced by its participation in the MESL project, the George Eastman House changed its mission statement, placing more emphasis on "scholarly and recreational inquiry." Another participant pointed to a shift in focus from the mechanics of digital imaging as the "big deal," to the value of the information itself and the importance of the infrastructure that makes that intellectual content more widely available.

Staff at the National Gallery of Art speculated that the current NGA Web site (offering kiosk access to thousands of NGA thumbnail reproductions of images—a much less controlling approach to information about holdings than is currently embraced by most cultural institutions) might not have happened as quickly had it not been for MESL. Several others commented that by taking the bold step within the framework of the MESL project to make images available in digital form outside their institutions, they learned that nothing really terrible happened to these images after all. In fact, there were numerous advantages—many of them unanticipated—particularly in education. For example, museums were surprised to learn that people wanted to see images about which little was known, and that they were very forgiving of incomplete or cursory textual data.

The MESL project provided abundant opportunities for museums to learn more about their data—both image and text—and its potential uses. Sometimes there were new insights about the educational value of museum image databases as something more than internal collections management tools. Needless to say, such shifts in perspective led inevitably to discussions about requisite "next step" improvements in database content, design, and standards.

"MESL has been a great learning experience for The Museum of Fine Arts, Houston. It has been interesting to see how the data looks on the Web with different interfaces, how electronic teaching techniques can be used in the classroom, and to learn more about the mechanics of digital imaging. The project has met the Museum's goals of sharing information about our collections more broadly, while teaching staff a great deal about the nuts and bolts of networked information."

JEANNETTE DIXON
THE MUSEUM OF FINE ARTS, HOUSTON
Participants' Meeting

▶ Technical Impact

Perhaps the biggest questions the museums grappled with in the beginning had to do with what was "big" enough and what was "good" enough to export. In the end, many reported that the MESL project stimulated significant progress in both technical knowledge, especially the process of capturing and exporting images, and institutional practice. Five of the museums created their first institutional Web sites as a result of their MESL participation (the Library of Congress and the National Museum of American Art already had them), and all reported marked improvement in staff skills with regard to capitalizing on Internet access and tools.

▶ Content Selection

The issues surrounding content selection for the MESL project produced strong sentiments all around. The participants wanted to provide images that would generate interest and use.

They hoped to identify materials that would be appealing to faculty members willing to experiment with MESL images, even though the project was, by design, very limited in the number of images that could be provided.

In general, the project's impact on content selection strategies highlighted the fact that a successful project requires a "critical mass" of images—in other words, enormous databases—that can be browsed far in advance of course planning cycles. Further, faculty and students really want to see all of the images that particular institutions own. For example, if they know a particular work is at The Museum of Fine Arts, Houston, they want to be able to access it for a course or for study purposes. They also want to be able to supplement these images with additional images from other sources to which they have access, and to be able to merge them easily into a digital presentation. Although the MESL project was not big enough to satisfy these needs, it did provide university faculty and museum curatorial staff with important insights that could help shape future database services. It was enlightening for curators to see the specific ways in which images were used, as well as the excitement that the images generated in several courses.[1] This was especially gratifying with respect to the close collaboration between the District of Columbia museums (the National Museum of American Art and the National Gallery of Art) and the University of Maryland, which linked classroom use of the images to subsequent site visits to see the originals. (This success led participants to recommend increased use of local museum/university teams in future projects.)

In the course of the project, the participants tried a number of different techniques to support the selection process and encourage communication between museum staff and university faculty. At the conclusion of the project, this was an area that all participants felt still needed improvement. Although the project experimented with several online tools to support dialogue between curators and faculty, these didn't solve the problem. Further, the *a priori* limitations on the available universe of materials (existing digital images or slides that had no intellectual property restrictions) meant that museums were unable to make significant portions of their collections available for faculty selection. Museum curators were disappointed by the process because this was an area in which they felt most competent to assist, yet the tools and communication channels were not effective. Faculty were discouraged because they wanted to select from a broader universe that covered their teaching needs. A notable exception—one that had perhaps the greatest success with the content selection aspects of MESL—was the Fowler Museum of Cultural History. The Fowler posted thumbnail images of its entire imaged collections (approximately 37,000 items) on a local Web site and allowed faculty members to browse it and choose specific items for the MESL data set.

The Library of Congress also took a different approach from the fine art museums model whereby curators presented a cross section of individually selected works. Instead, it offered two coherent collections (1,300 photographs by Carl Van Vechten and 700 political prints from 1780–1876), in order to learn the degree to which university faculty and students found whole collections to be of value. Both the student and faculty surveys, conducted by the University of Illinois during the MESL project, supported this approach by indicating a strong preference for the capability to browse entire databases of museum collections.[2]

▶ Cataloging and Documentation

The text that accompanied the images generated some of the most profound project outcomes. The MESL data dictionary that was developed to "normalize" project data for more or less standardized output represents a significant outcome. Further experimentation with the data dictionary will inevitably lead to further modifications, streamlining, and simplification.

In general, the MESL project enabled more sharing of data and allowed institutions to experiment with making information, previously intended only for internal use, much more broadly available. From that, they learned a great deal about the ways in which people use the data and look for images. They also learned of some of the creative uses that people had for the data when they were given access.

Harder to grapple with were the ways that the MESL project underscored the inadequacy of the data for widespread use, particularly given the lack of standardization in descriptive terms and practices. For many museums, particularly for their curators and registrars, standardization issues are new concepts. The MESL project pointed out the necessity for data uniformity, as well as ongoing data maintenance (and mechanisms for tracking the history of record). A few institutions (such as the National Gallery of Art and the National Museum of American Art) that were further along in standardizing their data found that the MESL project validated their approach and made them more confident about releasing their data in the future.

The Library of Congress was the most vociferous critic of the approach taken. The Library staff who prepared the cataloging for its two collections said that it was burdensome to make all data conform to a narrowly defined structure. They suggested that in future projects an information architecture be selected that would permit the compilation of a variety of data types or forms (commending the approach found in the so-called "Dublin Core" structure under discussion in the library community).[3]

"Indirectly, MESL emphasized the importance of making our collection data publicly available. This paved the way for putting our collection database with images on the Web."

DON MCCLELLAND
FOWLER MUSEUM OF CULTURAL HISTORY
Technical Report

▶ Legal Issues/Site Licensing Lessons

Over the course of the project, major shifts in thinking occurred on topics related to intellectual property ownership and the notion of site licensing. Simply put, many museums entered the project with the idea that they could get a site license for their images and make money. By the end of the project, several were speculating that there might not be any real potential for profit from site licensing schemes. As the project wore on, discussions focused more on the merits and risks of making images available on the Web (without charge), as well as on whether site license schemes could generate enough revenue to enable museums to add value to the data (and therefore do a better job of making the information available, perhaps on a "break-even" economic model). For some, the site license approach represents a mechanism to control and regulate access and use, even more than a source of revenue. For others, it offers support for improved service and increased efficiencies for both content providers and users of the database(s). The Library of Congress reports that the experience of the MESL project informed their own plans for an educational site license.

The MESL project prompted a few to postulate a "so what" scenario: that is, what if someone takes all of a museum's images off the Web for some unauthorized purpose—what awful thing could happen? There was further discussion concerning the importance of authoritative data and the fact that no one can really steal a museum's authority/imprimatur (although there are disturbing examples of counterfeit and deceit on the Web). Others felt that museums needed to be more realistic about the extent to which they could control access on the Internet, even in a site licensing scenario, and that instincts to "control" access should be discouraged. As a follow-on to the MESL project, the Fowler Museum of Cultural History plans to make its thumbnail and moderate-resolution images available without charge, with the caveat that it may reconsider if a viable licensing alternative comes along.

During the American Memory pilot, the Library of Congress investigated a revenue-generating model, but determined that it was preferable to make the Library's online collections freely available via the Internet. This approach, the Library found, attracted financial support from other sources (mainly private) and permitted the digitization effort to continue as a provision for the public good. The project has evolved into the National Digital Library Program, and fundraising has thus far kept pace with production.

The significance of the Terms and Conditions document that came out of the MESL project cannot be overemphasized. Such a collaborative document, outlining the essential elements of an agreement between museums and universities with regard to use of images, was a direct result of the relationships of mutual respect and trust that evolved between the museum and university participants over the course of the project. Both communities achieved a better understanding of their respective concerns and points of view and, during the project, moved much closer to a compatible vision of how to make images more widely accessible.

► Notes

1. In April 1997, the University of Maryland MESL team hosted an event that brought museum staff together with faculty to see and discuss the ways in which the museums' images were used in a variety of courses.
2. Beth Sandore and Najmuddin Shaik, "The Use of an Art Image Database in the Classroom: Instructor and Student Evaluation Report," submitted to the Getty Information Institute, October 1997: 73.
3. The Dublin Core is a 15-element metadata element set intended to facilitate discovery of electronic resources. Originally conceived for author-generated description of Web resources, it has also attracted the attention of formal resource description communities, such as museums and libraries. For more information about Dublin Core, visit *http://purl.oclc.org/metadata/dublin_core/*.

MESL Impact : University Perspective

PATRICIA McCLUNG

The MESL project caused repercussions within universities and museums, the two major participant subgroups, and had an overall impact on the entire cultural heritage community as well. Perceptions about the MESL project's impact on each of the participating universities were often related to the reasons that motivated the institutions to participate in the first place. University attendees at the final MESL working meeting in May 1997 reviewed their institutions' original motivations as background for further discussions about changes in those goals over time, project impediments, significant outcomes, and how the collaborative process affected the results. This article is based on those May 1997 discussions, supplemented by input from various other project forums and documents, including the MESL project technical reports that were completed by each institution.

▶ American University

REASONS FOR PARTICIPATION The MESL project appeared just as American University was preparing to launch a new digital and fiber-optic network intended to support and enhance on-campus information delivery. At the same time, there was keen interest in bringing the art history department into a project employing new technologies. As time went on, the emphasis shifted from mounting the images and making them accessible to incorporating them into the curriculum. Equipment was purchased, workstations made available, informational flyers and newsletters distributed, and faculty training sessions held. The primary focus was on delivering the images in useful ways. The MESL images became part of a bigger effort at AU to increase the availability of electronic resources for research and teaching.

"We have trained a lot of faculty as a result of this refocusing, but I don't think we've fully realized the payoff from that yet. It takes time for faculty to develop something new, get noticed, and have others fall in behind them once they see the benefits."

DIANA VOGELSONG
AMERICAN UNIVERSITY
Participants' Meeting

EFFECTS The MESL project enjoyed high visibility on campus and exemplified how technology can enhance teaching and learning (the Provost mentioned the MESL project in this context in his annual address to the faculty). It interested many art history faculty members in the challenges of teaching with digital images and provided the impetus for the development of a related faculty training program that will have lasting effects. Faculty in the School of Communication who were already familiar with digital technology found that the MESL project provided interesting content for student projects, thus allowing them to generate new assignments that exploited the curricular advantages of the medium. The kinds of changes the MESL project initiated take time to mature, but it was catalytic: It gave the library, the art department, and the academic computing group the chance to experiment with making a new online product available—learning as much from what didn't work as from what did.

▶ Cornell University

REASONS FOR PARTICIPATION Cornell was attracted to the collaborative nature of the MESL project, and to the fact that the issues it targeted had already been identified at Cornell as problematic, especially rights clearance and management. Cornell also saw MESL as a chance to experiment with existing content, as opposed to other projects in which the content needed to be created before the work on developing interactive tools—a Cornell priority—could get under way.

EFFECTS The MESL project stimulated cross-campus collaboration as the project took shape and enhanced the technical skills of project staff. Cornell's participation also benefited other similar digital projects on campus. Each of these projects seemed easier than the last, particularly once the initial challenge of mounting the MESL data (and providing a search interface) had been met. The MESL project is credited with contributing to an improved institutional infrastructure for supporting digital imaging initiatives. It fit well with several other projects under way at Cornell and helped stimulate cross-disciplinary use of digital images on campus. It also helped expand the library's role from that of a distribution center to the locus of new digital services and online collections.

The fact that Cornell was conducting compatible research (in its Interactive Media Group) permitted using the images in new ways and testing them in different classroom situations with various delivery mechanisms. The MESL project also provided a "real content" database (as opposed to a test database) for a computer science professor and graduate student who are building a new multimedia database engine.

▶ Columbia University

REASONS FOR PARTICIPATION Columbia was involved with several initiatives to deliver digital images on campus, including a project to create an image reserve collection for a course required of all undergraduates: "Masterpieces of Western Art." When MESL participation emerged as an option, Columbia was already grappling with intellectual property rights, primarily obtaining permissions, and confronting a number of technical issues related to quality control. The MESL project also provided a nice follow-on to Columbia's contributions to The Research Libraries Group (RLG) Digital Image Access Project, which had been focused on search and retrieval issues.[1]

The MESL project became an opportunity to test several local infrastructure assumptions and experiment with them on a large scale. It also helped staff address key issues concerning the collection and delivery of visual information, including experimentation with multimedia processing techniques and content-based image query systems. The project provided a concrete example for librarians, academic computing specialists, and faculty to explore alternative forms of building an image collection in lieu of (or as a complement to) the traditional on-demand production of copy slides for study and teaching.

EFFECTS The MESL project contributed to the beginning of an online catalog of Columbia's digital library. The MESL images, and accompanying metadata, served as a test bed for the development of revised methodologies for assimilating huge amounts of information into the catalogs, and for the design and implementation of a new infrastructure to accommodate these collections. As a result, students now have access to images for "home" study (from their dorm rooms, lounges, libraries, and a variety of other places). At the same time, the project demonstrated the difficulties of making the iterative process of image selection in such a short span of time match the needs of course content and faculty schedules. The MESL project took place at a critical time, well synchronized with Columbia's investment in providing Internet connections to all campus dormitories and in deploying a series of electronic classrooms throughout the campus. It served as a catalyst in the evolution of Columbia's digital library (and more efficient delivery of large quantities of information through the campus network), as well as for the creation of a media center for the art history department.

▶ University of Illinois

REASONS FOR PARTICIPATION When the opportunity to participate in MESL presented itself, the University of Illinois was already devising mechanisms to support arts, humanities, and social sciences faculty in their use of technology in the classroom. Digital image databases incorporating related lecture notes and other pertinent materials were being assembled. The MESL project offered the prospect of a large image database, complete with metadata that Illinois could use in experimenting with organizing, supporting, providing and controlling access (using different types of search engines), and designing user interfaces. The MESL project could also serve as an incentive to interest the slide library in digitizing its collections.

As the MESL project took shape at Illinois, it matched up well with other efforts to improve and test electronic information delivery tools. A technical person who had been hired to enable faculty in the College of Fine and Applied Arts to use images in the classroom migrated to the library to report to the MESL Project Coordinator. This link facilitated timely responses to feedback from users of the MESL database and allowed the library to experiment with assuming responsibility for services that had previously been dispersed among departments all over campus.

EFFECTS The MESL project provided new ways for traditionally "nontechnical" units—like art history—to use technology, teach with digital resources, and use them in their research. Illinois recognized the importance of these contributions and provided support for related efforts. MESL proved to be the necessary catalyst for the slide library to begin digitizing its collections. It also galvanized an influential group of people across campus to decide that homegrown, desktop databases (emerging all over campus) should be discouraged in favor of an integrated resource that deposits, manages, tracks, and allows for sharing the merged collections of images campus-wide. An unexpected benefit relates to the impact on visitors who come from all over the world to see Illinois's National Science Foundation digital library project. The MESL images have proved most effective in capturing visitors' imaginations and illustrating the power of the online tools, which come alive because of the exciting visual component that just isn't possible with traditional text project illustrations.

"The significant outcome that we can point to is that a strong foothold has been gained in the area of enabling traditionally non-technology units, like art history, to use technology, teach with digital resources and to use them in their research. And I think that has been recognized institutionally as something important."

BETH SANDORE
UNIVERSITY OF ILLINOIS
Participants' Meeting

▶ University of Maryland

REASONS FOR PARTICIPATION Administrative officials at the University of Maryland (UM) were drawn to the MESL project because it presented an opportunity to bring innovative technological support to the College of Arts and Humanities, especially to the Department of Art History and Archeology. There was also an expectation that funding for new tools and infrastructure would be associated with the project. Support for MESL within the department came from several faculty members who wanted to learn more about clearing intellectual property rights to images for teaching purposes.

As the MESL project was launched, the project team coalesced at UM and the potential benefits in the classroom (and beyond) became apparent to all. The availability of museum digital images created incentives for technical people to work with faculty using the images to enhance teaching, research, and student work.

"I found that my students and I became involved in a collaborative educational effort of a sort not generally possible with more conventional technologies for teaching art history. The project team at Maryland also functioned in a collaborative fashion—that was supported by others around the University in many ways. By this I don't mean that someone was leading and others were following. In fact, this project worked because every member of the team was there."

SALLY PROMEY
UNIVERSITY OF MARYLAND
Participants' Meeting

EFFECTS The University of Maryland had a particularly successful MESL implementation. The project team made some critical early decisions that contributed to this outcome. Technical staff, working closely with involved faculty members (especially Sally Promey, who was also the project team coordinator at UM), developed software tools that supported search, retrieval, and display of the images in electronic classrooms. Professor Promey devoted more than 200 hours to developing a course that made full use of MESL images. She and a few of her colleagues took advantage of the opportunity to experiment with an innovative classroom style that engaged the students more actively in the learning process, often with much higher levels of participation and creativity than had been experienced in regular classrooms. No doubt the MESL project contributed to the fact that the Department of Art History and Archaeology received the university's award for teaching excellence in 1997. The kind of technical support and collaborative approach used in the MESL project to enhance interactive teaching and its extension outside the classroom inspired other related efforts in the department and college, and served to break down barriers that had existed between campus units before the advent of MESL.

Staff already see signs of the lasting effects of the MESL project at the University of Maryland. A recently funded project to share architectural images among five universities will use many of the tools created for the MESL project, including the data dictionary concept and the image search and retrieval software.

▶ University of Michigan

REASONS FOR PARTICIPATION The University of Michigan was attracted to the MESL project because of an interest in licensing as an economic model for managing intellectual property. Licensing, in terms of understanding the issues in the context of instruction, was also a compelling area for investigation within the MESL project. Providing digital image content for instructional programs was appealing, as was increasing the university community's interest in digital media. There was a sense that the MESL project could encourage art librarians, faculty, and students to work together on developing digital resources, as well as on defining and testing methodologies necessary to incorporate digital media into the classroom and the curriculum.

Use of the images in courses during the project was constrained by the fact that MESL didn't supply the critical mass of images required to attract faculty interest. Consequently, the university's focus shifted from an emphasis on classroom teaching using MESL images to identifying a process for providing image database access on campus (and to remote users). However, Michigan's interest in licensing continued throughout.

EFFECTS The impact of the MESL project at the University of Michigan was an increased interest in making digital image content available, either via licensing agreements or by capturing digital images in other ways (e.g., purchasing/obtaining them from other sources or scanning them locally). The MESL project contributed to Michigan's planning effort for implementing a digital image production service that would include local content development as well as contracted digital services. These plans feature various ways to involve faculty in strategies to build digital visual resources. Michigan's experience as the central distribution point for all of the MESL images taught staff a lot about infrastructure needs and what it takes to deliver images on campus to serve teaching, study, and research needs.

"One obstacle to using [MESL images] seems inevitable: those of us who are not at ease using computer technology will need a lot of time to master it and to explore. Unfortunately, time is scarce for faculty at UM, and despite the many encouragements to dedicate more time to innovative teaching ideas, for most of us the priorities remain research and meeting the immediate needs of students and administrative assignments."

REBECCA ZURIER
UNIVERSITY OF MICHIGAN
Technical Report

▶ University of Virginia

REASONS FOR PARTICIPATION Because the University of Virginia had been engaged in scanning images to build online databases for several years, staff there were already dealing with complex intellectual property and metadata issues. The MESL project seemed like a good way to experiment with expanding the existing image database by adding "licensed" content. There was also an expectation that additional funding would flow into the MESL project, helping to support the local efforts that were being operated with a skeleton staff. The MESL project came along when Virginia was ready to explore other means of access than its proprietary database manager software, and it fit with other campus initiatives in which individual faculty are identified and encouraged to use technology in new ways.

As the project developed over time, the University of Virginia used the MESL project as a model for treating standards issues, metadata, and image database construction. MESL became a point of reference for a number of people on campus, as Virginia continued to implement a host of related initiatives that employed electronic tools to support curriculum development and teaching.

EFFECTS A significant project outcome at Virginia occurred in a class that a faculty member in religious studies taught with MESL images. He found that using the images as the centerpiece of the course transformed the relationship between teacher and student. Technology leveled the playing field, and students took more responsibility for the content and success of the course because of the ways in which images were used. (This happened in a class in which the teacher had never taught with images before.) In the Art Department, graduate students were drawn into service to help capitalize on the availability of the MESL images, which they used for undergraduate study sessions and other outside-of-class assignments. MESL sparked an increased awareness that digital images are going to be

"We had some extraordinary early successes with MESL. A Religious Studies faculty member, Ben Ray, taught with MESL images and found that they totally transformed the relationship between teacher and student. It may have happened so readily because he had never taught with images before and didn't have preconceived notions of quality or a particular kind of functionality. . . Another significant outcome was the extent to which we were able to involve the graduate students in art history in using the MESL images, because in a sense we think that's a place where the payoff will be very great. Those are our future customers. . . "

JUDY THOMAS
UNIVERSITY OF VIRGINIA
Participants' Meeting

created all over campus, both by traditional units such as the academic departments and the library, and by individuals. The project underscored the necessity for mechanisms that integrate all of these resources coherently, and also provided models for how creating and managing these resources might be allocated between the library and technology support staffs.

▶ MESL Challenges and Collaborations

While there was considerable variation among institutions as to their reasons for participating, the challenges the MESL project posed were felt across the board. They are summarized here to inform those who follow, making special note of the fact that we learned as much from the problems encountered along the way as from the successes.

COLLABORATIONS Perhaps owing to the universal nature of the challenges presented, all seven institutions used similar approaches to tackle them—namely, interdepartmental teamwork and collaboration. Virtually every participant credited the MESL project with bringing experts from different campus units together to work in new and productive ways. For example, at the University of Illinois, the project stimulated increased support for a campus-wide image and multimedia database which was implemented in the summer of 1997. In addition, the library and the school of information studies got together to teach part of a course on system evaluation using the MESL database as an example for close study. At the University of Michigan, the information technology division and the library have teamed up to produce new digital imaging services for the campus. And the University of Maryland pioneered new software tools and teaching techniques that are already finding applications in other projects and courses.

This same spirit of collaboration eventually characterized the entire project: "Project staff worked together as a balanced team, and a rewarding kinship grew up among all the project staff from other institutions [as well,] which was extremely motivating and effective in creating a sense that the MESL community was interconnected and working towards the same end."[2] In the classroom, students became involved in a collaborative educational effort with their teachers that wouldn't have been possible with conventional art history teaching technology.

The universities in the Washington, D.C. area found that the MESL project enabled new kinds of cooperation with project museums in the area (the National Gallery of Art and the National Museum of American Art). The MESL project provided the impetus for an ongoing series of conversations and collaborations that are likely to continue. Among the most significant outcomes of the project are the ways in which overlapping concerns and shared interests of the academic and museum communities have been identified and highlighted, and further, that the project has had (and will continue to have) an impact on the solutions that are crafted. In particular, the mutually negotiated MESL Terms and Conditions document can serve as the basis for future site licensing agreements. A critically important benefit of the project, it represents a breakthrough in communication and mutual understanding between the academic and museum communities.

TIMING While the MESL project achieved remarkable success in only two years, the project could have benefited from an extended period of time. The ambitious schedule meant that the start-up phase of the project—including creation of the data dictionary; development of all of the technical procedures; selection, preparation, documentation, and distribution of database content; as well as deployment on local systems—needed to occur within the first six months of the project.

The extraordinary efforts of all participants came very close to meeting this goal, as the MESL database was mounted on campus servers just after the fall 1995 semester was under way. However, this meant that faculty only began using the images during either the winter of 1995–1996 (when the database was still incomplete) or the fall or winter semesters of 1996–1997 (by which time the project was entering the home stretch and faculty were often unwilling to commit the time and effort to redesigning a course for only one semester).

"I think our participation spurred interest in building digital image content—both in just licensing more from other sources as well as trying to get additional content that we already have on campus digitized and online . . . We learned a lot about infrastructure and how to develop the technologies we need to deliver images on campus . . . and we are prepared to move on to the next level."

JOHN WEISE
UNIVERSITY OF MICHIGAN
Participants' Meeting

LACK OF CRITICAL MASS The number of images (9,319 total images) represented a relatively limited resource. Such a small sample made it difficult for all but the most determined faculty members to incorporate MESL images into their courses. Those few professors who took the time to tailor courses—and participate in the less than optimal content selection process—had dramatically encouraging results. We learned from the MESL project that there must be a critical mass of pertinent images available before faculty will cross the technical Rubicon.

TECHNICAL ISSUES Even more daunting for faculty than the limited content in the database were the many types of technical challenges that the MESL project presented. Inadequate electronic classroom facilities, technical equipment, training programs, promotional materials, and preparation time seriously limited the scope and nature of the project's impact. Projection equipment is still prohibitively expensive, and if it exists anywhere on campus, it is rarely found in arts or humanities departments. Experience showed that students and faculty were reluctant to trek to borrowed classrooms in engineering departments; jury-rigging works to an extent for determined pioneers, but will not scale. Major financial investment in redesigning and retrofitting classrooms are necessary prerequisites.

In short, the technical and operational infrastructures necessary to support widespread and effective use of digital images are not yet in place. Nevertheless, MESL participants demonstrated how much can be accomplished under such "real world" conditions, and provided invaluable practical experience that can help set priorities and streamline subsequent improvements to the requisite infrastructure.

▶ Notes

1. In 1994–1995, The Research Libraries Group sponsored this project, which involved nine RLG institutions. In partnership with Stokes Imaging Services of Austin, Texas, it explored ways to catalog and index large photographic collections as well as to make them more accessible via electronic technology.
2. University of Maryland, MESL Technical Report (1997).

Findings of the Instructor/ Student Survey

BETH SANDORE

▶ Introduction : Purpose of the Evaluation

The purpose of the instructional evaluation was to establish a baseline of the use of digital images among students and instructors. Critical components of that baseline included demographics, technology background, and the attitudes of students and instructors at the seven MESL universities toward the use of digital images in the classroom and for individual learning in the study of fine arts, humanities, and other subjects. The instructional evaluation was carried out as a series of two surveys, the first administered at the beginning of the term between January 1 and February 17, 1997, and the second administered at the end of the term between April 10 and May 23, 1997. This summary is intended to report on the results and findings of these preliminary and post surveys that were administered to both students and instructors.

▶ Survey Design and Administration

Population

The focus of the project was limited to courses at the following seven universities for spring term, 1997:

- American University
- Columbia University
- Cornell University
- University of Illinois at Urbana–Champaign
- University of Maryland
- University of Michigan
- University of Virginia

Number and Type of Participants

Eighteen instructors at the seven universities offered a total of 11 courses that incorporated MESL images during the spring term 1997; all of these instructors agreed to participate in the evaluation study. The results presented in the instructor evaluation are based on data collected from the 18 instructors from all seven universities in the preliminary survey and 15 instructors from six universities in the post survey. In some cases, more than one instructor participated in teaching a course (see Table 1).

▶ **TABLE 1 Courses, Instructors, and Students Participating in the MESL Surveys—Spring 1997**

University	Course	Faculty (Pre)	Faculty (Post)	Student (Pre)	Student (Post)
AMERICAN UNIVERSITY Professor Katherine Ott	History in Images & Objects Course No. 29.387.01/ 29.687.01	yes	yes	14	12
AMERICAN UNIVERSITY Professor Jean-Christophe Hyacinthe	Introduction to Digital Imaging Course No. 17.519.01	yes	yes	13	14
COLUMBIA UNIVERSITY Preceptor Kim Dramer	Masterpieces of Western Art Course No. C1121 Sec 8	yes	yes	23	22
COLUMBIA UNIVERSITY Professor Alexander Vergara	Masterpieces of Western Art Course No. C1121 Sec 18	yes	yes	19	21
COLUMBIA UNIVERSITY Teach. Asst. Ethan Roberts	Masterpieces of Western Art Course No. C1121 Sec 17	yes	yes	19	17
COLUMBIA UNIVERSITY Professor Thomas Dale	Masterpieces of Western Art Course No. C1121 Sec 15	yes	no	17	16
COLUMBIA UNIVERSITY Preceptor Sean Sawyer	Masterpieces of Western Art Course No. C1121 Sec 13	yes	yes	14	12
COLUMBIA UNIVERSITY Professor Alexander MacGillivray	Masterpieces of Western Art Course No. C1121 Sec 12	yes	no	16	19
COLUMBIA UNIVERSITY Professor David Rosand	Graphic Arts of the 18th Century Course No. G8573	yes	yes	8	7
CORNELL UNIVERSITY Professor Laura Meixner	Impressionism & Society Course No. 362	yes	yes	20	26
Teach. Asst. Susan Newbury		yes	no		

(continued)

▶ **TABLE 1** *continued*

University	Course	Faculty (Pre)	Faculty (Post)	Student (Pre)	Student (Post)
UNIVERSITY OF ILLINOIS Professor Katherine Manthorne	Early American Modernism 1900–1945 Course No. ARTH 351	yes	yes	17	18
UNIVERSITY OF ILLINOIS Professor Jean-Philippe Mathy	History of French Civilization II Course No. French 336	yes	yes	23	22
UNIVERSITY OF MARYLAND Professor Sally M. Promey	American Art to 1876 Course No. ARTH 453	yes	yes	31	26
UNIVERSITY OF MARYLAND Professor Terry Gips	Art Theory: Digital Imaging Seminar Course No. ARTT 468/689	yes	no	15	0
UNIVERSITY OF MICHIGAN Professor Diane Kirkpatrick	Problems in 20th Century Art Course No. HA 773	yes	no	6	0
UNIVERSITY OF VIRGINIA Teach. Assits. Kim Therault Howard Blazzard, Melanie Kirschner, Johanna Bauman	Modernist Art Course No. Arth 254	yes no yes no	yes yes yes yes	96	46
TOTAL		**18**	**15**	**351**	**278**

Approximately 351 students who were enrolled in courses at the seven MESL universities during the spring term 1997 participated in the preliminary instructional evaluation. A total of 278 students who were enrolled in courses participated in the post-instructional evaluation.

Both instructors and students who either taught or were enrolled in the courses using MESL images completed a series of two survey questionnaires—a preliminary and a post survey. Two separate types of questionnaires were designed to elicit information from the two different perspectives: (1) from instructors about teaching with the MESL images, and (2) from students about using the MESL images in conjunction with their course work and assignments (see Appendix E, "Instructor/Student Surveys," pages 186–200).

Survey Instruments

Survey instruments were developed that polled both instructors and students in their classes about their current use of visual resources, their intended use of MESL images, their attitudes about using digital images, and their preferences for future image database development and delivery of cultural heritage information. Information was collected in three areas on both the student and the instructor surveys: (1) personal information (demographics), (2) technology background (including current use of visual resources), and (3) the use or intended use of the MESL images.

The surveys were administered in two waves—a preliminary survey at the beginning of the term and a post survey near the end of the term. Both surveys were administered to instructors and to students in their classes. Further information about the guidelines for the implementation of the surveys on each campus, and about the human subjects review that occurred on each university campus can be found at the MESL Evaluation and Base Measurement Working Group Web site (*http://www.gii.getty.edu/mesl/eval/eval.html*).

The survey instruments were developed initially by a group of MESL colleagues at the University of Maryland, in conjunction with the MESL Evaluation and Base Measurement Working Group. The University of Maryland group crafted a survey based on internal surveys that were administered in early 1996 at the University of Maryland, and other surveys were developed and used at American University and the University of Michigan. In the fall of 1996, six institutions tested the draft survey developed by the University of Maryland team. A University of Illinois group collected the completed surveys in late fall and performed an informal analysis of the responses. This cursory analysis indicated that the replacement of open-ended questions with multiple-choice questions had the potential to increase response rates. A number of other changes were drafted by the University of Illinois group and reviewed by the MESL Evaluation and Base Measurement Working Group at the December 1996 meeting. These changes were approved and finalized by January 1997.

Survey Structure and Content

The preliminary survey was designed to gather information that would enable us to build a profile of students and instructors by asking questions or obtaining opinions on their technology expertise, their current use of visual resources, their use or intended use of the MESL images, and what type of impact they believed their use of digital images would have on the way they (1) pursued their own research, (2) taught in the classroom (in the case of the instructors), and (3) completed course assignments (in the case of students). Before the surveys were administered, a set of evaluation questions was extrapolated from all of the survey instruments combined. This set of questions was used as the framework for the analysis in this report.

The post survey, which was administered near the end of the term on each campus, was designed to elicit information about a number of topics related to the use of MESL images:

- Changes in the attitudes toward using MESL images
- Comfort level with using computer technology
- Ratings of the quality and the use of digital images
- Preferred characteristics of a future image database
- The relationships between participants' attitudes, comfort levels, ratings, preferences for an image database, and factors such as their institutional affiliation and status

STUDENT PRELIMINARY AND POST SURVEYS

The two main questions that were explored in the student preliminary survey were:

- To what extent is technology expertise, comfort level with using computer technology, attitude toward using digital images, and the current use of digital images associated with demographic characteristics including gender, status, choice of major, and institutional affiliation?

- Are there significant differences in these variables across these demographic characteristics?

The questions that were explored in the student post survey included:

- Did the participants' attitudes towards using MESL images and their comfort level with using computer technology change over time, and to what degree are they associated with race, gender, status, major, and institution?
- Are the ratings of the quality and the use of digital images associated with race, gender, status, major, and institution?
- What kinds of functions and information are important to include in a future image database? Are these preferences associated with race, gender, status, major, and institution?

FACULTY PRELIMINARY AND POST SURVEYS

The purpose of the MESL evaluation study for the instructors was to:

- Determine if instructors' technological backgrounds and attitudes toward using computer technology influenced their use of MESL images for instruction.
- Describe participants' ratings of the quality and the use of digital images.
- Identify characteristics of an image database appropriate for instruction and research.

▸ Methods Employed in the Presentation and Analysis of Results

Demographic Information

Simple frequency distributions were performed for each variable in both the student and the instructor surveys. Aggregate data is reported here, and some discussion of individual institution data is also included. A full complement of data-reporting information for the aggregate as well as the individual universities is accessible on the MESL Evaluation and Base Measurement Working Group Web site, under the heading "Current Activities" (*http://www.gii.getty.edu/mesl/eval/eval.html*).

For the instructor preliminary information, a data set of 18 observations was analyzed. For the instructor post information, a data set of 15 observations was analyzed. For the student preliminary descriptive information, a data set of 351 observations was used. For the student post descriptive information, a data set of 278 observations was used. Since the data collected for the instructor group included a small number of observations, only descriptive information was reported. The higher number of observations from the student surveys permitted us to perform statistical analysis of relationships between independent and dependent variables.

Open-ended Questions

A number of open-ended questions were posed on the student and the instructor surveys, both preliminary and post. The responses to these questions have been assembled in appendices that are included in the full, unpublished Instructor/Student Evaluation report.[1] The responses have been reviewed but have not been formally analyzed as part of this report. The student responses, with individual student identification numbers, are sorted by institution.

Tests of Significance: Student Preliminary and Post Surveys

CHI-SQUARE ANALYSIS

An initial exploratory analysis using the chi-square analysis method was performed on a number of the variables in both the student preliminary and post survey questionnaires to identify relationships among dependent and independent variables. For the preliminary survey, a data set of 345 observations (omitting the University of Michigan) was used. For the post analysis, a data set of 278 observations was used.

T-TESTS

Finally, t-tests were performed on nine variables matched for similar or identical questions posed on the preliminary and the post surveys, using the merged file of preliminary and post data, which contained 357 observations. These questions elicited opinions and attitudes from students about using the MESL images and other digital images, as well as technology. The objective of the t-tests was to determine whether there had been a significant shift in the attitudes or opinions about using digital images of the aggregate student group from the preliminary to the post survey.

FURTHER ANALYSIS OF INTERACTIONS

Regression analysis was attempted using the preliminary student survey data set. However, the composition of the data set made it impossible to perform further analysis (e.g., regression analysis using several variables) to determine the extent of interaction among variables that would show which variables affect digital image use habits, and to what degree those variables affected those behaviors. In a number of cases, the values within cells were too small to determine significant effects. On a test basis, we were able to perform chi-square analysis controlling for one independent variable at a time with some useful results. This area of examination is recommended for future analysis of this data.

▶ Results : Student Preliminary and Post Surveys

Objectives

The objective of the preliminary survey analysis was to establish a baseline profile of the students who completed the surveys and who were enrolled in courses where MESL images were going to be used in the classroom. While that information did *not* enable us to describe the "average student" in this group, it did enable us to construct a profile of the aggregate group across the seven institutions, and to examine the areas where sectors of the group differed in statistically significant ways. The results of the analysis of the preliminary student survey suggest that there were significant differences across the participant group in their technology backgrounds, use of visual resources, access to computers, and the intended use of the MESL images. The composition of the data set made it impossible to perform further analysis (e.g., regression analysis using several variables) to determine the extent of interaction among variables that would show what affects use habits, and to what degree that variable affects those use habits.

The objective of the post survey analysis was to examine and further extend the baseline profile of the students who completed the surveys, to analyze significant relationships among the independent (status, major, gender, institution, etc.) and the dependent variables in the post survey questionnaire, and to recognize attitude statements that were either similar or identical across the preliminary and the post surveys.

While both the preliminary and the post survey questionnaires were administered to the same classes for each institution, not all of the same individuals may have been present for both of the surveys. In essence, the preliminary survey and the post survey represent two separate sets of individuals, some number of which are represented in both the preliminary and the post surveys. For this reason we reported the demographic information for the post data in addition to that for the preliminary data. There are strong similarities. However, one will find that, in comparing the preliminary and the post frequency data, there are slight differences in the category percentages of students who responded to the questions. These differences are either due to the fact that the same students responded to the questions differently than they did in the preliminary survey, or due to the fact that there were simply different students responding to the post survey in some cases. No attempt at analyzing these differences is made in the presentation of the information below, unless there is a marked difference in the percentage of responses from the preliminary to the post surveys.

Demographic Profile: Preliminary Survey

Students were roughly divided into several categories of majors, of which Fine Arts (18 percent) and Humanities (25 percent) comprised a total of 43 percent of the population on the preliminary survey. Social Science/Other majors comprised approximately 57 percent of the group. More than half of the students were women (62 percent), and less than half were men (38 percent). In terms of status, undergraduates made up the largest part of the group (91 percent), with 47 percent lower- and 44 percent upper-class undergraduates. Graduate students comprised 9 percent of the participant group. Across institutions, there was some variability on the makeup of the student populations depending on the type of class taught. A significant minority of students (40 percent) who registered for the class indicated they had done so out of personal interest. Another 36 percent indicated that the class was a general requirement, and 24 percent enrolled in the class as part of a major/minor requirement. In terms of race/ethnicity (an optional response) a majority of the students (77 percent) enrolled in the MESL courses indicated they were "White," 15 percent indicated they were "Asian," 4 percent "African-American," 3 percent "Hispanic," and .33 percent "Other."

Technology Background and Access to Computing Resources

Overall, 69 percent of the students in the preliminary survey rated themselves as having "average experience" with computing technologies. Just over half of the students (53 percent) indicated they had "average experience" with office applications such as word processing and spreadsheet software. Internet applications proved to be the area where most students had the highest level of technology experience. Forty-nine percent of the students indicated they had a high level of experience with the Internet, and another 45 percent indicated they had an "average level of experience." Most students indicated that they had "none to low" experience with advanced computing applications such as digital video editing or Web programming (see Figure 1).

A vast majority of the students (98 percent) indicated that they felt comfortable using technology in their course work. Further, over half of the students (58 percent) indicated that they owned a computer from which they could access MESL images. An

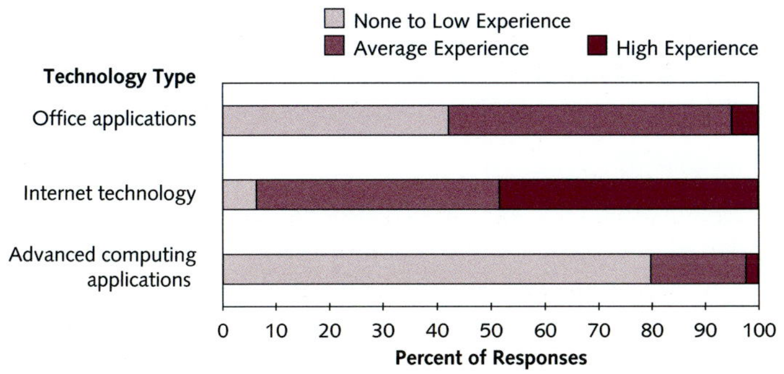

▶ **FIGURE 1** Technology Background by Level of Experience

overwhelming majority of the students (92 percent) indicated that they used computers on campus, while 58 percent indicated that they used computers in an office, a dormitory, or from home. Over half of the students (65 percent) indicated that it was not difficult to get help on campus to learn to use various computing technologies.

The chi-square analysis revealed that there were significant differences in the technology backgrounds of the students. The largest dichotomy across the board appeared with the independent variable "gender." In all three of the areas, and in the combined area of technology background, significantly higher percentages of men ranked their experience at higher levels than did women. These differences have been identified in other studies, and it appears that a gender/technology gap that favors men exists in the group of students who participated in this study as well. One possible reason for this result is the tendency of women to underestimate their skills when assessing themselves. What was surprising about this documented difference was the fact that after approximately ten years of access to computers and networked computing resources on college and university campuses, as well as the widespread popularity of grade school and high school computing programs, significant gender differences persist among students at both the undergraduate and graduate levels with respect to their technology experience.

Further analysis of technology background revealed that there were significant differences across institutions in technology backgrounds of the students. Several factors appear to be involved in this overall technology background picture, and it is clear that further exploration of the data set should be done in order to determine the causes for differences in technology backgrounds. As a rough summary statement, specific areas of technology experience appeared higher at the two private universities (Columbia and Cornell), but the data is simply not sufficient to support more detailed analysis of whether this trend is borne out. Students at Cornell also indicated a higher percentage of "average experience" with office applications (see Figure 2 on page 108).

However, when analysis on these variables was performed controlling for student status, it was found that student status played a mitigating role, creating a different picture where technology background varied first by status, then by institution. Access to their own computers could be a factor in enhancing students' technology backgrounds. A significantly higher percentage of students at Columbia University and a similar percentage of students at the University of Maryland indicated that they owned their own computers from which they could access the MESL images. It is difficult to determine from the resulting data whether a particular institution or group of institutions provide their students with more comprehensive technology tools than others in the group, and whether that in fact influenced the technology background levels at which the students ranked themselves. In terms of specific technology backgrounds, the results revealed that across the board, students ranked themselves as having the most experience in the area of Internet applications.

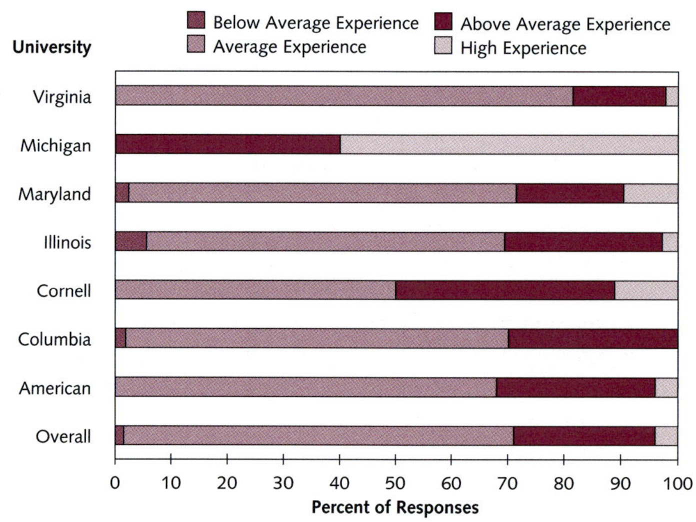

▶ **FIGURE 2** Technology Background by Institution

Use of Visual Resources

Print and film representations of visual resources are still heavily used in the study of art works. Over half of the students (64 percent) indicated that they used prints or textbooks "regularly" to study art works. Thirty percent of the students indicated that they use slides "regularly," and 47 percent "sometimes." *However, the use of digital images to study art works has established itself unmistakably, with 65 percent of the students indicating that they used digital images "sometimes"* (see Figure 3).

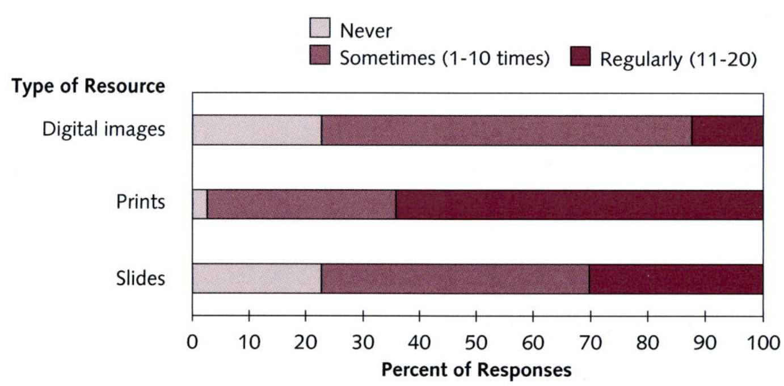

▶ **FIGURE 3** Current Use of Visual Resources

It is important to note that, while the majority of the classes taught were categorized as Art History, the students' use of visual resources and their intended use of the MESL images for the courses varied significantly across institutions, by student status, and by major. No real gender differences resulted in these areas. These results suggest several potential causes, and most likely the results can be attributed to a combination of factors.

It was apparent from the survey results that the MESL institutions differed in the ways in which they required students to obtain access to visual resources for classroom use or for individual study. These differences are most likely contingent on the infrastructure that each institution had set up for using visual resources. For example, the University of

Maryland used the locally developed Caprina and the Slidesearch online systems that enabled instructors to project digital images of art resources on classroom screens, as well as enabled each student to have simultaneous access to a monitor with the same image on his or her desktop. Thus, in the analysis, the University of Maryland, as well as American University, had a higher percentage of students who indicated that they "never" used slides to study visual resources than those at the other institutions. Students at the University of Illinois relied heavily on slide collections in their slide library, although the university was in the process of converting slides to digital images in order to make them accessible from instructors' Web pages (along with the MESL images). While the frequency distributions indicated that 63 percent of the students used digital images "sometimes" to study visual resources, there were no significant relationships that resulted in the chi-square analysis with that dependent variable and any of the demographic independent variables.

Student status appears to have some influence on the frequency of use of various formats of visual resources, with more graduate students using slides "sometimes" or "regularly" than lower- or upper-class undergraduates. This could be due to the fact that graduate students, particularly those enrolled in art history courses, are required to use slides as well as prints, photographs, and textbooks on a regular basis to study art images. Further, graduate students have been studying visual resources for a longer period of time and are more likely to have established use patterns of traditional print and film-based technologies for this purpose.

Use or Intended Use of the MESL Images

PRELIMINARY SURVEY

Over half of the students (56 percent) indicated that they had not used the MESL images, while nearly half (44 percent) indicated that they had already used the MESL images, either in the class that was surveyed, or in previous classes, or through personal browsing and discovery. Most students indicated that they intended to use MESL images for fairly traditional purposes—mainly to write a paper—but students also indicated that they intended to search the collection online to examine the images.

Use or intended use of the MESL images, like use of visual resources, proved to be subject to the influence of the particular university environment, and most likely a particular function of the types of assignments and research that students were asked to complete within the scope of a course (primarily art history classes) (see Figure 4).

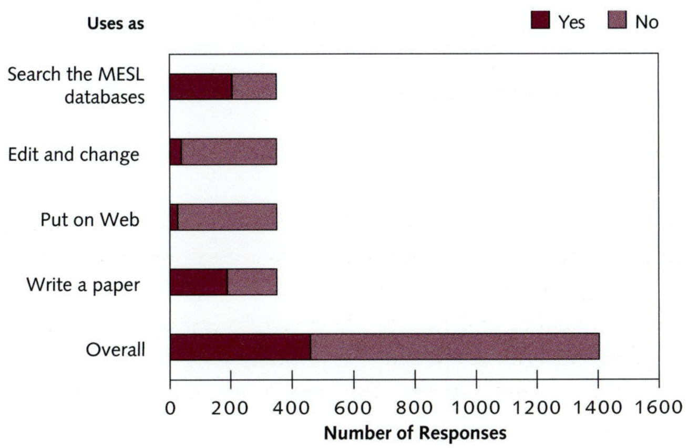

▶ **FIGURE 4** Use or Intended Use of MESL Images

Significantly more students at the University of Virginia than at any other institution indicated they intended to write a paper in which they analyzed the MESL images. Students at both American University and the University of Illinois indicated this choice the least of all six institutions. The analysis also revealed that more lower- than upper-class undergraduates or graduate students chose this as an option for how they intended to use the MESL images. In constructing the surveys, the MESL Evaluation and Base Measurement Working Group classified "writing a paper" as a more traditional use of the MESL images. On the spectrum of possible uses ranging from "writing a paper" to "editing and manipulating MESL images," writing a paper represents a traditional use of visual resources.

The remaining three options for using MESL images (searching, editing/manipulating, and incorporating images into a Web page) addressed the more technologically oriented aspects of digital image use. Searching the MESL collections was an intended use that was chosen significantly more often at Cornell University than at other institutions. The option of searching the collection may not have been applicable at some institutions where the images that were selected for a class were already linked from an instructor's Web page. Therefore, students may not have needed to search the MESL collection in order to identify images for study. Status appeared to play a significant role in whether a student indicated he or she intended to edit and manipulate the MESL images as part of a project, with more upper-class undergraduate and graduate students indicating they intended to use the images in this way. Gender also influenced whether or not a student indicated an intention to edit and change the images, with more men than women indicating they intended to edit and manipulate the images for a project.

POST SURVEY

Over half of the students (65 percent) enrolled in the courses taught with MESL images indicated that they used MESL images during the term in conjunction with that course. Further analysis revealed that significantly more Fine Arts/Humanities majors than Social Science/Other majors used the MESL images in conjunction with the course. Additionally, upper-class undergraduates and graduate students were more likely to have viewed the images for the course than lower-class undergraduates. Approximately 40 percent of the students indicated that they had used digital images other than the MESL images during that term. An overwhelming majority of the students (81 percent) at the six institutions used the MESL images from 1 to 11 times during the term. Approximately one-fifth of the students (19 percent) noted that they used the images more than 11 times during the term (see Figure 5).

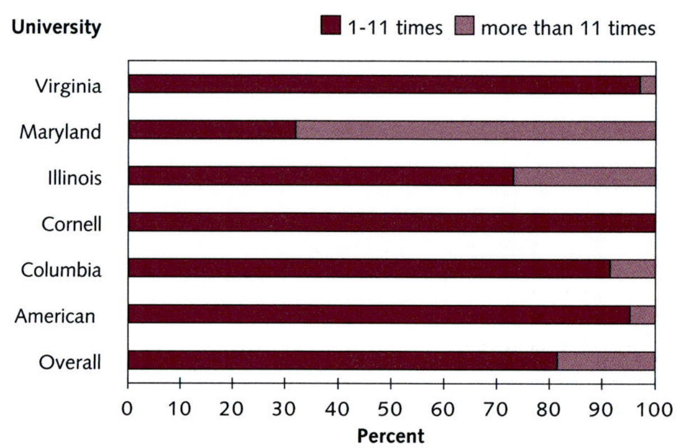

▶ **FIGURE 5** Frequency of Student Usage of MESL Images

MESL images, as well as other digital images, were clearly used by a majority of students in the six institutions who were enrolled in the participating classes. MESL images were used most often in assignments that used visual resources in traditional ways. The most frequently cited use of the MESL data was for the text information describing the images. Other uses included side-by-side comparison of two images during lectures and reviews for tests. Use of the images in more advanced technology applications (e.g., in Web page construction or a multimedia presentation) was infrequent. A number of significant interactions were observed between the independent variables and the variables that described how students used MESL images. Significant variations in the types and frequency of uses were found across institutions. Student status was also found to be a significant factor in the frequency and the types of uses of the MESL images.

Over half of the students participating in the survey indicated that they owned a computer that they could use to access MESL images from home. An overwhelming number of the students (94 percent) indicated that they were comfortable using computer technology in conjunction with their course work. Students obtained access to MESL images most often from (in order of frequency): computer labs (22 percent), the library (16 percent), a residence hall (15 percent), a classroom (13 percent), or home (11 percent).

Opinions About Using MESL Images

PRELIMINARY SURVEY

Students' responses to the attitude statements in this section of the survey indicate overall positive attitudes toward the use of MESL and digital images in conjunction with course work. The important positive factor about access to MESL images appeared to be that students could access them from remote locations (92 percent). A majority of students (66 percent) disagreed with the statements that using digital images would involve more work and that using digital images would be less convenient than using print images (75 percent). An overwhelming majority of students felt that having access to MESL images would give them access to art works which they had not seen previously, and that it would be easy to integrate images into their papers and projects (see Figure 6).

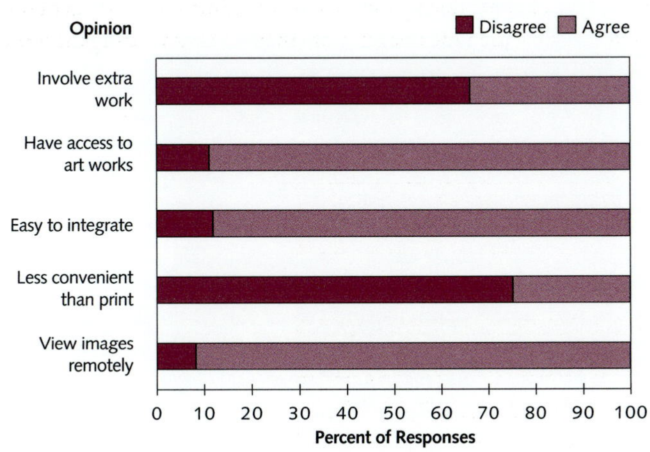

► **FIGURE 6** Opinions about Using MESL Images

The only area in which significant differences occurred among students about using MESL images was revealed when the survey data was examined by the variable "major." Fine Arts/Humanities students disagreed significantly more often than did Social Science/Other majors with the statement that using MESL images would give them access to images that they could not otherwise use. As was noted earlier, it is likely that students who were Fine Arts/Humanities majors had more knowledge about where they could locate visual resource materials that are not easily found in mainstream resources.

POST SURVEY

Students' overall attitudes about using MESL images were positive. Most students (72 percent) did not feel that using MESL involved more work, and most of them (80 percent) felt that MESL provided them with access to images of art works to which they would otherwise not have access. They found it easy to incorporate MESL images into papers and projects (68 percent). An overwhelming majority of students (95 percent) felt it was advantageous to be able to view the images from a remote location. An overwhelming majority of the students (96 percent) indicated that it was easy to use the MESL database at their institution. A majority of the students (72 percent) indicated that using the MESL database enabled them to do things with images that they could not do with slides, prints, or textbooks. More than half of the students (63 percent) agreed with the statement that using digital images made the study of art more interesting than using slides, prints, or textbooks. Students indicated in a majority of cases (72 percent) that the MESL images were presented with enthusiasm in class (see Figure 7).

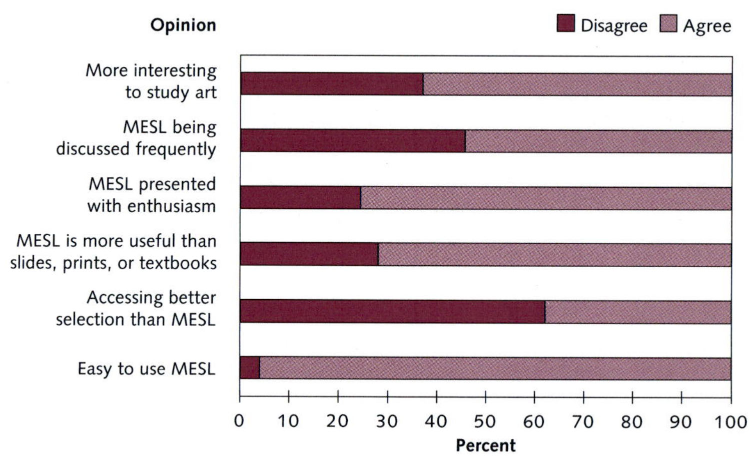

▶ **FIGURE 7** Opinions about Using MESL Images (Post Survey Only)

Students appear to be pleased with the ease of access to the MESL database, and with the fact that it provided them with access to unique and valued digital images. *The survey findings suggest that, while most of the students recognize the flexibility of digital images to enable them to accomplish things that print and film counterparts cannot, it is only a small group of early technology adopters who have begun to use digital images in innovative ways.*

Usefulness of the MESL Data

Overall, a majority of students rated all aspects of the MESL data at their respective institutions to be useful. Screen-size (97 percent) and highest-resolution images (93 percent) were the most frequently noted useful aspects of the MESL database. The search capability (88 percent), the availability of thumbnail images (86 percent), and the text information describing the images (83 percent) were functions that were also selected as useful by a majority of the students (see Figure 8).

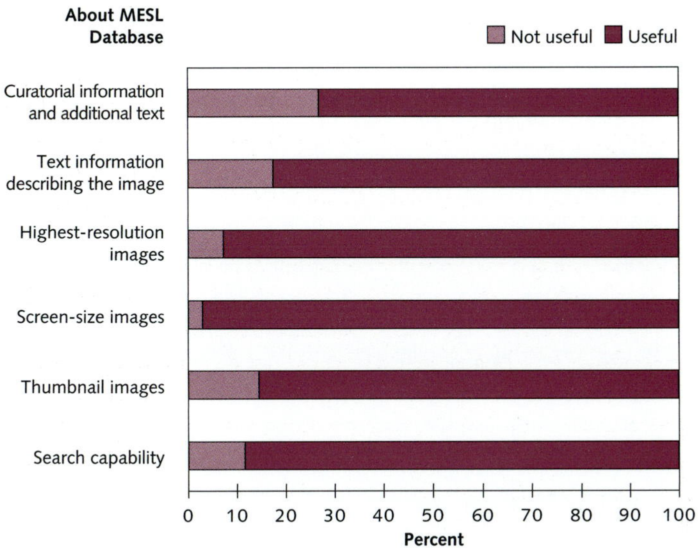

▶ **FIGURE 8** Usefulness of MESL Data

In general, the basic information that was supplied in the MESL database at each campus was considered to be useful by the majority of student users in the classes that used MESL images. More analysis revealed that a slightly higher percentage of Fine Arts/Humanities majors than Social Science/Other majors found the screen-size images to be useful. Further, more women than men found the text information describing the images to be useful.

Quality of MESL Images Viewed on a Computer Screen and in the Classroom

Overall, students rated the quality of MESL images when viewed on a computer screen as "above average." Color (90 percent), size (78 percent), clarity/resolution (75 percent), and detail (74 percent) were rated "above average" by the majority of students. The "time to load images" on the screen was rated "above average" by over half of the students (65 percent). Color quality ratings of "excellent" at two institutions were noted as significant, which might be an indicator of the institutions' commitment to quality imaging technology.

Students' ratings differed slightly for the various components of quality when the MESL images were viewed with classroom projection equipment. Fewer students (64 percent) rated clarity/resolution or detail "above average" than those who viewed the images from a computer screen. Color received a lower percentage of "above average" ratings (72 percent) for classroom projection than for on-screen computer display. Interestingly, most students (79 percent) rated the time to load images as "above average" when images were viewed on classroom projection equipment, whereas they rated time to load images lower when they viewed them on a computer screen. Ratings of the detail of images when viewed with projection equipment varied significantly across institutions. Again, this variation could well be due to the variability of projection equipment.

Attitude Shifts: Paired Questions from Preliminary to Post Surveys

Several interesting and significant shifts occurred in the attitudes of the two groups of students who completed the preliminary and the post surveys. First, there was an increase (32 percent) from the preliminary to the post survey in the percentage of students who indicated they had used MESL images. This increase bears out the assumption that exposure to the images in the classroom promotes usage. Next, the number of students who felt it would be useful to integrate MESL images into their papers and projects increased by 23 percent from the preliminary to the post survey. There was a slight increase (10 percent) in the number of students who believed that the MESL database provided them with access to images of art that would not otherwise be accessible. And finally, the percentage of students who had indicated that they were *not* comfortable with computer technology became slightly *less* comfortable in the time that elapsed between the preliminary and the post survey. This interesting shift could be due to the fact that students who were introduced to new technologies during the term were still developing these skills.

▶ Results : Instructor Preliminary and Post Surveys

Demographic Information

In the preliminary survey, eight male (44 percent) and ten female (56 percent) instructors participated in the survey. In the post survey there were eight male and seven female instructors.

Technology Background and Access to Computing Resources

The majority of the instructors indicated that they were familiar with the basic applications required to comfortably use the digital images on the Web, and about 50 percent of the instructors in the sample indicated that they had knowledge of software in the advanced applications category. In the office applications category, 78 percent of the instructors rated themselves as having "average" experience, 17 percent with "above average" experience, and only 6 percent indicated "no experience." In the Internet tools category, 56 percent rated themselves as having "above average" experience and 44 percent indicated "average" experience. In the advanced applications category, 44 percent indicated "no" experience, 50 percent "average" experience, and 5.6 percent "above average" experience.

To successfully integrate computer technology into curriculum and instruction, instructors require, at the minimum, the existence of the following components:

- A technology support system to facilitate the process of integrating technology into curriculum and instruction
- A comfort level with using the technology in curriculum and instruction and for research purposes
- Adequate access to the technology resources

A majority of the faculty (61 percent) indicated in the survey that it was relatively easy to get help on their campus to learn to use computer technology. Approximately 89 percent are comfortable using computer technology as part of their daily work, and

67 percent are familiar with using computer technology to develop instructional material. More than half of the instructors (56 percent) indicated that they are not comfortable using computer technology in the classroom. Even though instructors were comfortable with using the technology, more than half indicated that they were not ready to use the technology in the classroom. Slide and print technologies are considered to be relatively more dependable than digital technology. One possible explanation could be the time lag required for the instructors to gain confidence using the new technology before fully integrating it into instruction.

A majority of the instructors (78 percent) indicated that their department provided access to computer technology that would enable them to use MESL images; 41 percent had a computer in their office to access the digital images. Eighty-two percent indicated that students in their class had easy access to computer labs where they could use quality digital images, and 44 percent indicated that these computer labs were also conveniently located to their departments.

Use of Visual Resources

All of the instructors indicated that they used slides "regularly." A majority (89 percent) indicated that they used print/photographs "regularly," 6 percent using them "sometimes," and 6 percent "never" using slides at all. Online digital images were used "regularly" by 39 percent of the instructors, 28 percent used them "sometimes," and 33 percent "never" used the digital images (see Figure 9).

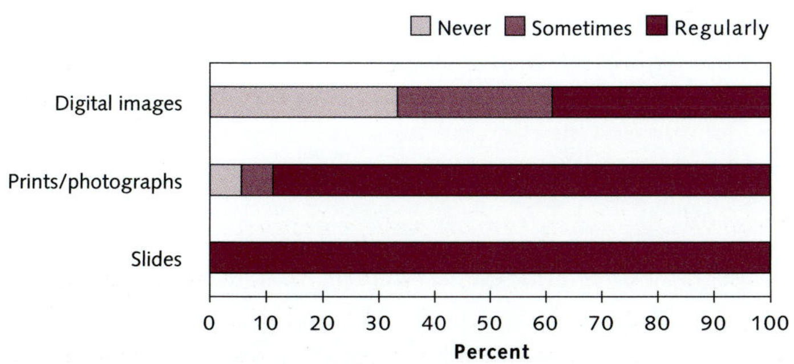

► **FIGURE 9** Use of Visual Resources

Use (or Intended Use) of the MESL Images

Digital images were used for a variety of purposes in curriculum and instruction. Six common uses of digital images were identified, and the instructors were asked to select the common uses of digital images from the following:

- Search/browse the MESL collection to determine its contents
- Select images for class
- Display the images in class
- Incorporate the images into an electronic (Web) page
- Create assignments for student projects
- Use images for research

The participants rated the six categories in the order shown in the following table (see Table 2 on page 116).

▶ TABLE 2 Common Usages of Digital Images and Related Frequencies of Occurrence

Category	Frequency
Search/browse the MESL collection to determine its contents	14
Select images for class	11
Create assignments for student projects	11
Display the images in class	10
Incorporate the images into an electronic (Web) page	10
Use images for research	6

The instructors, in general, were aware of the overall content of the MESL database. Their intentions are reflected in their ratings of the six categories and conform to the overall sequential process of using images for curriculum and instruction: One has to first search and browse the image database, select the images, display them in the class, and use them for student assignments. Instructors are also becoming more comfortable with the Internet and are beginning to provide instructional resources on the Internet. The frequencies for these categories reflect this process.

USE OF MESL IMAGES BY MUSEUM COLLECTION

Overall there was a close match between instructor expectations for the collections they would use and their actual usage of resources from respective museums. Not all of the museum resources were used equally. Some museums were more heavily used than others. The visual resources at the National Gallery of Art was used most often, followed by The Museum of Fine Arts, Houston, and the Harvard University Art Museums. The intended use (13) and the actual use (13) was equal for the National Gallery of Art. The actual use (9) was higher than the intended use (7) for The Museum of Fine Arts, Houston. For the rest of the museums, the actual use fell short of the intended use by a very small margin. The following table presents the order in which the resources from museums were used:

▶ TABLE 3 Usage Frequencies of Digital Images Supplied by Participating Museums

Museum	Intended Use	Actual Use
National Gallery of Art	13	13
The Museum of Fine Arts, Houston	7	9
Harvard University Art Museums	9	8
George Eastman House	6	5
National Museum of American Art	6	5
Library of Congress	6	4
Fowler Museum of Cultural History	3	2

FREQUENCY OF USE AND POINT OF ACCESS

A majority of the instructors (64 percent) accessed MESL images between 2–10 times, 21 percent accessed the images once, and about 7 percent accessed them more than 11 times for the term. The instructor's office and the campus library were rated as the most frequently used sites, with a frequency of 7 for each site. Classrooms, computer labs, and off-campus locations were the next preferred sites, with a frequency of 4.

Opinions About Using Digital Images, Technology, and MESL Images in the Classroom

Instructors were asked to indicate their opinion about using technology and whether digital images had affected their work in research and teaching. Instructors were also asked to indicate their opinion on whether online access to digital images is useful for student use.

All of the instructors agreed that online availability of digital images would enable students to have remote access to the digital images. About 80 percent indicated that students would be able to integrate the digital images into their class projects, and 94 percent agreed that online availability of digital images would provide access to art work that is normally not available to the students. In general, instructors agreed that online access to digital images was beneficial to the students.

All of the instructors agreed that online availability of digital images would complement their traditional source of images. Whether or not instructors will actually use the digital images depends on how they perceive that the use of digital images will affect their time and other resources. About 61 percent felt these images would provide an additional perspective, and that they had to put in extra work to use the online images. To the question of whether MESL images will be used to design assignments that are not possible with slides/print images, about 76 percent of the instructors responded that they would not. MESL digital images were provided to the educational institutions as an additional resource to supplement visual resources from conventional sources such as slides, prints, and the textbook. The data from the survey support this intention. In the early phases of online technology, it is natural for instructors to view the digital resources as a supplement. With continued availability of online digital resources, instructors will be able to find innovative uses of digital images in their daily work.

Instructors were asked to indicate their opinion about how the use of the MESL images affected their work and their teaching. A majority of the instructors (86 percent) indicated that it was advantageous to view the MESL images from a remote location. Half of the instructors (50 percent) indicated that using online digital images was less convenient than using images from slides or books, and 71 percent indicated that the classroom setup was not convenient for using digital images. A majority of instructors (79 percent) indicated that the MESL database was easy to use, and 64 percent indicted that they were able to access a larger collection of digital images. About 43 percent of the instructors indicated that the selection of digital images from the MESL database was adequate for their use, and 64 percent indicated that they can get a better selection of digital images from other sources. About 50 percent indicated that digital images make the study of art more interesting than using slides, prints, and textbooks. Since digital images were used as an additional resource along with images from slides, prints, and textbooks, a majority of the instructors (71 percent) indicated that using digital images involved extra work.

More than half of the instructors (57 percent) indicated that they could not have achieved the same objectives in their class by using images from conventional sources such as textbooks, prints, and slides. A majority of the instructors (71 percent) stated that their students were able to integrate digital images into their class projects.

HOW MESL ASSISTED IN TEACHING

MESL images were mostly used for projects outside the class and for research. The next most frequent use was for in-class projects and assignments. MESL images were less often used to accompany class lectures. A majority of the instructors (85 percent) indicated that they used the MESL digital images to complement the slides and images in the textbook, and 62 percent indicated that they were able to design assignments with digital images that were not possible with slide and print resources. About 46 percent indicated that they used the MESL digital images to provide an additional perspective on a given concept.

Usefulness of the MESL Database

Online digital image databases present the most complex challenges for presenting and manipulating visual and textual information. A digital image database with search capability and high-resolution, screen-size, and thumbnail-size images were rated high (13–14). Instructors indicated that both the text and the curatorial information accompanying the image provide important additional information about the visual resource and are a standard and often useful feature of the database. The instructors (9 in one case and 10 in the other) rated these features as relatively important.

Quality of MESL Images Viewed on a Computer Screen and in the Classroom

Instructors were asked about the quality of the MESL images when they were viewed on a computer screen and on classroom display equipment. The overall ratings for the quality of the images when viewed on a computer screen was good to excellent in terms of color, details, clarity/resolution, size, and the time to download. The overall rating of the quality of the images when viewed on classroom projection equipment in terms of color, detail, clarity/resolution, and time to download was poor to fair. Forty percent of the instructors (5) selected the "Not applicable" option, implying that either there was no projection equipment available in their classroom or they did not use it for the class.

▶ Student and Instructor Observations Side-by-Side

Future Image Database Preferences: Student and Instructor Ratings Compared

The preferences of students and instructors for image database features were compared. Four categories of image database features and functions were examined: content, search, display and manipulation, and communication. Both groups most frequently cited content features in their preferences, followed by communication, search, and display and manipulation. Both groups recommended including "more images" and "more artists" as the top two choices. "More cultures" was a content feature that appeared in the top five rankings of both faculty and student groups. Faculty chose "more genres" and "more styles" more often than did students, ranking them higher than did students. Students as a group ranked "more text information" as a higher priority than did faculty. In terms of search access points, both instructors and students chose search by artist most frequently, with search by genre, date, and culture cited less frequently. The most frequently noted image database display and manipulation features suggested by instructors and students were "zooming in and out" and "comparing two images." Beyond that point, it appears that students and instructors prefer slightly different functionality. Instructors were more interested than students were in functions that would enable them to create and save sets of images. Both instructors and students indicated that the top communication functions of an image database ought to be "browsing museum collections" and "asking museums questions".

Instructor and student choices for the search functions they would prefer to see in an image database differed slightly (see Table 4). Students chose a search by "artist's name" as the most important search feature. "Genre" and "style" appeared as more important features for students than for instructors. Instructors chose searching by "date" the most frequently—far more often than did students. Instructors chose "geographic place" as an important search function more often than did students. Both students and instructors chose "culture" infrequently as a preference for an important search feature.

▶ **TABLE 4 Search Function Preferences**

Instructor Choices	Student Choices
Date	Artist's name
Geographic place	Style
Artist's name	Genre
Genre	Date
Culture	Geographic place
Style	Culture

As shown in Table 5, a comparison of instructor and student preferences for image database display and manipulation features suggests that instructors and students prefer the same functionality—"zooming in and out" and "comparing two images." Beyond that point, it appears that students and instructors prefer slightly different functionality. Both groups frequently chose the features "higher resolution images" and "high quality print capability," but students chose these two features more frequently than instructors. Instructors chose data and set manipulation functions such as "sort search results" and "save search results" more frequently than did students. This is most likely due to the fact that instructors devoted more time than students to searching the MESL database in order to locate the appropriate images for their classes. Both groups chose the "annotate images with comments" and "image editing tools" infrequently on their lists of preferred display and manipulation features for an image database.

▶ **TABLE 5 Display and Manipulation Preferences**

Instructor Choices	Student Choices
Compare two or more images	Zooming in and out
Zooming in and out	Compare two or more images
Sort search results	Higher resolution images
Save search results	High quality printing capability
Easy export of images	Save search results
Higher resolution images	Sort search results
High quality printing capability	Image editing tools
Annotate images with comments	Easy export of images
Image editing tools	Annotate images with comments

Both instructors and students chose virtually the same communication features with the same relative levels of frequency—with one exception. It is clear that both groups find "browsing online museum catalogs" and being able to "ask museums questions" are important communication functions (Table 6). Neither group appeared to select the group communication features "online chat" or "post notes to a shared database" with much frequency. It is probable that in this phase, users are more interested in finding out what kinds of information museums can make accessible in digital format.

▶ TABLE 6 Communication and Feedback Preferences

Instructor Choices	Student Choices
Browse online museum catalogs	Browse online museum catalogs
Ask museums questions	Ask museums questions
Online chat	Post notes to a shared database
Post notes to a shared database	Online chat

Conclusions : Instructor and Student Opinions About the Impact of MESL Images

Both students and instructors responded to eight identical opinion statements about the impact they felt the MESL database had on their teaching and their course work. A side-by-side comparison of how each group responded to these attitudinal statements reflects some of the findings of each individual group. A review of both groups' attitudes provides a salient overall summary of the scope of this analysis (see Table 7).

▶ TABLE 7 Users' Opinions about the Effects of Using MESL Images on Their Teaching and Learning

Opinion	Instructors	Students
Access to art work not available elsewhere	94%	80%
Easy to integrate images into class projects	80%	68%
Convenient to view images from remote locations	100%	95%
Could do things not possible with slides/prints	77%	72%
Involves extra work	71%	28%
Less convenient than print	50%	27%
MESL database easy to use	70%	96%
Could get access to a better set of images	64%	62%

A higher percentage of instructors than students felt that the MESL database provided them with access to works of art that were not available elsewhere. A lower percentage of students than faculty felt that it was easier to integrate MESL images into their course work. Perhaps the faculty felt that students ought to be able to complete assignments using MESL images with more ease, while in actuality, fewer students shared this opinion. Interestingly enough, a much higher percentage of instructors than students felt that using the MESL database involved extra work. This sentiment was expressed informally among faculty at several of the universities and appears to have been reflected in the surveys. More instructors than students found the use of MESL images to be less convenient than print. This attitude could perhaps be related to the fact that faculty overall were not fully comfortable using technology to teach with digital images in the classroom. It was clear from their informal comments that instructors were more geared to using prints and slides, and thus making that transition meant more effort and new learning for them on top of the already demanding pressures of teaching and research. Further, display technology for digital images on large screens does not yet compete with that for slides. However, similar percentages of both groups felt that they could accomplish goals that were not possible with slides or prints.

The results of this study provide clear indicators that students and instructors have begun to integrate digital images into their research, teaching, and assignments. The results suggest that both groups appreciate remote online access to images and that they have similar preferences for the features and functions of systems that provide access to images and their descriptive metadata.

▶ Note

1. Beth Sandore and Najmuddin Shaik, "The Use of an Art Image Database in the Classroom: Instructor and Student Evaluation Report," submitted to the Getty Information Institute, October, 1997.

Findings of the MESL Casual User Survey

GERALDINE GAY, ROBERT RIEGER, AND AMANDA STURGILL

▶ Introduction and Objective

From January to June 1997, the Interactive Media Group (IMG) at Cornell University collected data from informal users of university Web sites that were part of the Museum Educational Site Licensing Project (MESL). The survey was one of several evaluation efforts coordinated by the MESL Evaluation and Base Measurement Working Group.

The primary objective of the Casual User Survey was to hear from users who were accessing MESL Web pages, but who were not among the audiences formally identified by university project participants. The survey instrument (see Appendix F, pages 201–203) was authored by the IMG with review by the Evaluation and Base Measurement Working Group. It included a mix of open- and closed-ended questions.

▶ Methods

The survey was administered electronically using a Web survey form. Users reached the survey by clicking a teaser button on each of the participating MESL sites. MESL administrators offered incentives (drawings for an art poster and twenty-five dollars cash) to encourage users to complete the questionnaire. Upon completion of the questionnaire, respondents clicked "Submit" to send their data to a Sun workstation maintained by the IMG. The processor calculated new statistics and updated a spreadsheet, which was available in HTML for viewing by MESL site administrators (*http://testing.img.cornell.edu/mesl/MeslTemplate.html*).

Seventy-five users completed the survey and submitted their data. Twenty-one percent of these were from the University of Virginia, 19 percent from the University of Illinois, and 15 percent were from Cornell. Most of the respondents were undergraduates (37 percent) or graduate students (27 percent). No one major field of study dominated, relatively speaking, with representation from the fine arts, humanities, social sciences, and sciences. A majority (55 percent) were age 30 or under. Sixty-three percent were female.

▶ Summary of Findings

Listed below is a summary of the findings of the Casual User Survey. (For complete frequency statistics and responses to the open-ended questions, see the Findings section on page 124.) Even though users were seeing and experiencing different interfaces at the various university MESL sites, there were considerable parallels among the responses. The most common responses included:

- Need for standardization.
- Various inadequacies of the search interface, including lack of useful browsing features (to compensate for frequent failure of the keyword searches due to lack of standardization).
- Lack of context, insufficient information.
- Poor quality of many of the images (e.g., too grainy, poorly cropped).
- Limitations on access (particularly the inability to access the site from dialup modems).
- Potential of MESL (most respondents urged further development, expansion, and improvement).
- Most respondents learned about the MESL Web site they were evaluating through a friend's recommendation or class assignment. A few respondents said they found the site using a Web search tool or an electronic mailing list. Only two respondents said they learned about the MESL site through links from another Web site.
- Forty-four percent of respondents said they have visited the MESL site only once, and another 29 percent said they have visited two to three times. Sixteen percent have visited more than 10 times.
- Nearly half (46 percent) said "curiosity" was the reason they visited the MESL Web site. Another 19 percent came for "research," and 18 percent came for a "class assignment."
- Respondents rated interface characteristics of the MESL sites on a one to five (poor to excellent) scale. Ratings from all sites were then combined to calculate an average score for all sites. "Image quality" received the highest average, with a mean of 4.14. Respondents rated "Ease of browsing" the lowest, with a score of 3.46, and "Effective search" next lowest, with a score of 3.65. Other scores include "Screen appeal," 3.76; "Clarity," 3.83; "Information quality," 3.86; "Ease of searching," 3.87; and, "Speed," 3.87. For "Overall appeal," respondents rated an average of 3.93.
- Asked to identify the subject of their searches, respondents reported such specifics as "Info on painting titled 'Master of Saint Lucy,'" "Matisse-related works," or "'Buddha and Cambodia' from Harvard." Many identified more general categories, such as "American landscape paintings," or "Images for class assignments."
- Although 33 of the 75 respondents said they were "Just browsing," more than half the respondents said they either "Found what I was looking for" or "Found something that interests me." Only 9 of the 75 said they were "Unable to find what I was looking for."
- Asked what they will do with the information they found, 40 percent of respondents said "Nothing." Twenty-three percent said they will "Use it in a report, research, etc." Five of the 75 respondents said they will "Copy and paste it in another program," and 11 said they will "Refer/link other users to it." In the "Other" response category, users said, for example, they will "visually compare to my painting," "I use the images as my wallpaper," or "Talk to my art director."
- Fifty-seven percent of respondents reported that, before MESL and other Web resources brought digital images to their computers, they seldom or never used images in class assignments or research. The remainder (43 percent) said they occasionally or frequently used images.

- Eighty-four percent of respondents rated the value of the Web site as "Excellent" or "Good."
- Open-ended comments were generally positive, with many comments and suggestions regarding interface design, image quality, and use of sites in teaching.

Findings

0. Which university MESL site are you evaluating?

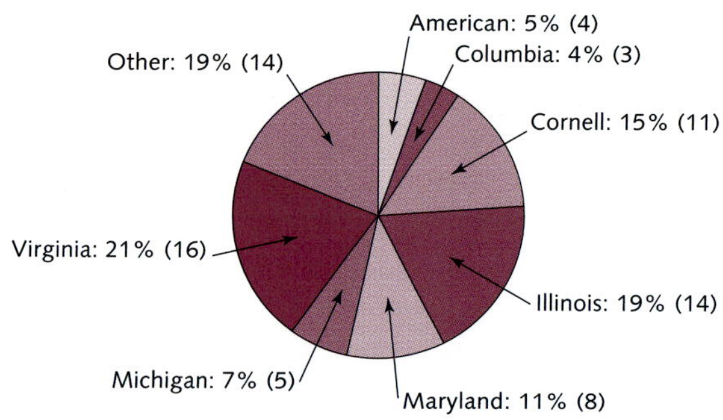

1. Where did you learn about the MESL Web site? (Check all that apply.)

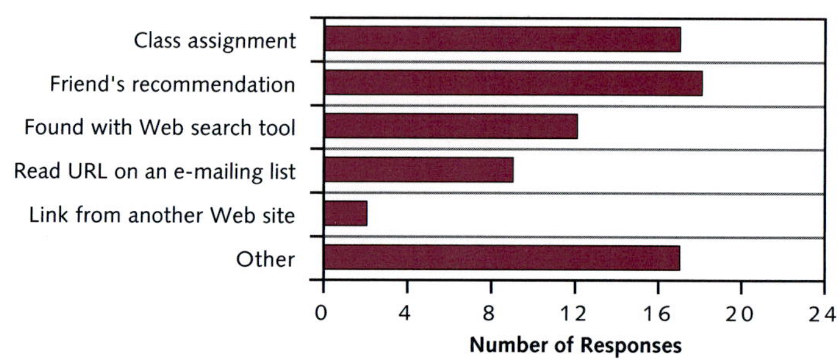

2. Approximately how many total times have you visited the MESL Web site?

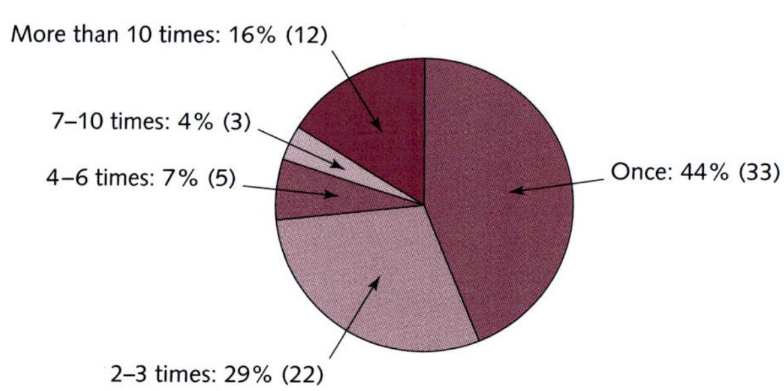

3. What is the main reason you visited the MESL Web site this time?

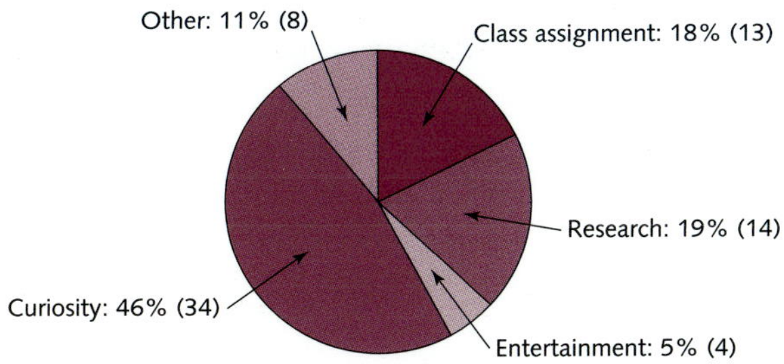

4. Please rate the following aspects of the MESL Web site:

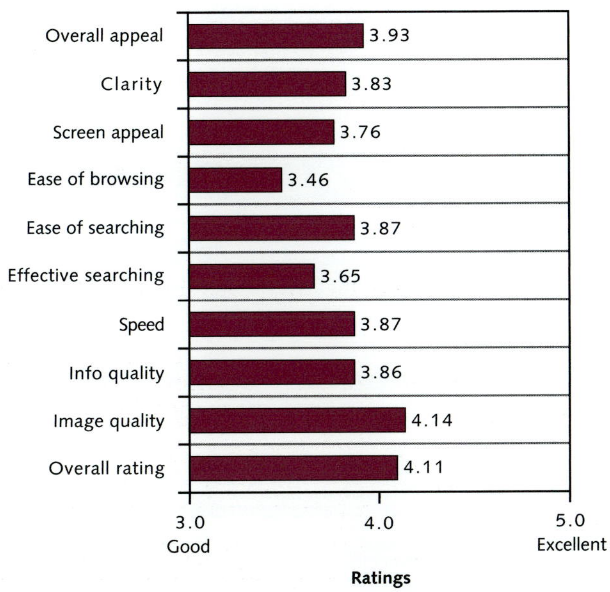

5. What were you looking for? (Optional)

- Info on painting titled "Master of the Saint Lucy"
- Northern
- Matisse-related works
- Books of Hours (medieval devotional books)
- Both one-to-one name or title hits and subjects
- History of Niagara Falls artworks
- Wanted to find out how I could donate some art
- Architectural info
- Just browsing
- Predominately photography
- French art
- Stuff about museum education
- Class stuff
- American landscape paintings
- Images for class assignments
- Joseph Cornell

(continued)

5. *(continued)*

- How well a novice could find anything without knowing much
- Favorite paintings
- Images featuring technology
- Just enjoyed browsing
- Search
- Possible use of images for wallpapers on pc
- Graduate Schools in Architecture
- Italian-American art
- Just checking out the site
- Info on 18th-century painting
- Searched for "Buddha and Cambodia" from Harvard
- Performed several test searches
- Information about virtual reality world

6. Did you find what you were looking for? (Check all that apply.)

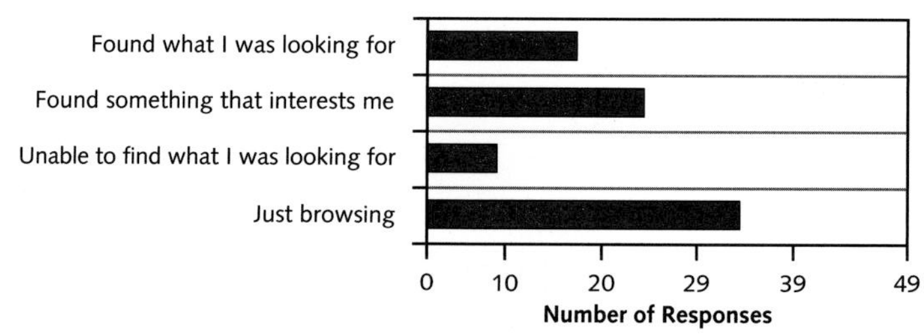

6a. What will you do with the information that you found? (Check all that apply.)

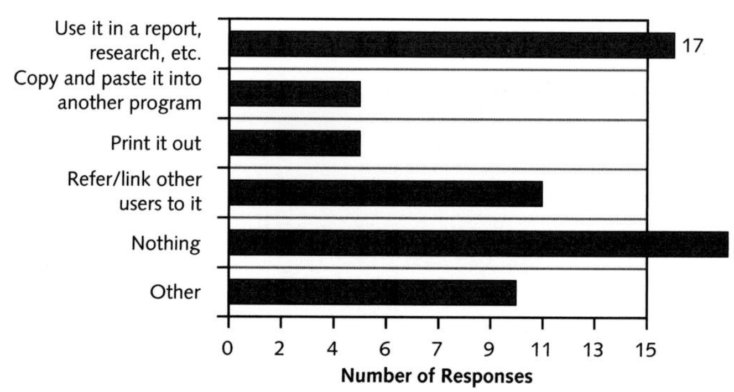

OTHER, please explain.

- My own information
- Talk to my art director
- I use the images as my wallpaper
- Tell my friend, who has an interest in such things
- Use it for teaching
- Evaluate the UIUC site
- Look at it
- As reference for studying
- I could not get anything; your browser is not working
- Visually compare to my painting

7. Before MESL and other World Wide Web resources brought digital images to your computer, how frequently did you use images in your class assignments or research?

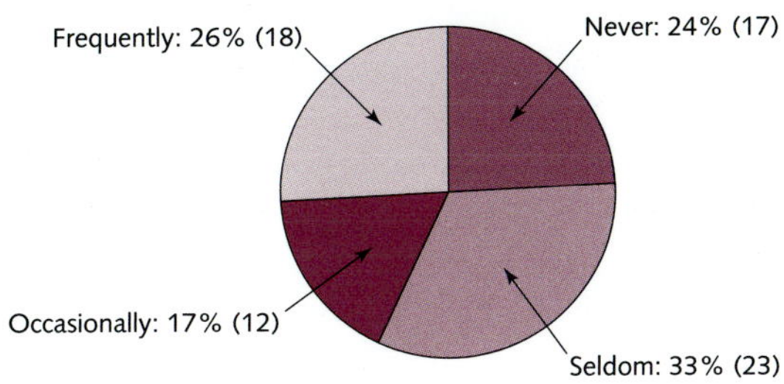

8. Tell us about you.

a) Status

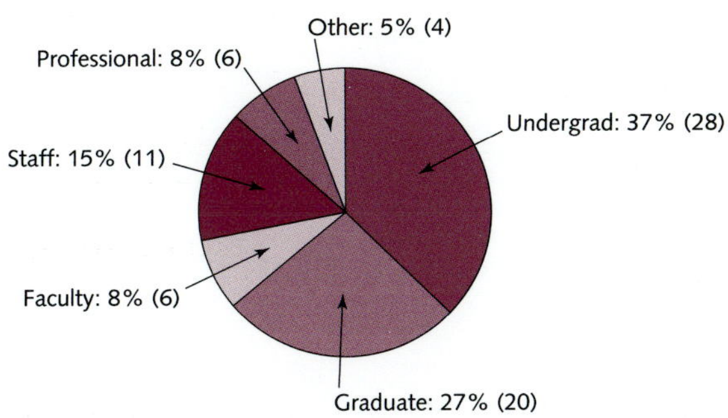

b) Major field of study

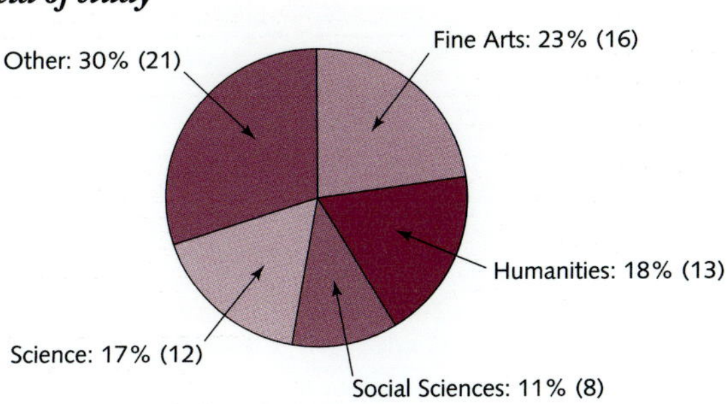

c) Age

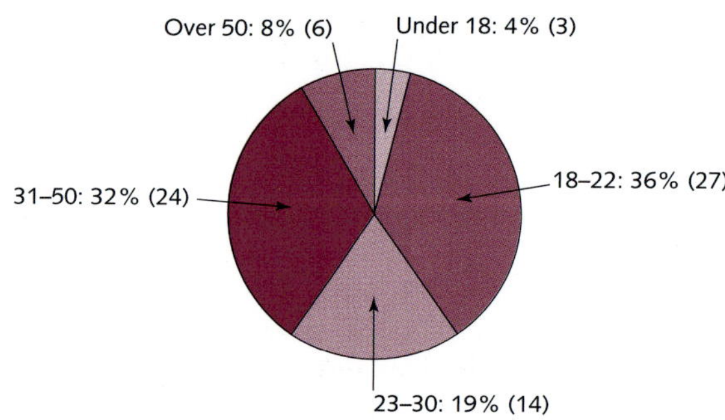

d) Gender

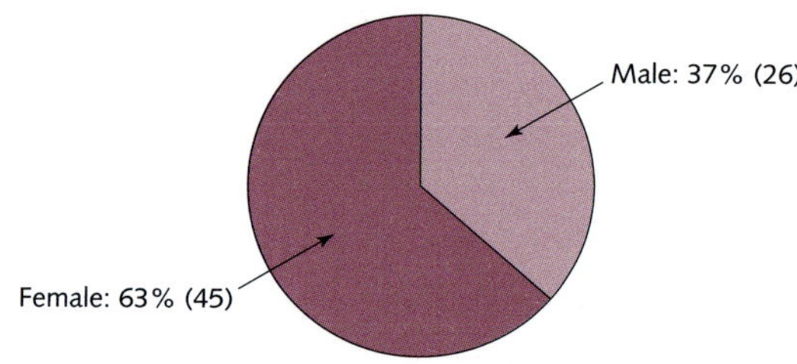

9. Overall, please rate the value of this Web site.

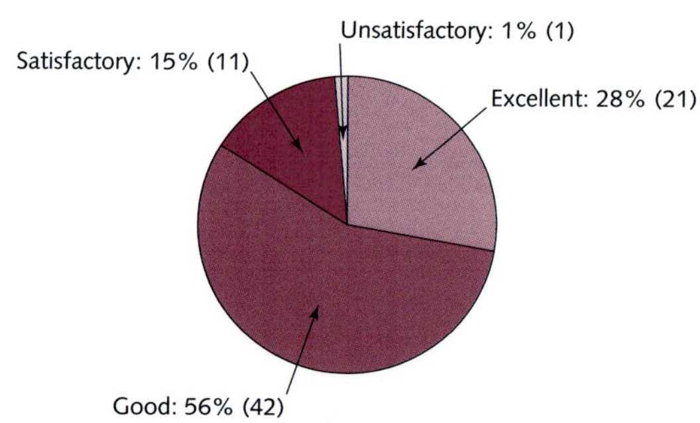

10. Please enter additional comments here. We are particularly interested in learning if MESL helps you use digital images in new or different ways.

COLUMBIA UNIVERSITY

- I wish more museums would lend their images to this collection!

CORNELL UNIVERSITY

- I didn't find much that would help me place images in a broader cultural context. The things I looked at were useful primarily for students in a particular course. As with most sites, I'm frustrated by the lack of info that would provide more detail.

- I would like to be able to access images from the listings of artists from the specific museums. While I like the idea of the galleries, I think it would be interesting if users could create their own galleries based on their own ideas about unifying concepts. It would be good if there was more flexibility in accessing and manipulating the images.
- MOA should use several MESL features; actually, I recall recommending that there be an overview screen (which is beautiful in MESL), basic search, etc. Overview screen's images should be linked to institutions. When receiving search results, the image should be at the top of the screen, with the text at the side. Shouldn't have to scroll down to see image. High res. image link should give size in K (or at least approximate size: 1 MB). System not really usable from home over modems.
- MESL is fine just for browsing; the images are of very good [quality?]

University of Illinois at Urbana–Champaign

- I have watched the progress of this database since it began. It is much more user friendly now than when it started. A lot of hard work has gone into this project. Congratulations.
- I wish I had a better handle on what kind of controlled vocabulary/ thesaurus was being used for subject access. Although I did find one item related to what I was looking for (Book of Hours), that heading did not appear. I was able to locate the item using the term 'book,' but that search yielded a large number of unwanted and unrelated items (sketchbooks, studies, etc.). Of course, the fact that the MESL database didn't seem to hold images of Books of Hours could explain why the term was not used.
- I found this quite useful when I knew the title or artist of the image I wanted to retrieve. For subject searches it was not useful unless your subject was very general. For example, I wanted to look at pictures of pears. Although there may not have been any in the database, I was surprised to retrieve images with words like "spears" and "pearson" in the description. I also did a search on flowers and retrieved many, but when trying to find a particular flower like poppy or rose or violet, my search was unsuccessful. I also found it frustrating that you could not choose to only hit one field at a time (i.e., title and subject). It was frustrating to bring up items that had my subject search term in the artist's name. I would use MESL again if I needed an image, but, as stated before, I would pretty much have to know the title beforehand. I think the concept of MESL is great and when completed, will be a valuable source.
- It's great to have it all, without bulky art books, and to have it so seemingly close-up, somehow. There might need to be a good index with this though. Also, if computers could really get good, clear images (not so blurry and muddy), that would be even more useful.
- I teach predominately photography students. While I find the potential for this technology exciting, the photographic material available, particularly what was made available by the Eastman House, was not particularly useful. I would be much more inclined to utilize this resource if the photography offerings were more extensive and/or less obscure.
- The search engine needs to cover more ground.
- MESL has improved the quality of the images. I can use the images to study for exams, instead of looking at a stamp-sized image in our slide case. In addition, I can give the information to my interested students, who want to learn more than what we tackle in class.
- The MESL images make it easier to view artwork.

University of Michigan

- This needs standardization!!!

University of Maryland

- The images are well digitized, but it would be better if the images weren't cropped.
- The MESL site allows for the student to go back and review a picture from class lecture when needed, plus provide additional background information needed from time to time.
- Very frustrating at times as images not available when thumbnails clicked on. Also, not the easiest site to navigate. Home page not illuminating. Would be useful to have an overall list of images available in glossary (by artist's last name?) form. (Maybe I missed this.)
- The MESL site was definitely helpful in doing my research and writing of several papers for my History of American Art class this semester.
- Having digital images is very helpful to me as a resource for studying. I am an Art History student and it is often hard to find images that we have looked at in class because they are usually on slides.

University of Virginia

- Great site!
- I'm a computer support person, and as such, am more interested in the Web methods used. I do enjoy viewing the art of course.
- Fast loading makes for a good site. Images grainy (both thumbnails and large)—maybe need some comment as to quality of the original. In the Search Results screen, it would be good if the images were brought back as live links, not simply URLs. Great site in general.
- I mentioned that the speed of delivery was not applicable because I am lagged due to dialup already, so I cannot judge the actual speed of the page. IT seems fine as far as dialup speed goes though!
- A little drab in overall page appearance, but the images are very good as resource materials.
- The whole site did not work; I did a search and all my results were, ACCESS RESTRICTED, SITE NOT YET COMPLETED!!!!!!!!!!!!!
- I've been trying to research an old watercolor painting of Niagara Falls. I've been looking at other paintings and mine is one of a very few with no man-made structures in it. If there are any experts who like to solve old mysteries, [e]-mail me and I'll send info on my piece. So far, I'm certain it was done before 1800 so that puts it in a rare category of paintings. And I think it might be attributed to James Cockburn, the 18th- and 19th-century English artist.
- Discovered some broken links in the example assignment about American Landscapes. Also, some links opened unrelated sites. Search functions are a high priority and need to be implemented at all sites to make the data more useful.
- Will need to explore the site further before I know whether or not it will be useful to me.
- Need category browsing/searching—keyword search was not effective due to too many or too few hits—a search result with 2500 hits was put onto a single page. This would croak most browsers. Results like this need to be broken out into groups of 25 or 50. Thumbnails in the search results page are different sizes making the page hard to read. The checkbox scheme is a

questionable user interface and is not well implemented: it is easy to confuse which checkbox goes with which thumbnail; requires lots of scrolling; difficult or impossible to get an overview of which images are checked. Browsing is impossible since the images are not linked via next/previous, and apparently very few images are available outside the search engine. It's not clear whether or not the search engine understands 'and'; it's not clear what the search engine was searching. With no example data records, I could not tell that there were more than a few dozen images until I tried a search. Need to be able to browse by category: collection, culture, date, subject, artist, media. Need consistent thumbnail display. User interface would benefit from Javascript or Java, and perhaps frames, but only if implemented by someone with a strong background in user interface design. It is generally good to have at least two ways to search and browse, and to use methods which complement each others' strengths and weaknesses. Pages should be short and concise, with well organized clusters of links, and toolbars for navigation. This site has many pages that are 5 or [more] screens long. This site would be very hard to browse at dialup speeds. The permitted uses seemed to be obscured by too much fine print. This site has a wealth of imagery and biographical information. It is clear that a great deal of work was put into the site; I think work should continue on this valuable concept.

OTHER

- I can't wait to come back to this Web site. It was very useful. Thanks so much.
- I have a Max Beerbohm collection and I wanted to find out if the museum would be interested in receiving it.
- The need to be on a machine at one of the participating universities severely restricts the utility of this site.
- Very much disliked having browsing categories split by museum collections. The browsing chart is confusing and unnecessarily detailed. If I were interested in browsing the art of a particular period, I would not have the patience to go back to the chart and repeat the browsing process for each museum collection separately. This scheme is already awkward and very unlikely to scale well as the number of collections increases. The search form is better, especially with the option for simple or complex searches. Make sure you include an option to search all fields, since users may not be sure which particular field is likely to contain the information they are searching for. Search results page looks sharp and the images are impressive!

Introduction

In the fall of 1996, the School of Information Management and Systems at the University of California, Berkeley received a grant from the Andrew W. Mellon Foundation to study the costs and use patterns associated with the networked distribution of museum information for educational purposes as reflected in the MESL project. The goal of the study is to identify the economic parameters of a distribution system for digital images and compare them with existing modes of analog distribution. The Mellon Study is due to be completed in mid-1998.

While not strictly a part of the MESL project, the Mellon Study was inextricably intertwined with MESL in its final year. In some cases, the two projects worked together to create instruments for data collection, such as the museum and university technical reports. In other cases, such as the evaluation efforts reviewed in the previous section, the MESL participants shared their results with the Mellon Study investigators.

The Mellon investigators hypothesize that digital distribution models will supplement, rather than replace, analog distribution (slides) for some time. Their investigation will test this hypothesis. They will analyze data relating to the cost and use of cultural heritage information in digital form in the MESL project and compare these costs and uses to those found in traditional systems for analog image delivery at universities. Central to their investigation will be the identification and examination of the critical cost centers for distributing images in general (for example, rights administration in museums) and the cost centers unique to digital and analog distribution systems, respectively.

In the following article on the Mellon Study, Bob Yamashita focuses on methodological issues. He deals with the very difficult challenge of identifying the major cost centers—those which are likely to exist in any digital distribution model—and distinguishes them from those that were unique to MESL as a demonstration project. From this formulation, he identifies the primary data sources for establishing the economic parameters within each cost center.

As more and more cultural institutions begin to make image collections available for licensing in the coming years, the results of the Mellon economic study should prove to be an invaluable tool. Institutions will be able to draw on the study's data and conclusions to further their understanding of the economic impact that licensing digitized cultural heritage information may have on their overall plans for information delivery.

VI
ECONOMIC ISSUES

The Costs of Digital Image Distribution: Theory, Methods, and Preliminary Results of the Mellon Study

ROBERT YAMASHITA

▶ Introduction

The Museum Educational Site Licensing Project (MESL) was designed as a prototype demonstration project, using "digital imaging and network technologies" to "make cultural heritage information more broadly available." It consisted of two basic objectives: (1) to develop, test, and evaluate procedures and mechanisms for the collection and dissemination of museum images and information, and (2) to propose a framework for a broadly based system for the distribution of museum images and information on an ongoing basis to the academic community (see Appendix A, page 165).

The MESL project provides us with a unique opportunity to examine costs and uses of digital images delivered over campus networks. The social and economic cost evaluation of MESL is supported through a grant from the Andrew W. Mellon Foundation (referred to as the Mellon Study) to the University of California at Berkeley. The Mellon Study was started in the fall of 1996 and will be completed in mid-1998. Its overall goal is to compare the costs of digital image distribution within the MESL framework with the costs associated with the existing analog distribution methods found in slide libraries. The goal of the evaluation of the MESL project is to identify the infrastructure requirements and the social and economic resources needed to distribute digital images. Understanding the costs associated with particular steps in the MESL distribution process is critical, not only for understanding the relative success of MESL, but also for framing the future direction of the digital image distribution concept.

This article presents the Mellon Study's framing of the MESL project. It identifies the major structural relationships, central practice environments, and delivery and usage practices in the production and distribution of digital images, then outlines the methodology used in the economic evaluation. It tentatively identifies the key cost centers within these environments and outlines some provisional "critical paths" required for the effective creation and distribution of digital images.

▶ Background

An analysis of costs across different projects requires a model of the distribution of digital images. As a higher-order representation, the model should establish a cognitive map, or schema, that *provides a **theoretical** picture of the production and distribution of digital images.* Such a map permits an examination of project design and actual practices.

However, in order to create a model of the MESL distribution process, we must first identify the elements involved in the process. This, in turn, requires us to review and understand the goals and objectives of the MESL project. The first MESL objective defined a feasibility study, i.e., identifying whether the networked distribution of a large number of images from museums to universities was possible. This objective suggests a basic distribution model in which digital images and their accompanying text documentation are created by museums and distributed to universities, which make them available for use in the classroom and for research. The second objective of the MESL project sought to define the underlying character of the relationship between the museums and universities—the conditions for using the images.

The penultimate goal of the MESL project was the *packaged* distribution of digital images of museum objects and their associated text as a new *digital entity.* In principle, a digital entity is a package that links distinct data elements. In MESL, this consisted of a digitized image and text data, but digital entities could also include audio and/or video. The technical hurdle in MESL was combining two sets of digital information: relatively new digital images and text data held primarily as legacy data in local information systems which were designed for other purposes. Extracting legacy data from systems designed around a local culture into a shared database demands a certain degree of standardization. At minimum, this requires determining the appropriate classification categories and translating the local terminology into a shared vocabulary. In the MESL project, the shared vocabulary needed to be negotiated between seven distinct providers.

Based on these goals and objectives, the MESL project has two basic procedural elements: image and text producers (represented by museums), and image and text distributors (represented by universities). In addition, the MESL project is predicated on two other framing components. First is the formal "terms and conditions" of usage. These permit museums to create digital images and offer universities the right to use them. The second component is the sense of relevance of the images provided. This determines what is accessed and how it is used. This component, in turn, acknowledges a third element: the end user. While the fundamental principle in conditional use presumes end user control, actual distribution practices limit formal controls. This creates an asymmetry between the formal terms and conditions of use and actual practice. The management of this asymmetry was sought in the underlying technology, where procedural controls could limit direct access to the image and text database.

The number of sender institutions, combined with a large number of digital entities and different digital imaging skill levels, introduced a final procedural element: the management of data records and error. While each university could theoretically manage different data file structures (and errors), it was recognized early on that having each institution perform the basic processing of images, texts, and aggregation would result in unnecessary duplication of effort. While several solutions were proposed, the MESL participants opted to have a central processing site with limited duties, the extent of which evolved over time. The responsibilities included basic quality assurance file checking of digital images and associated text data sets for noticeable errors (e.g., field delimiters), standardization of the data sets into a uniform digital appearance, and packaging and delivery of this data to the universities. This model recognized that the integration of data elements into functional digital entities and the aggregation of the multiple data sets would require each university to perform additional processing in order to develop its local database.

These objectives and modifications established the MESL distribution pathway and its operational framework (see Figure 1[1] on page 136). The distribution pathway consists of four physically distinct elements, or zones: museums that produce the images and text, a central processing facility for error checking and quality control, universities that deliver the images and text, and end users who access the images for particular purposes. Activity within each zone is framed by two additional elements: the terms and conditions of use and the usage preference and relevance.

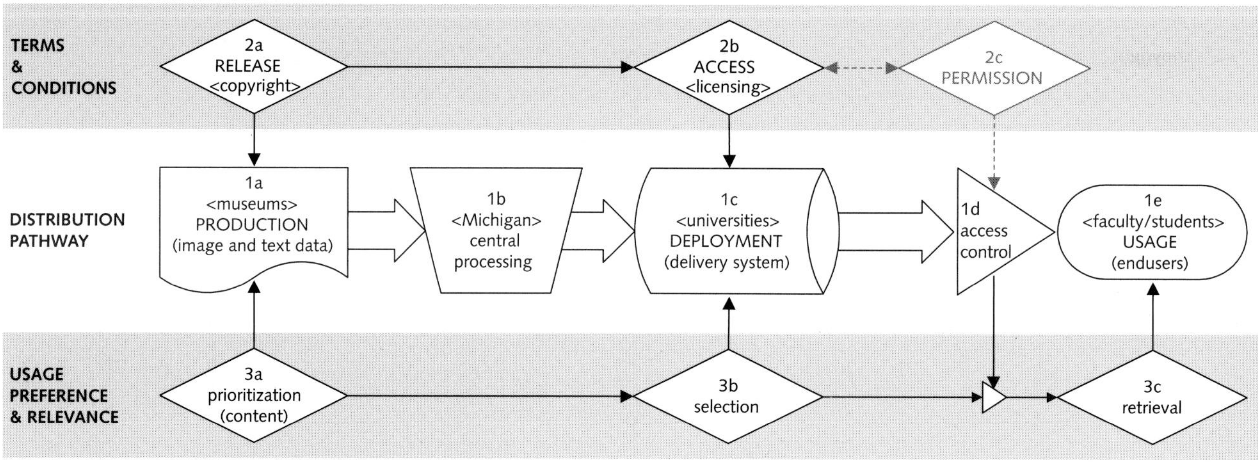

► **FIGURE 1** MESL Distribution Model

► Economic Framing

The economic evaluation must recognize that the MESL project constitutes an experiment in digital entity production and distribution. The MESL model was developed under a set of limitations and constraints, and needs to be understood as only one of many possible models. Because of its experimental character, the MESL model will most likely not be replicated in production environments. The analysis therefore has to move beyond the specific workings of the MESL project to an examination of the functions needed to distribute digital entities in general.

The MESL project's structural organization highlights the segmentation of processes that form a distribution pathway in the delivery of digital images. This segmentation groups together the fundamental operations that any digital image delivery model must address. There are physically distinct zones: the production of images and associated text, the processing of image and text data and the creation of functional digital entities, the deployment of entities through a distribution system, the security system to control access, and the usage of these entities by end users. Each zone constitutes an "environment" that contains technical activity required for digital image delivery. Collectively these environments form a distribution pathway. Figure 2 illustrates this digital image delivery pathway. Each zone in the delivery pathway is described in detail below.

(1a) *Production environment.* The production environment entails the organizational and technical processes needed to produce a digital object and associated text. Production involves the physical digitization of images from a source, the identification and extraction of the relevant text documentation, and the transfer of this data to a site where it can be checked and processed into digital entities. The digital production of images requires legal permission (copyright clearance). It is also contingent on some form of prioritization of the content.

(1b) *Processing environment.* The processing environment is composed of the organizational and technical processes required for creating a basic digital entity. An entity consists of an image and associated text (and audio, audiovisual information), encased within a sequential database container. Processing the data elements received from a producer requires conducting basic quality control, aggregation, and delivery of the entities to distributors. Quality control efforts focus on basic file checking of both

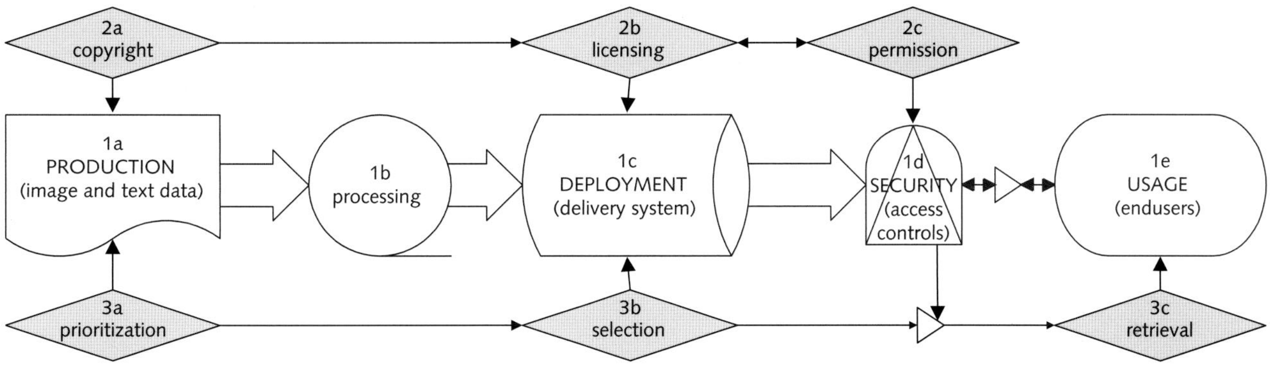

▸ **FIGURE 2** Basic Digital Image Distribution Model

image and text records from individual producers (e.g., delimiter errors, data record problems, etc.). Problems need to be corrected in conjunction with the image producer before further processing can take place. The data structures must also be standardized. After image and text data elements are checked, they need to be aggregated, that is, the data packages need to be parsed and integrated into a locally defined database. The integration of digital entities from multiple producers then requires more extensive record checking for errors and consistency, and usually requires the manipulation of records. The processing facility then delivers the raw database container to the deployment environment.

(1c) *Deployment environment.* The deployment environment gives end users access to the digital entities. This environment focuses on the digital delivery system and includes the network infrastructure, physical storage, interface, and the "backroom" work of providing a mechanism to access the database. This environment requires both licensing permission and interest in the data.

(1d) *Security environment.* Security (access control) is located between the deployment system and the end user. Its primary purpose is to limit access to the database to a specific community. Importantly, the security system needs to be transparent enough to the end user so that it does not become an obvious prohibition to access. Permission to use the images needs to be granted by the museums, and formal access is determined by the university access control system.

(1e) *Usage environment.* The usage environment is where end users access the digital entities for a specific purpose. Functional usage is framed by the capabilities of the deployment system. Individual preference or sense of relevance also determines what end users access. Ultimately, the primary determinant of use appears to be framed by content—the set of available images.

While the distribution model presented above mirrors that of the MESL project, the functional components for the economic analysis are different in several respects. Under MESL, each environment was institutionally discrete—museums produced, universities deployed. In other models, responsibilities for processes can reside inside an institution or they can be shared or contracted out among several institutional sites. (However, as in the MESL project, the terms and conditions of use and the preference and sense of relevance of end users will also frame processes in other models.) Organizationally, the functional model shown in Figure 2 first identifies a processing environment which includes both MESL's central processing facility and a portion of the work done by universities (the integration of data elements into functional digital entities, and the aggregation of the multiple data sets into a cohesive sequential database container). Second, the functional model adds a formal security environment because the implementation of any security apparatus tends to engage actions that are distinct from either the deployment or usage environments. The need for a distinct security environment was reinforced by the MESL project, when, during the later stages of MESL, several institutions began to move away from simple access controls to more formal security implementations (e.g., authentication).

Each environment in the functional model encapsulates a production process comprising multiple component tasks. One of the goals of the economic evaluation is to identify all these elements and determine their relationship and relevance. Identification requires evaluating their economic impact, since the costs of these tasks range from continuous direct charges to one-time charges, indirect assessments, or simply technical concerns.

▶ Methods

One of the unique features of the MESL experiment was the willingness to create a situation from which standards for the digital distribution of images could emerge, rather than imposing them and seeing how they worked.[2] By design, MESL was a many-to-many experiment: multiple museums sending a large set of digital images to multiple universities for distribution. More importantly, there was an effort to introduce a heterogeneous mix of institutions with different characteristics, different experiences with digital imaging, and different visions of image delivery. This willingness to encourage and explore the possibility of emerging standards within a broad mix of institutions makes it difficult to statically assess cost estimates and usage outcomes.

The technical problem of the economic evaluation is to *reconstruct* the full range of activity—both formal and informal—that was needed to accomplish MESL. At the outset, the economic evaluation was confronted by practical problems in data collection. First, although the digital objects were similar, their production and distribution environments were theoretically different at each institution. This meant that specific commonalities and cost centers along the production and distribution chain (from the museums' creation of the images and accompanying text, to their distribution to the universities, to their use by individuals) needed to be derived from diverse project implementation designs. This heterogeneity makes standardized data gathering problematic. Second, at all institutions, MESL was understood as an experiment in the electronic distribution of digital images and data. MESL participants were on a steep learning curve, caught in a web of solving specific technical problems in order to accomplish the overall goals of the distribution. Thus, although individual sites were asked to keep accurate logs of what was happening during the course of MESL implementation, most did not do so. Understanding much of the MESL experience therefore depends on recreating experiences from memory. Finally, there was a significant learning curve as each site determined how to distribute digital objects effectively. Thus, many of the costs are likely to be higher than they would be during a true production mode.

Recognizing this institutional heterogeneity and experimental mindset, the MESL–Mellon evaluation team identified data collection points at which experiences could be triangulated. Figure 3 illustrates the relationship between the basic digital image distribution model and the primary data sources of the MESL project.

For the economic evaluation, the primary data collection device was the technical report. It was jointly developed by MESL and the Mellon Study and solicited from each participating institution as part of its project reporting. Supporting data came from the

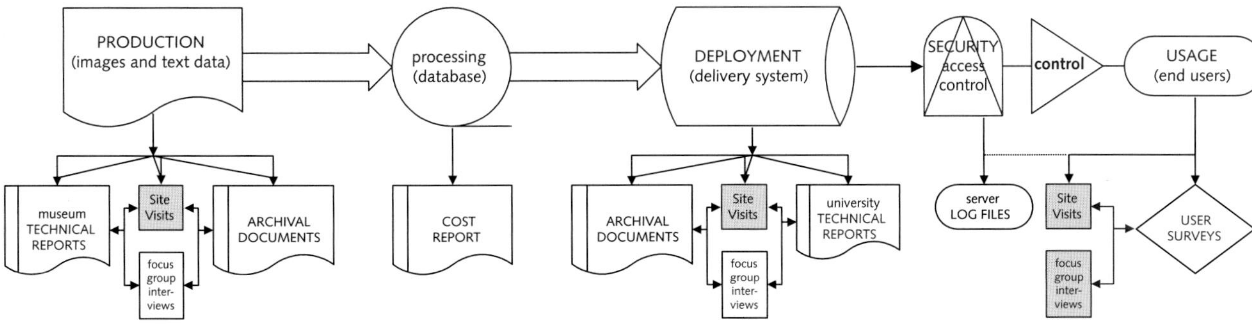

▶ **FIGURE 3** Data Sources of the MESL Project

MESL project archives, site visits, focus group interviews, surveys of MESL participants and end users, and Web server log files.

1. *Technical reports.* The reports review the implementation requirements of MESL and document the associated economic costs. Parallel reports were developed for museums and universities. Each has three sections: an institutional profile, technical implementation, and reflections on experience. The profile section documents the resources of the institution, general procedures, and staffing for the MESL project. The final section asks open-ended questions so that project team members could expand on their experience.

   The heart of the report is the technical section, which documents procedural moments. For museums, this includes information about collections management systems, content selection, and image and text processing. For universities, this includes system architecture, data preparation, functionality, and support.

   Each question in the MESL technical report can be linked to a specific production environment and mapped to a logical procedural moment in the digital imaging distribution path. For example, Section 2.1.4 in the museum technical report asks about the digital imaging process. The series of questions under this section include interrogation about past experience, prior resources, and MESL experience and resource commitment. On the other side, Section 2.1.3 asks the universities about data preparation requirements and requirements for loading MESL data onto their systems. Questions under this section interrogate resource needs and expenditures for different kinds of data preparation (e.g., images and both structured and unstructured text). The cost reports include an assessment that ranges from "highly accurate" to anecdotal estimates. The individual moments can be collected into functional "cost centers" in the workflow.

2. *Cost report from the central processing facility.* The University of Michigan's central processing facility submitted its own cost report on its activities in text and image aggregation and correction. It evaluated the types of problems and included cost estimates. This report provides insight into the technical hurdles confronted by the museum image production environment. It provides the core data for understanding the entity-processing environment.

3. *MESL archival data.* These data include project announcements, calls for participation, project proposals, MESL electronic lists, and published reports.

4. *Focus group interviews.* Group interviews are useful devices for eliciting data on individual experience that otherwise might go unreported. The group setting allows

"personal" experience to be expressed in a situation in which individual experiences might be collectively affirmed as common ones. The focus groups were conducted during the final MESL project meeting.

5. *End-user surveys.* Objective measures for the end-user environment came from a cooperative effort of several teams working with different instruments that target distinct features of the MESL project. The University of Illinois at Urbana–Champaign was charged with an evaluation of the classroom experience at the MESL academic sites. Cornell University conducted an evaluation of end-user response at the MESL Web sites and a survey of MESL participant experiences.

6. *Site visits.* The Mellon team members have conducted six formal and informal site visits to MESL institutions to evaluate the impact of the project. These site visits are informative because they allow participants to discuss and demonstrate their own MESL experience. Specific meetings with faculty during the visits to universities provide important clues about the creation of courses and impediments to use.

7. *Server logs.* A few of the MESL university sites that use Internet Web servers have made their log files for a single academic semester (spring 1997) available for further investigation. Log files provide useful information about how the image server was accessed. Data mining of these files can reveal when the site was accessed, where users came from, where they entered, and where they left. The files may provide some insight into what functions were tried, in what order, and how long they took.

The economic evaluation recognizes the variation in kinds and qualities of the data. Interpretation requires linking "hard" or "objective" data to softer, experiential, or qualitative evidence. The sections in the technical report (hard data) can thus be mapped to supporting documentation (soft data). Site visits and focus group interviews help to interpret the technical reports. Supporting evidence for data in the background sections of technical reports are derived from the request for applications and proposals submitted by each applicant. Supporting material for the technical implementation comes from meeting notes and listservs, as well as data from the central processing cost report. The reflection section of the technical reports receives support from the various participant surveys. These relationships are illustrated in Figure 4.

The formal design of the MESL project saw the deliberate bringing together of different institutions with distinct strengths and interests. Although general cost center analyses and cost trajectories are instructive, the disparities between institutions are as important as their similarities. The heterogeneity of institution means that any individual site can be viewed as an archetypal example of a specific type rather than a member of a collective. The analysis thus must be both an intra- and an inter-institutional exercise situated within a context and examined in terms of local social organization and local culture. This requires a two-step examination of costs that compares not only the data quality across institutions (correspondence) but also its link to accounts in individual experience (coherence). At this stage of the Mellon Study, we can only report on formal schematic aspects of the MESL digital delivery system.

▶ MESL : The Digital Distribution of Images

The examination of the various environments in the delivery pathway can be broken out into three distinct areas that define the economics of the digital distribution of images: formal cost centers, technological infrastructure, and the institutional organization. Each

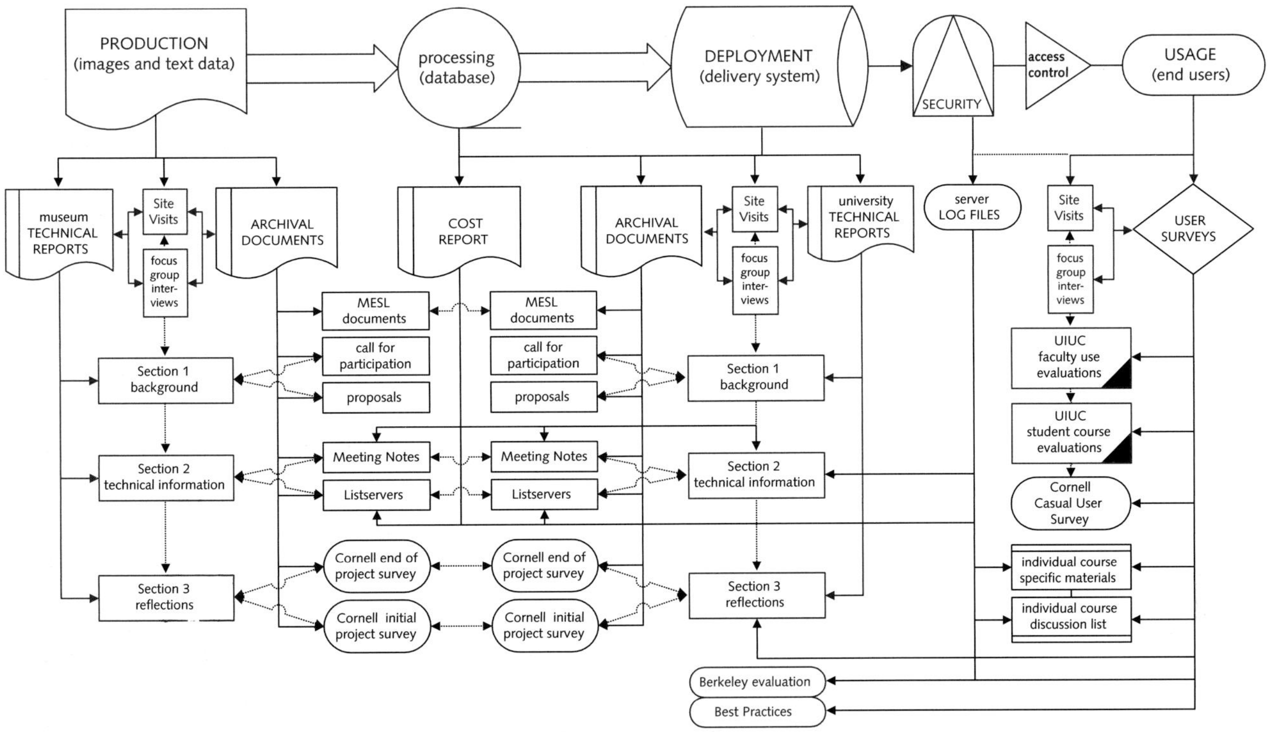

▶ **FIGURE 4** Interrelationships between Data Sources

environment consists of a number of cost centers. A *cost center* constitutes a collection of linked activities that appear to be required to accomplish a particular task. For example, the process of identifying the legal rights to digitize and license an object would be a necessary cost center for an image producer. This cost center would be different from the process required to identify images that consumers might want to use, or the center that involves the actual digitization of the object. There are different kinds of relationships between cost centers within environments. Some are procedural with linear dependencies (e.g., one step requires another), others operate as parallel processes (e.g., they happen simultaneously), and some are discrete either/or operations. The *technological infrastructure* constitutes the ambiguous connections between the various environments or between clusters of specific activity. For example, the connection between the production environment and processing environment could be the Internet or a mail/package delivery system. Similarly, the connection between the selection of an object to digitize and the digitization process could be personal knowledge, notation on a card or in a database, a phone call, or electronic mail. *Institutional organization* is the defining social structure that affects and shapes the environment. This includes the distinct participation of operational units and sponsorship. For example, in both museums and universities, the department that housed primary responsibility shaped how the project operated. The functional relationship can also be top-down or bottom-up. In most cases, the functional relationship determines the commitment of actual resources rather than simple "in-kind" contributions.

Internal Cost Centers

A number of discrete cost centers can be identified for each environment. A cost center encapsulates a set of processes and activities and results in a distinct end product. Economic evaluation requires identifying and measuring the resource commitment to accomplish the task and includes calculating the costs of machines, mechanical processes, skilled personnel, and the necessary infrastructure. Figure 5 provisionally outlines these cost centers.

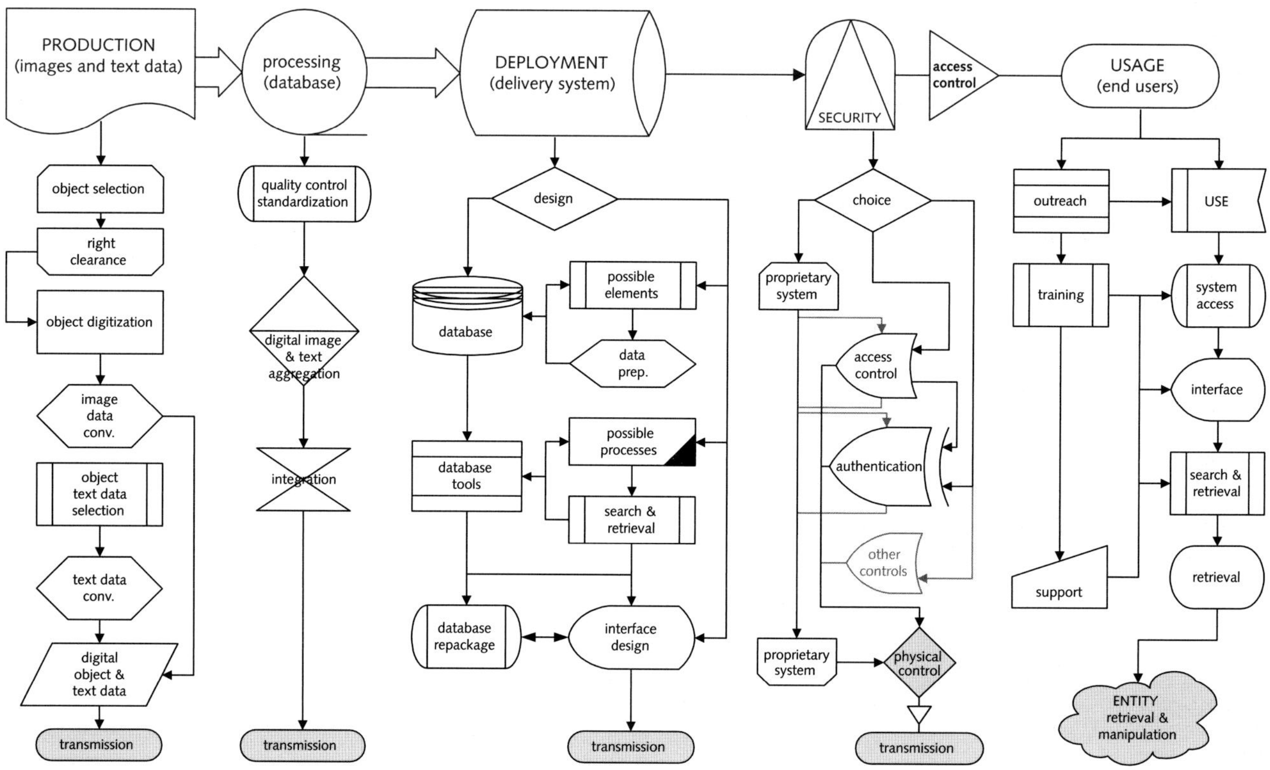

▶ **FIGURE 5** Provisional Outline of Key Cost Centers

Analyses of these cost centers for MESL are difficult. The technical reports ask for information on automation and personnel requirements. These resources form the key data for determining hard economic costs. A review of the data in these reports reveals wide discrepancies in the number of persons (or person-hours) required to accomplish the same task. It could be that the specific differences are an artifact of institutional culture (it is done that way), data quality, or projection of the number of bodies in a given unit. Assessment of the numbers therefore needs to begin with an internal examination of the institution, before making comparisons across sites. Finally, specific questions as to the infrastructure requirements were not asked. In many instances it can be assumed that some minimal set of technical elements needs to be in place before a task can occur. The different level of existing capabilities can result in different qualities in results. Nonetheless, their physical impact on the overall cost picture needs to be documented. Specific assessment will come through selected follow-up interviews and inferred across sites. What follows is a preliminary overview and summary of data for the key cost centers in each environment.

PRODUCTION ENVIRONMENT

The production environment creates raw digital images and their associated text. The specific requirements for these images and text can be determined by third parties. In the MESL project, the primary producers of digital images and text were officially restricted to museums. However, each university reported the need to produce its own set of additional digital images and texts to fulfill the specific interests and course needs of local faculty. The cost centers in the production environment include selection, digitization, documentation, data conversion, and object transfer (summarized in Table 1).

The production environment was examined in Section 2 of both the museums' and universities' technical reports. This environment includes a number of distinct activities: selection, permission, digital imaging, text data selection, and transmission. An additional activity, not identified in the museum technical report, was the effort required to fix inadequate images or data files. Each activity within the environment constitutes a cost center.

▶ TABLE 1 Production Environment—Outline of Cost Centers and Primary Data Source

Cost Center	Description	Source
SELECTION	Identification of objects for digitization. This includes collection specifications and rights clearance.	Museum technical report, sections 2.1.2, 2.2.3, 3.2
RIGHTS CLEARANCE	Gather permissions to (a) create digital representations of object and (b) distribute these representation in specific ways.	
DIGITIZATION	The actual creation of a digitized object—requires the digitization of either the object or a representation. Usually consists of two processes. First an analog photograph of the object is taken and then this photograph is digitally captured.	Museum technical report, sections 2.3.1, 3.3
IMAGE DATA CONVERSION	Ensures that the digital images correspond to the required specification.	
DOCUMENTATION	The intellectual mapping of the existing collections management and curatorial information systems into the proposed data dictionary and file exchange specifications.	Museum technical report, sections 2.3.2, 3.4
TEXT DATA CONVERSION	Ensures that the content and labels of text data fields correspond to required specifications.	
ERROR CORRECTION	Working with the processing facility to rectify errors in transmitted data files. May require re-accessing the local information systems or re-digitizing the image.	
OBJECT TRANSFER	The physical sending of a set of digital images and an accompanying delimited file consisting of the text documentation. It requires some form of data file compilation, writing it to some transportable form (e.g., tape or CD-ROM), then physically shipping the data (electronically or via U.S. Postal Service or package delivery service).	Museum technical report, sections 2.3.3, 3.5

One of the important tasks in the production environment is selection of the images—from deciphering the range of possible objects available for imaging and the processes used to select objects (including permission to digitize them), to actually selecting them. Image selection and gathering permissions present the starting point for establishing the cost of the MESL process. Section 2.1 of the museum technical report described the collections, and Section 2.2 collected data on the selection and permission processing. Image selection is reported as a matter of fact. It either occurred through a solicitation of interest by participant faculty members, or was simply mandated as part of the data the museums provided. In order to establish the significance of specific costs, the use of these different kinds of selection criteria for the various sets of images will need to be explored.

Assessing actual digitization cost in the MESL project is difficult. While MESL image producers offered over 9,000 images in two distributions, the vast majority of digital images were captured prior to the MESL project (see Table 2).

▶ TABLE 2 Number of Images Delivered

Institution	*Distribution (Section 2.3.1.1.1)*			*Processing (Section 2.3.1.1)*	
	1995	1996	*Total*	Pre-Existing	Newly Created
Fowler Museum of Cultural History	584	765	*1,349*	701	648
George Eastman House	500	500	*1,000*	0	1,000
Harvard University Art Museums	527	509	*1,036*	875	161
The Museum of Fine Arts, Houston	496	515	*1,011*	0	1,011
Library of Congress	1,400	750	2,150	2,150	0
National Gallery of Art	739	825	1,564	1,548	16
National Museum of American Art	541	459	1,000	1,000	0
Total	*4,788* *54%*	*4,325* *46%*	*9,110*	*6,275* *69%*	*2,835* *31%*

Critical assessments of cost need to separate real costs (specific for the project) from those which "recapture" previous expenditures. Such evaluation needs to extend beyond the simple notion of having digital images for an external audience. Other internal units could benefit and use the images for new purposes (automating and integrating registrar, collections, and curatorial information, etc.) and could lead to new internal digitization efforts.

Critical assessment also needs to account for not only the physical costs of digital imaging, but also the costs of any "intermediate" items such as an analog slide or transparency. If an analog slide is digitized, questions of costs associated with the photography need to be addressed. Another intermediate item is actual experience with digitization. The theoretical costs of gaining experience are always higher than subsequent efforts. In addition, the efforts to implement digital image production at the museums ranged from well-developed internal procedures to outsourcing of work. Another intermediate item is whether the existing digital image was offered "as is" or whether a "derivative" generated from another digital version of the image was supplied. While the "value" of the derivative would be lower than the original image, an additional cost would be incurred in creating the derivative (one that is probably acceptable).

Another final set of issues is to define the costs of producing accompanying text documentation. The MESL technical report addressed the cost incurred for other data such as structured text derived from the collections systems or unstructured data from other information systems. The most significant, and probably the most costly, technical issue focuses on taking existing digital versions of text documentation and putting it in a form that could be used by the MESL participants. This seemingly simple conversion process can pose some interesting and complex problems. Most collections data exists in legacy systems and its extraction into a usable shared form is not necessarily a simple and mundane transaction. The substantive question of translating the local classification vocabularies clearly had some impact on the quality and quantity of the associated text. The cost of the technical implementation of merging these different data systems in the production environment needs exploration.

Processing Environment

The processing environment is the creation of a sequential database container containing the accessible digital entities. Processing includes cost centers for quality control, aggregation, and integration (see Table 3). In the MESL project, processing was divided between the central processing facility at the University of Michigan and the individual university deployment sites.

▶ TABLE 3 Processing Environment—Outline of Cost Centers and Primary Data Source

Cost Center	Description	Source
QUALITY CONTROL	Object checking, documentation checking, and data standardization (bit checking).	Other report—University of Michigan cost report
AGGREGATION	Entity creation: the merging of image and text data to create a sequential data file consisting of all the data elements for each individual site. This primarily requires the parsing of the data units and their organization into distinct data structures.	University technical report, section 2.1.3
INTEGRATION	Cross-site entity linkage, which requires ensuring that the structure of data elements from the sequential data files match. The linking of these data files into a single collection constitutes the basic sequential database container.	University technical report, section 2.1.3
TRANSFER	The sequential database container is made accessible for formal database development and deployment.	

The relationship between cost centers tends to be procedural. Under most distribution models, individual producers will provide initial sets of digital images and text information. The individual data files will need to be processed to ensure quality and structural standardization, then integrated into a larger data container that will include files from other providers. Provision will also have to be made for replacing or updating data elements and subsequent reintegration.

The *processing environment* for MESL was located at the University of Michigan. The activities of the site included basic quality control, data standardization, and the delivery of objects and text to the deployment sites. The deployment sites needed to create digital entities through an aggregation of the data received from individual providers, then integrate these entities into their database so they could be manipulated. Additional processing was required at the university deployment sites. Raw data files needed to be parsed into a single database container, then aggregated with other digital objects.

In terms of assessing the cost of ensuring data quality, the University of Michigan submitted a cost report on its distribution activities. The report compared costs over the two distributions. It showed a sharp reduction in overall costs (over 50 percent) due to having processes in place for the second distribution. Table 4 summarizes these data.

► TABLE 4 Error Checking Costs

Distribution	Number of Images	Costs	Average Cost per Image
1. 1995	4,789	$32,498	$6.79
2. 1996	4,325	$13,938	$3.22
Total	9,110	$46,436	$5.10

The average cost for error checking was $5.10 per image (direct costs), with the second distribution averaging $3.22. Subsequent deliveries would probably only see a slight decline. It is important to distinguish between the types of errors incurred and their source. It is important to distinguish errors related to corrupt individual files from errors created by operators ("human error") or errors that are a function of merging data from different information systems. Another issue is to determine the cost estimates of "fixing" errors by individual museums. A final issue is to distinguish between what was checked by the central processing site and what additional efforts had to be made at each university in order to make the collected database usable.

DEPLOYMENT ENVIRONMENT

The deployment environment results in the production of a functional database system and the mounting of the database to a local delivery system. Deployment consists of three fundamental activities: database creation, database tools, and database interface. Within each of these activities there are a number of distinct cost center elements. For example, under database creation, there is database element specification and data preparation. Table 5 summarizes these cost centers.

► TABLE 5 Distribution Environment—Outline of Cost Centers and Primary Data Source

Cost Center	Description	Source
DATABASE	Create the physical structured database from selected elements and processed data.	University technical report
Database elements	Select field to use from database. This is linked to the general concept of what kinds and level of capabilities are desired for the system.	University technical report
Data preparation	Prepare data for the physical database. Can include converting data elements such as images to meet the required specifications of the database (e.g., thumbnails, resolution).	
DATABASE TOOLS	Develop the capabilities to manipulate the database.	

▶ **TABLE 5** *continued*

Cost Center	Description	Source
DATABASE TOOLS		
Process identification	From the database structure, identify the kinds of processes desired.	University technical report, section 2.1.4; Other report
Search and retrieval	Design and provide functionality for the kinds and types of tools provided to managers and end users for the manipulation of the data.	University technical report, section 2.1.4; Other report
DATABASE INTERFACE	Design and build the front end for accessing the database. Develop access methods to the database tools.	University technical report
TRANSFER	Mount the database to an information retrieval system.	University technical report

The university technical report requested information on the implementation of the MESL deployment system. The development and implementation of this system required several distinct procedural activities ranging from simple acquisition of data storage capacity to the formal design of the database, and implementation of the deployment system to the required support of end users. Each set of activities constitutes a discrete cost center.

The server implementation at each deployment site varied from fairly robust dedicated servers to modified workstations (or a combination). While all sites received the same data set, some sites reported the need to acquire additional storage resources. These substantive differences in hardware infrastructure requirements need to be linked to the formal organization of MESL within the university system. A second infrastructure issue emerged in assessing both the anticipated clients and the MESL implementation in the classroom. Many sites were forced to address the formal limits of their infrastructure—even though they all reported having dedicated digital laboratories or classrooms.

Six of the seven sites developed their MESL delivery under Web-based strategies. Different operating systems and approaches dictated formal differences in interface design and possible differences in functionality (Section 2.1.4). These subtle differences in design based on formal infrastructure choice have a potentially significant cost impact. This relationship needs to be explored in greater detail. The seventh site (University of Maryland) used a proprietary system that added greater functionality for specific classroom activities. Interestingly, they also had a Web version of MESL under development, but that system lacked the enhancements that made the system classroom friendly. The different Web implementations were explored by the University of California at Berkeley's cross-site experiment, and is reported by Howard Besser in the article "MESL Implementation at the Universities," page 70.

SECURITY ENVIRONMENT

The security environment restricts access to the database. Although this can take many different forms, we can loosely group it into three categories: proprietary systems, general access controls, or authentication (see Table 6 on page 148). Unlike other environments, the security environment tends to be discrete—where the choice of system embodies a set of defined procedures (although some systems can include "features" found in others). Table 6 lists the basic security environments.

▶ TABLE 6 Security Environment—Outline of Cost Centers and Primary Data Source

Cost Center	Description	Source
PROPRIETARY SYSTEMS	The restriction of direct connections through limited physical access. This can be done through a closed network system, common in many early computer laboratories, or through proprietary network operating systems that only recognize specific protocols.	
ACCESS CONTROL AND AUTHENTICATION	The limiting of access to the database through a simple system of network domain restriction. Additional limits can be achieved by restricting physical network access with authentication and other enhanced digital security schemes.	University technical report, sections 2.1.5, 2.1.6

Several of the original MESL delivery formulations sought to use "closed" systems (e.g., computer laboratory running proprietary systems). Some early efforts (release 1) reported on these efforts. At most institutions, proprietary systems were abandoned for more open Web-based systems. Efforts to control access to the database varied. Section 2.1.5 of the technical report summarizes the local security efforts. Most institutions reported using an IP domain control, and most did not report "problems" with their security system. Significantly, several sites reported moving to explore additional or alternative security implementations.

USAGE ENVIRONMENT

The usage environment addresses how individual images or sets of images are acquired for a particular purpose. It consists of four basic elements: outreach to inform end users of the database, training in how to use the database, support for ongoing use, and actual access. Table 7 summarizes these areas.

▶ TABLE 7 Usage Environment—Outline of Cost Centers and Primary Data Source

Cost Center	Description	Source
OUTREACH	The effort needed to promote and educate potential end users about the availability and the capabilities of the system.	University technical report, section 2.2.1
TRAINING	The need to train potential end users on the system. This takes two different forms—training for faculty who want to use the system in the classroom and training for students who want to use it for research or coursework. Faculty training requires a more extensive effort, given what needs to be done in the classroom.	
SUPPORT	Support includes two sets of distinct activities. The first is training (or additional training and hands-on walk-through) on using the system. The second is further technical development of the system and system tools.	University technical report, section 2.2.3

▶ **TABLE 7** *continued*

Cost Center	Description	Source
USAGE	The factors that influence the extent to which the database is accessed.	
Interest	Relevance of the database.	Other report: UIUC surveys and Cornell Casual User Survey
System access	The kinds of available access are critical issues for determining how the database is accessed and used.	Other report: UIUC surveys
User interface	The kind of user interface is a critical issue for determining what the naïve end user can do with the system (and how the informed end user can interact with it).	
Search tools	The kinds of tools provided to the end user for searching and manipulating the database. This includes the number of searchable fields and the kinds of tools.	
Retrieval	What is the form of retrieval.	University technical report, section 2.2.2

End-user economic issues are difficult to ferret out. Infrastructure appears to be the biggest concern. Existing electronic classrooms appear to be limited by their ease of use and functionality. Public access via public terminals and the Internet offers new challenges to distributors. The costs of providing or improving infrastructure—especially as it applies to digital imaging—is difficult to ascertain.

The formal costs for providing the database to end users fall into the first three areas: outreach, training, and support. Outreach, under the MESL initiative, mainly consisted of staff introducing the MESL distribution concept and technology to faculty and providing special seminars and training sessions. Training required walking individuals through the system. The final critical issue is the costs of support. Section 2.2 of the technical report asked about outreach efforts to encourage faculty usage, direct support for instruction, and additional effort needed to further develop the system for faculty and other end users. While there appears to be a significant investment in outreach and education at all MESL sites, the actual usage outcome (developing courses, etc.) does not appear to be high. A number of factors could be at work, including the lack of a critical mass of images or the barriers imposed by the lack of, or problematic, infrastructure. This needs greater exploration.

Assessing the cost of the fourth area, usage, is more difficult. As reported above, many of the applications for which the database is used require department and faculty involvement, but the technical reports do not represent them. Anecdotal information from individual faculty suggests a large time commitment required for course setup using digital images (one reported 200 hours). These large time commitments are, however, probably one-time expenditures (presuming the image database remains relatively stable). Student or casual user access is also difficult to define. For the most part, formal design by most of the MESL sites distributors looked to general Web-based architectures as a means to manage the variety of different machine architectures on the university campus. The Cornell Casual User Survey (see "Findings of the MESL Casual User Survey," page 122) notes that a number of non-students accessed the system looking for specific information. The best way to begin to assess the resource requirements is probably to explore the log file usage patterns. At another level, access or ownership of machines capable of using the images could affect broad usage of MESL images. UIUC data suggest that 40 percent of students who used MESL images as part of their course work did *not* personally own computers capable of accessing and utilizing digital images, which meant that they had to go to an on-campus facility to work with the images. Even those with the physical capabilities to access the images could be limited by how they are connected to the system. Low bandwidth at off-campus or dialup sites could slow image access to the point at which system functionality was negated.

Technology Infrastructure

The technological infrastructure is the ambiguous connections between environments or activity clusters. Infrastructure includes issues such as physical space, communication modalities, shared computing environments, information network or highway connections, and time. The technology frames what is feasible. It arranges objects and machinery and shapes the kinds of relationships producers, managers, and users have to them.

For example, one critical area that is affected by the changing character of the technological infrastructure is the fundamental concept of exchange. An object's representation constitutes a value that is at once distinct from the actual object but also strongly correlated to it. The physical representation helps to determine the core units in the technology infrastructure. There are several distinct representation layers. At minimum there are the "print" values such as transparencies that can be associated with print publications; there are also other analog images such slides; and there are digital images. Values could be attached to these layers by the individual institution that "owns" the rights to the object or wants the rights. For example, each provider institution has a price point for the sale of a slide or rental of a transparency (and, conversely, each end user has a price point for the purchase or rental). The values of digital representations are only now being explored, the most apparent issue being the notion of "image quality." In the MESL project, the definition of "quality" was clearly different for museums (using an analog framing) and universities (using a digital framing). In practice, the distinction between a high-resolution digital image and a low-resolution video display image was made. The substantive issue was framed by the ability to manipulate digital images easily to produce "derivatives" with varying characteristics (e.g., thumbnail-sized to full-screen representation). A significant secondary issue is the subtle technical issue of what is represented—is it the object itself, or is it a surrogate for the actual object such as an analog slide?[3] Any discussion of digital distribution needs to disentangle the varying values found in operational concepts.

Determining the formal infrastructure requirements is critical in any evaluation of the economic viability of a project, because they provide a baseline measure of the minimal formal context needed for the practical implementation and the successful achievement of a project's goals. However, actual infrastructure costs are always difficult to determine. For example, digital distribution presupposes that a set of reasonable technological capabilities already exists and is in place: there are objects; there are mechanisms to digitize them in the appropriate form; there is a means to transmit them; and there are mechanisms to retrieve them. While transmission under this model ostensibly means using a seamless "electronic digital network," transmission can also mean using the "sneaker network," where digital records are handed from entity to entity. In the MESL project, the appropriate transmission of both the set of digital objects from the museums and the raw data to universities was tape or CD-ROM, U.S. mail, and FTP, and the appropriate transmission of individual digital entities was the electronic network. This means that while digital networks are required for the delivery of specific end products (an individual digital entity) they aren't necessary for all parts of the process. Furthermore, an end-product delivery can be achieved through direct dialup access.

The formal network thus needs to be evaluated in terms of its functional relationship to those who use it. For example, the MESL project operated under a dual set of presumptions about institutional technological capabilities. MESL assumed that the universities had a technological infrastructure capable of delivering digital images. When each institution applied to join the MESL project, it was required to outline its technical capabilities and competencies. On the other hand, not all museums were expected to have such infrastructure. Among provider participants, digital-imaging experience ranged from fully implemented digital projects to a museum whose personnel did not yet have electronic mail. This created different experiences in actual procedures such as digitization and the transfer of images. Institutions with fully developed digital projects had specific procedures to follow and established cost structures, while less experienced institutions had to climb a learning curve on the digitization process.

These differences also resulted in varying calls for formal digital standards, where less experienced institutions wanted procedures and image quality specifications spelled out. The different experiences also translated into varying resource expenditures on the MESL project as a whole. At universities, the infrastructure issues in image delivery included changes in primary network protocols that affected the character of the physical network—sites that had proposed Novell solutions shifted to more open TCP/IP and Web applications. These evolutions in formal organization reflect, in part, general changes in the technology. At the time MESL was being implemented, a new commercial interest in the Web and whole sets of Web-based applications were being deployed.

Finally, an analysis of the technical infrastructure needs to address the general costs of actual physical capabilities. As reported above, all universities reported having digital classrooms, but all saw limitations in these classrooms affecting the overall adoption of the technology. Physical electronic classrooms clearly had different capabilities, ranging from multiple interactive networked terminals to a simple single network connection to a general display. The different capabilities clearly shaped the possible classroom access to the MESL database and influenced an instructor's willingness to teach with MESL material.

The technological infrastructure established formal limits to what was possible for MESL. Many participants identified the kinds of infrastructure questions the project raised. These ranged from looking for new collections management systems at museums to rethinking digital classrooms in the universities. On the museum side, MESL suggests that general distribution of digital images could be viewed as a collateral benefit rather than a primary one. Digital images—at the level of quality used in MESL—offered internal benefits for collections and management systems. The distribution of these "screen quality" images also led students close to MESL sites (Washington, D.C. area) to travel to the museum to actually see the artifact of interest. For universities, the definitions of access, enabling faster access, and limiting access were critical issues that appear to be progressively explored.

The range of technological infrastructure costs and benefits are difficult to ascertain, but need to be acknowledged. For the purposes of the Mellon Study, we will simply identify the central infrastructure issues that are critical for digital entity distribution. This includes real objects (such as physical computers and digitization devices, and actual classroom equipment) as well as critical concepts that affect distribution (such as digital networks and connections). We will take as natural constants (and will therefore ignore) issues such as power consumption or physical building space.

Institutional Organization

The institutional organization clearly has an impact on formal implementation and shapes the outcome. In the MESL project, there was a clear effort to select different kinds of institutions—both public and private organizations—as participants. All sites stressed varying degrees of participation from multiple internal units. The specific departmental unit that had overall MESL responsibility and the ability to mobilize resources appear to be critical factors for understanding the local outcome of the project.

Four private and three public institutions were selected as image providers. Each had a distinctive character to its collection and brought different technological sophistication to the digitization process and to the creation of fixed textual descriptions. Proposals from participant institutions to join the MESL project originated from various internal departments—information services, education centers, new media initiatives, and the registrar. In the museum proposals, a number of additional departments were identified as participating units. Importantly as the project progressed, operational control was shifted in three institutions from one internal unit to another. Table 8 summarizes these data for museums; data sources came from individuals or units named as part of the original project proposals and from the technical reports (section 1.4 staffing).

▶ TABLE 8 Museum Proposals and Operations: Lead and Participant Units

Location	Submitted Proposal		Actual Operation		
	Sponsor	Other Units	Lead Unit	Other Units	Change Notes
Administration		5		3	
Collections		1	0.5	2	National Gallery of Art—50% publication
Computer/IS	4	1	3	3	George Eastman House, Fowler Museum of Cultural History, Library of Congress
Curatorial		2		2	
Education	1	4	1	2	National Museum of American Art—new media
Legal				3	
Library		1	1		The Museum of Fine Arts, Houston—education
Photography		3		3	
Publications	1	1	0.5	2	National Gallery of Art—50% collections
Registrar	1	4	1	2	Harvard University Art Museums
Research		1		1	

Named participants from other units appear to cover the major operational entities with varying participation among institutions (range of two to seven participating units). The most interesting observation is that legal counsel was not identified as a required resource in any of the proposals. In practice, legal counsel became a formal part of the MESL operations at three sites—the other sites self-consciously excluded legal counsel by only distributing images they knew they had full rights to. Thus, while all MESL producers did not formally involve legal counsel, it was clearly part of the production process.

Among the image deployers, there were three private and four public universities. Among these institutions, there were distinctive differences in size, and each had a distinct technological sophistication in digital imaging. Because the primary mission of the MESL project was the development of "practical mechanisms to distribute electronic images," universities were required to demonstrate that digital images would be used in the classroom as part of their application. Six project proposals originated from the library. The seventh came from a department. Table 9 summarizes these data. Data came from named individuals or units as part of the original project proposals and from the technical reports (section 1.4 staffing).

▶ TABLE 9 University Proposals and Operations: Lead and Participant Units

Location	Submitted Proposal		Actual Operation		Change Notes
	Lead Unit	Other Units	Lead Unit	Other Units	
DEPARTMENT	1	6	1	0	University of Maryland
INFORMATION TECHNOLOGY	0	7	3	7	Columbia University, University of Michigan, University of Virginia
LIBRARY	6	7	3	7	American University, Cornell University, University of Illinois at Urbana–Champaign

In the course of the project, control of three library projects shifted to computer and information services units. Significantly, while all proposals invoked departmental sources, practical operations did not need their direct participation. In fact, departmental faculty appears to be construed as client end users for the delivery team. Table 10 summarizes the number of full time equivalents (FTEs) involved in the MESL project at each of the participating institutions. All sites include those who simply participated in "advisory roles." These distinctions would decrease the number of actual working participants. This data came from the MESL technical reports and includes personnel reported as either MESL or those "Doing the work of MESL." The issue of personnel can be used as a crude indicator of overall resource commitment by the local institution. Places with a low body-count could be construed as having little institutional support, while those with larger staffing suggest greater support.

▶ TABLE 10 MESL Personnel by Institution

	Year 1		Year 2	
	Over 50%+ FTE	Under 50% FTE	Over 50%+ FTE	Under 50% FTE
MUSEUMS				
FOWLER MUSEUM OF CULTURAL HISTORY		8		7
GEORGE EASTMAN HOUSE		2		3

(continued)

▶ **TABLE 10** *continued*

	Year 1		Year 2	
	Over 50%+ FTE	Under 50% FTE	Over 50%+ FTE	Under 50% FTE
HARVARD UNIVERSITY ART MUSEUMS		6		6
THE MUSEUM OF FINE ARTS, HOUSTON		13		11
LIBRARY OF CONGRESS		6		5
NATIONAL GALLERY OF ART		6		5
NATIONAL MUSEUM OF AMERICAN ART		8		7
UNIVERSITIES				
AMERICAN UNIVERSITY	1	9		10
COLUMBIA UNIVERSITY		11		11
CORNELL UNIVERSITY	1	6		4
UNIVERSITY OF ILLINOIS AT URBANA–CHAMPAIGN	2*	4	2*	4
UNIVERSITY OF MARYLAND	3*	11	3*	11
UNIVERSITY OF MICHIGAN	2	8		12
UNIVERSITY OF VIRGINIA		7		3

* Denotes students.

The reported numbers appear to be formal under-reports of how many resources were actually committed to the project. The cost of doing the work of MESL appeared to decline during the second year at all sites. An important understanding of overall personnel commitment for MESL is the fact that much of the project was completed with a low number of individuals employed over 50 percent. Many of the individuals identified as less than 50 percent had only a few hours for the entire year committed to the project (different Year 1 and Year 2 commitments).

The distinction in participant unit layers and personnel resource commitment gives us a frame for deciphering differences (if any) in MESL cost structures. The variety of institutions involved and the general success of the project suggests that digital image distribution is feasible for relatively low costs. However, one of the critical questions that needs to be explored is the differences between low resource commitment and overall quality of either image provided or interface. It permits an assessment of the practical differences and outcome of MESL. For example, viewed institutionally, the shifts in unit control could represent a cosmetic change in responsibility or de facto project control, or the change could be suggestive of a larger shift in organizational interest. Institutional sponsorship, defined by number of active participants, could also be significant for assessing how MESL was played out.

▶ Summary

The economic examination of MESL is still in process. The next step will be to attach summaries of resources needed and other costs associated with each cost center. The analysis is difficult not only because of MESL's innovative nature but also because of its formal design. The many-to-many experiment with varying institutional characteristics and different data collection points makes simple mechanical comparisons problematic at best. To date, many of the critical technical hurdles have been addressed, including defining methods to manage problems with data quality and comparability.

A comparative examination of analog image distribution/delivery systems (slide libraries) is in its opening stages. The analog model is an important comparative case because historically slide libraries have been the primary method for the mass distribution of cultural heritage information to the educational community. We have grouped cost centers in ways that expedite comparisons between analog and digital versions of each. We expect to find that a number of the cost centers for a slide library closely duplicate efforts already undertaken by museums, and that these costs might be greatly diminished in a more cooperative environment. (For example, the slide library's cost center for textual description of the object depicted in a slide might be replaced by a payment to a museum for conversion of their own textual description of that object into a form acceptable to the slide library.)

The analog distribution chain appears to be similar to that of the MESL distribution process. Every slide library appears to have a *production environment* where analog images are either produced or acquired. This usually includes some well-equipped physical space for the capture of analog images. There is also a *processing environment* where the finished images and their data are checked and entered into a physical record (and any additional information is also captured and entered). The *deployment environment* is the actual physical library and storage space for the analog images. This requires a number of additional resources, including check-in/out procedures and "reshelving" procedures. There is usually a *security environment* that restricts access by end users, usually determined by specific status (e.g., faculty, graduate student, or advanced undergraduate working on a project). There is usually a check-in process. There is also an *end-user environment* where individuals can physically access or use the images. This can range from physical removal of the images from the site to handling individual images on a light table or simply being able to view images in a backlit window. These processes permit a direct comparison to the digital distribution system outlined above. This study will provide significant comparative evidence for the overall effectiveness, strengths, and weaknesses in the digital image distribution model.

To date, the evidence suggests that the digital distribution model should not be viewed as a direct replacement of analog distribution systems. The lack of substantive infrastructure in the academic environment (e.g., digital classrooms, appropriate workstations and labs) and useful tools to help manipulate image sets makes reliance on only a digital distribution system problematic. In the Mellon Study, we will identify these barriers to widespread adoption of digital distribution/delivery systems, as well as advantages that have enticed faculty and students to use these systems despite their drawbacks. But for the foreseeable future, the digital distribution model should be understood as a supplement, rather than a replacement, for analog distribution systems for cultural heritage information.

We also expect to find that the value assigned to digital images by users will be relatively low. We surmise that museums should not expect an income stream from images in digital format, and (from a monetary standpoint) should at best hope for cost recovery. But we also expect that digital distribution will yield enticing benefits not related to a potential income stream. This can take forms as diverse as increasing the museum's public profile and attracting new use and attention; promoting new capabilities, work procedures, and staff relationships within the museum itself; and encouraging standard practices and cooperative ventures between museums.

▸ Acknowledgments

I gratefully acknowledge the financial assistance provided by the Andrew W. Mellon Foundation. Special acknowledgments and thanks to Howard Besser, the principal investigator, who shaped this set of studies and suggested changes to sections in this chapter. Many thanks to Christie Stephenson and Beth Sandore, who helped define the MESL evaluation side of the project. Special thanks to Christie, who provided many keen experience-laden insights (and corrections) to the observations, definitions, and technical points covered in this article. I gratefully thank the other members of the Mellon Project team: Rosalie Lack, Joanne Miller, and Lena Stebley. I also have to acknowledge the efforts of Jennifer Trant, David Bearman, and Maia Jin, who helped prepare the initial grant application to the Mellon Foundation.

Additional information on *The Cost of Digital Image Distribution Project* at the University of California at Berkeley can be found at the project Web site located at: *http://www.sims.berkeley.edu/research/mellon/.*

▸ Notes

1. Figure 1 uses standard flowchart shapes to symbolize decision making, processing, manual operations, documents, etc.

2. While the initial Call for Participation called for the use of "Getty AHIP Standards for Textual Information," the data model adopted was more flexible, based in part on examination of actual data in the museums' collections management systems.

3. Jennifer Trant, "Exploring New Models for Administering Intellectual Property: The Museum Educational Site Licensing Project," *Digital Image Access & Retrieval* (Urbana–Champaign: GSLIS, University of Illinois) (1997): 29–41.

Looking Ahead

CHRISTIE STEPHENSON AND PATRICIA McCLUNG

The preceding articles reflect the ambitious and multifaceted nature of the MESL project. Early in the project, the participants faced tremendous technical and logistical challenges to give the project a real existence. Later, individually, institutionally, and as a group of inter-institutional collaborators, they were able to reflect on their accomplishments and to think more deeply about the challenges and opportunities for the future that their participation had raised.

At the final participants' meeting, held in Charlottesville, Virginia, in May of 1997, the mood was both celebratory and reflective. There was a strong sense that the participants were unwilling to let go of this challenging and rewarding collaboration, resisting the need to move from the model of mutual cooperation to the next phase, where they would likely have to assume the mantle of business and fall more strictly into the roles of content provider and content user—licensor and licensee. More importantly, the group felt that their work was not finished, that the scope of the project had made it difficult to investigate fully many of the issues they had identified as critical components for the design of future projects. As a part of that final meeting, the group generated a lengthy list of topics for future investigation and extension of the MESL experience.

In summarizing the project's findings, it is useful to review our collective successes and to highlight some of those areas where we felt there was more work to be done. The MESL agenda was so broad that any one of its major areas of exploration could have occupied the participants for the two and a half years of the project. That our findings in some areas are less conclusive than in others is not surprising in a project of this type. They should be viewed as first steps in an iterative process to develop a new system for delivering cultural heritage information to educational users, as valuable for the new questions they raised as for the questions they answered.

▶ Legal and Administrative Issues

The "Terms and Conditions for Educational Institutional Licensing of Museum Images" is perhaps the most tangible outcome produced through the collective effort of the MESL participants. It represents the results of a long process of exploration and negotiation as museums and universities came to the table to explore their deeply held values. Together they were able to agree on a licensing framework which essentially embraces the principles of fair use within the terms of the license. This framework should prove invaluable both to the organizers of future licensing bodies and to those involved in negotiating licenses, as it represents a blueprint for the negotiation process. And the framework and process could well be extended to other arenas where the models for licensing digital content are still evolving.

Some readers may be disappointed that MESL did not reinvent itself as an administrative body to continue the experiment. But MESL was always cast as a demonstration project and neither the participants nor the sponsors were in a position to set up such an administrative structure. The Art Museum Image Consortium (AMICO) and the Museum Digital Licensing Collective (MDLC), the two groups currently being formed in the cultural heritage community to further the exploration begun here, are the first generation heirs of the MESL legacy. Others may yet emerge.

As the MESL participants reflected on topics for future research in the intellectual property arena, the difficulties that museums and universities have in clearing rights to images stood out. They recommended further study of rights clearance issues for contemporary art, including thorough documentation of practice and experience, for little of the content offered in MESL confronted these issues.

The MESL project demonstrated that even if a significant amount of content is available for licensing, users will need to supplement that content with additional images to support specific curricular and research needs. While some educational institutions may proceed to digitize images under a liberal interpretation of fair use, the MESL participants felt it would be useful to explore the real costs and outcomes if they were to seek permission to digitize images within the framework of the unadopted Conference on Fair Use (CONFU) guidelines.

"I would like to find ways to have easy access to images from other museums and make our images available to them. While I understand the importance of revenue, for schools and educators, the more images we can make available, the more teachers and students will see the museum as an important educational resource."

BETH B. SCHNEIDER
THE MUSEUM OF FINE ARTS, HOUSTON
Technical Report

▶ Content Selection

In the first fourteen months of the MESL project, more than 9,000 images and accompanying information were made available by the museum participants to the universities. In some cases, museums were able to respond to specific requests for content by potential users. In other cases, they were unable to respond because digital content was unavailable or intellectual property constraints restricted its use.

While the model for content selection used in the MESL project will most certainly not be replicated in the future, it did reveal some valuable insights and challenges for future content aggregators. It is useful to divide the universe into two kinds of users to explore this issue further—users trying to locate specific images and users looking for images on a particular theme or topic or to illustrate a style or time period.

Users trying to locate specific images will likely be frustrated by the absence of many of the images they are looking for in the corpora of available digital images. This was a major disincentive to use the MESL images and will likely continue to be an issue for some time.

Users with less well-articulated needs had a difficult time with the MESL data set, in part because the collections of the participating institutions were not necessarily well known to them. It was difficult to know what to expect and therefore difficult to attribute search failures to the absence of images in the collection, to failures of the data to adequately describe them, or to failures of the local indexing scheme and search engine. As long as the content of collective licensed collections is built around the holdings of specific museums, some intermediate method of gathering images into comprehensible groupings will need to be devised in order for users to effectively navigate the offerings.

Finally, the process of content selection points to the tension between the goals of the content provider and the needs of the content user. The MESL project attempted, in somewhat limited ways, to give the end user input into the selection process. If this model is abandoned, will users feel sufficiently satisfied by the available content to ensure their participation as licensees? If this model is adopted, how will the demands of internal museum priorities and the competing demands of an increasing large customer base be reconciled?

▶ Technical Issues

Knowledge Representation, Discovery, and Retrieval

One of the most challenging technical aspects of the MESL agenda was centered on the structured data about objects—its extraction from museum systems and its re-presentation to end users in the seven university implementations. That there were seven delivery systems in place within the first year of the project populated by over 5,000 merged data records from seven different systems was no small accomplishment. The obstacles encountered on the way to our successes brought many issues such as data standards and user interface design into better focus.

As we move from traditional systems of image delivery in education (slides and mounted reproductions) to very large digital corpora, there will be a number of significant hurdles to overcome in the interim. One of the MESL university participants summed up the experience by saying, "If you build it, they won't come. . . ." Users have tremendous difficulty comprehending the scope of a collection made up not of "greatest hits" but of the breadth and depth of specific collections that are joined together by virtue of the museums' agreement to cooperate. We are challenged to find more and better ways to contextualize the images and provide more predictable subject access.

Another area that warrants further investigation is knowledge representation about museum objects through structured and unstructured data records and its effects on discovery and retrieval. The MESL database was constructed in a very practical way, using existing museum collections management data. In contemplating a large-scale expansion of the MESL model, it is likely that the same type of readily available management information records will provide the core data set. More study is needed of the values that populate various data fields in order to structure and present the data in ways that end users, particularly those doing open-ended searches, can search effectively. An investigation of the mediating effects of the Getty Information Institute's vocabulary tools on retrieval results could also yield valuable information for the design of future systems. It would also be useful to compare search results using many very specific data elements as in the MESL Data Dictionary or more loosely structured textual data that aggregates related information.

"My hope is that we can distill from the MESL experience those common denominators that will enable creation of a shared database of museum information (much like a great national library) from which universities can easily tap, as needed, those images required for their teaching."

COLUMBIA UNIVERSITY
Technical Report

We need to design studies that investigate the interaction between data structure, data values, search mechanisms, and search behavior. Because of the heterogeneous nature of the MESL implementation model, these are very difficult to disentangle in our current systems. A more detailed study, similar to that carried out by Howard Besser's Berkeley students, conducting precision and recall tests of scripted searches in different university MESL database implementations, could prove a rich source of information on specific indexing and searching protocols. Replicating some of the existing studies of user behavior in seeking images using the MESL data set might yield some useful findings as well.

Standards and Quality for Digital Images

Images supplied in the MESL project varied widely in size and quality. Some of the museum participants were uncomfortable with the open-ended specifications for digital images to be supplied for the project. Future projects might want to be more prescriptive. There is a clear need for additional guidelines and best practices to provide guidance for future museum image capture projects.

While the technology exists to make publication-quality images available online, a key question that MESL engaged was what level of image quality was appropriate for an educational project such as this: How to offer "good enough" images (in a cost-effective manner) without threatening the museums' control of access to print-quality reproductions of the works in their collections.

Reactions to the quality of the images ranged from very dissatisfied to rave reviews. More research is needed on whether users can detect quality differences among various capture technology options and whether some sources or particular types of images have either exceptional value or serious problems. In addition, because of the paucity of adequately "wired" classrooms, we were unable to make definitive recommendations about the quality requirements for projection of digital images. This area needs further investigation.

System Architecture, Infrastructure, and Distribution Issues

At one point during the closing discussions on the impact of MESL, one of the participants remarked that MESL's impact related to three things: "infrastructure, infrastructure, and infrastructure." While everyone chuckled at this systems expert's bias, in fact many of the lessons from MESL have to do with institutional readiness and adaptability for incorporating digital images into existing collections of digital resources and providing the necessary infrastructure for their delivery in libraries, labs, offices, homes, and particularly the classroom. None of the participants believe that the MESL approach of locally loading image databases on campus systems is likely to be a viable option once the database size grows significantly. Nevertheless, there were persuasive reasons to consider models in which subsets of data from a remote or distributed image database might be incorporated into local campus systems on some kind of time-bounded arrangement—to improve response time in the delivery of frequently used images, as well as to allow seamless integration into local delivery systems.

The emerging model of the centralized distribution agency to perform the valuable functions of data validation and format standardization was validated by the MESL experience. In addition, for the foreseeable future, the centralized distribution agency can serve as an aggregator, a license validator, and a redistributor. This picture may change as standards for data interchange and interoperability evolve and become more widely deployed.

We were unable to conduct detailed study of the impact of campus network capacity on MESL performance. However, we are relatively confident in asserting that delivery from a distant server will not be a reliable means of serving images in a classroom setting. Perhaps the development of Internet 2 will provide a more reliable and rapid delivery environment.

"As it turns out, MESL's original goals were somewhat unrealistic. We haven't been able to achieve everything we set out to do. Although we came up with some innovative solutions, we didn't really come to terms with all of the technical issues. The MESL reports will offer leverage for influencing what happens next in this arena. The fact that there are already new opportunities (and organizations committed to rights management) on the horizon is a preliminary indication of MESL's success."

ROBIN DOWDEN
NATIONAL GALLERY OF ART
Participants' Meeting

▶ Museum Impact

The MESL project was coincident with an extraordinary growth in museums' access to the Internet, as well as in their understanding of the potential of the World Wide Web as a means of expanding their ability to reach established audiences and to attract new ones. It is therefore difficult to separate the impact of MESL in particular from the impact of the Web in general.

For the MESL museum participants, the most significant outcomes were a greater understanding of licensing issues both from their own point of view and that of their educational collaborators, a new view of the data in their collections management systems and its inconsistency, and the enormous opportunities that networked delivery offered them to extend and enhance their own educational missions. Museums are just beginning to understand their requirements for organizing and maintaining large sets of images and data, both structured and unstructured. Meeting this challenge will be critical for the future if they hope to manage and utilize their digital assets to meet a variety of needs.

There was a steep learning curve for museums with the least prior experience. This may preclude many smaller museums from participating in licensing initiatives in the near term. Even the museums with a higher level of technical experience struggled with various aspects of the work. As museum collections management systems develop and improve, more sophisticated support of authority control and export routines may ease these burdens.

▸ Educational Impact : Use, Training, and Support

Where MESL images were used extensively in classroom teaching and student assignments, the impact on the curriculum, teaching styles, and student engagement was dramatic. Faculty and students alike attested to a more interactive and energized classroom experience in which students took more ownership of course content.

While we should not minimize the impact of MESL where it was embraced, the project underscored the tremendous need for providing direct support to many of those faculty members committed to incorporating the material in their teaching. The costs for support, when coupled with licensing fees, may put these collections beyond the reach of some educational institutions for some time.

We need to know more about what motivated some faculty to use MESL images and why most did not. We need to understand what tools will enable faculty to master the technology learning curve, what or how many images need to be available so that digital images represent an attractive resource for faculty, and what kind of additional incentives, such as release time or specialized assistance, will entice faculty to take the time to develop new courses. MESL gave us some preliminary models and tools, such as the University of Maryland's ISIS software and collaborative development process. How can we build on these successes, making digital images easier to use and providing the support necessary to ensure expanded adoption in the future?

"Somebody suggested that we should just put everything up on our Web site and 'share, share, share.' That may not be practical, but it's certainly healthy."

ROGER BRUCE
GEORGE EASTMAN HOUSE
Participants' Meeting

▸ Economic Issues

While the Mellon economic study is still under way, we can say for certain at this point that it will be some time before analog image delivery systems are replaced by digital ones. The transition period will be a complex one, as a mix of newly created analog images, locally digitized images, and licensed digital images will all be components of the visual resources landscape. We can speculate that, in this time of scarce financial resources in higher education, the price point for licensing digital images and information will have to be low enough and the use and perceived value high enough to justify licensing bodies of digital images. On the museum side of the equation, demands for licensable digital content create additional strains on typically understaffed and underfunded institutions. It remains to be seen whether a sustainable economic model that acknowledges the strains on both sides of the equation will develop.

▸ Architecture for Networked Cultural Heritage

At their final meeting, the MESL participants pondered broader questions of how to build a more dynamic system for the delivery of networked cultural heritage information, making museum information widely available for students, scholars, and lifelong learners. Through the collaboration of museum and university personnel in the MESL project, we were able to think about these issues in a way that neither group would have done on their own. Together we identified certain features of mutual benefit for which we should strive for in modeling such a system, including:

- creating a mechanism for capturing feedback on the images and text from knowledgeable users and channeling it back to museum curators and educators.

- enabling a system that allows community database building, which facilitates the linking of related information in a distributed environment to truly provide a network of cultural heritage information. Such a system might link preparatory drawings held by one museum, a completed work held by another, correspondence relating to the commission residing in a library, as well as secondary source material and contextual information in a distributed database.

These final elements in our follow-on research agenda hint at a powerful transformative element surfaced by the MESL experience. They contain the suggestion of a new relationship between museums and higher education—a relationship where scholarship is advanced and shared collectively, where the educational missions of both kinds of institutions are enhanced.

In many ways, the MESL project was modeled on systems and relationships which exist in the analog world. The next generation of projects may follow these models as well, for this in an iterative process of exploration. What remains to be seen is whether new models will eventually emerge that are based on the creation of intellectual value rather than on the protection of intellectual property. In such a model value would reside in the authorativeness of image and information, as well as in the creation of value-added content. The relationship between museums and educational institutions would thus be defined not primarily in economic terms but in terms of a shared commitment to their educational missions in the networked world.

VIII
APPENDICES

- Appendix A : Goals and Objectives
- Appendix B : Cooperative Agreement
- Appendix C : Data Dictionary
- Appendix D : Chart of MESL Field Usage
- Appendix E : Instructor/Student Surveys
  - Instructor Preliminary Questionnaire
  - Student Preliminary Questionnaire
  - Instructor Post Questionnaire
  - Student Post Questionnaire
- Appendix F : Casual User Survey

Appendix A : Goals and Objectives

GOALS AND OBJECTIVES

Goal

The Museum Educational Site Licensing Project will define the terms and conditions under which digitized museum images and information can be distributed over campus networks for educational use.

Objectives

1. Develop, test and evaluate procedures and mechanisms for the collection and dissemination of museum images and information.

Tasks:

- Identify and test community standards for image information and associated texts, including guidelines for appropriate levels of image resolution and standards for associated documentation. Working with the broader community, develop guidelines and standards where necessary.
- Specify requirements for network transmission, security, image display, and quality control. Gather comparative technical data that will demonstrate whether certain systems architectures and topologies (such as compression techniques, disk caching, distributed storage, and secondary storage devices) deliver images within an adequate time frame for the user population. Compare and assess alternate technological solutions.
- Develop methods to ensure adequate levels of privacy and confidentiality, that are consistent with the need to track the use of the material.
- Devise an analytical framework for collecting information about image use and evaluating such use. Conduct and report on user studies that will document and assess the ways that images and their associated information were used. Data from these studies will further our understanding of searching strategies, image quality needs, user tolerance levels, and adequacy of access vocabularies, and provide a critical basis upon which to assess the standards employed or developed by the project.

2. Propose a framework for a broadly-based system for the distribution of museum images and information on an ongoing basis to the academic community.

Tasks:

- Define appropriate educational uses of museum images.
- Estimate costs for image assembly and distribution and examine levels of use as a basis for estimating the value of ongoing site licenses.
- Develop model site licensing agreements which govern the educational use of museum images and information on university and college campuses.
- Explore administrative and technical mechanisms for the ongoing delivery of museum information to academic campuses.

3. Document and communicate experience and discoveries of the project.

Tasks:

- Issue reports which document the procedures employed in the project and communicate the experiences of the project participants.
- Prepare and distribute a regular project newsletter.
- Establish a network of project observers.
- Establish a project listserve, WWW presence and network accessible archive site.

Last Revised: 1995/02/22
J. Trant, Manager, Imaging Initiative, Getty Art History Information Program†

†As of July 1996, known as the Getty Information Institute.

Appendix B : Cooperative Agreement

MUSEUM EDUCATIONAL SITE LICENSING PROJECT

Cooperative Agreement

PURPOSE AND GOALS:

The purpose of the Museum Educational Site Licensing Project (MESL) is to explore and promote the educational benefits of digital access to museum collections through campus networks maintained by academic institutions in order to help promote the development of computer-based learning tools for the study of art and culture. During this project, a small number of selected academic institutions and museums will collaborate in good faith to develop methods and guidelines for the educational use of digitized museum-owned materials at colleges and universities.

The participating museums and academic institutions will develop and test the terms of capture, distribution and educational use of images of works from the cooperating museum collections and their associated texts. MESL will serve as a laboratory for developing and testing the legal, administrative and technical mechanisms needed to enable the full educational use of museum collections through routine delivery of high-quality museum images and information to educational institutions.

The project will be governed by agreements made between the MESL Management Committee, which selected the participating institutions and is responsible for overall coordination of the project, and the participating Institutions, as represented by their appointed Project Coordinators, who are responsible for liaison with MESL Management Committee, liaison with participating institutional staff and/or faculty and liaison with Project Coordinators at other participating institutions.

PARTICIPATING INSTITUTIONS:

The following institutions are participating in this Cooperative Agreement:

Participating museums:

Fowler Museum of Cultural History at the University of California, Los Angeles
George Eastman House, Rochester, NY
Harvard University Art Museums, Cambridge, MA
Library of Congress, Washington, DC
Museum of Fine Arts, Houston, TX
National Gallery of Art, Washington, DC
National Museum of American Art, Washington, DC

Participating universities:

American University, Washington, DC
Columbia University, New York, NY
Cornell University, Ithaca, NY
University of Illinois at Urbana–Champaign, IL
University of Maryland, College Park, MD
University of Michigan, MI
University of Virginia, VA

Sponsoring organizations:

Getty Art History Information Program, CA†
MUSE Educational Media, New York, NY

DURATION:

The Museum Educational Site Licensing Project is a two-year effort, covering the academic years of 1995–96 and 1996–97. The term of this agreement shall be from the beginning of the planning session on February 7, 1995 until the end of July 1997.

(continued)

SPONSORS/PROJECT MANAGERS:

The Getty Art History Information Program (AHIP)† and MUSE Educational Media are the sponsoring organizations. They agree to provide project coordination and administration, to convene meetings of the project participants, to provide regular status reports to the project's participants and other interested parties and to publicize the results of the project.

FUNDING:

The Imaging Initiative of the Getty Art History Information Program will provide partial funding for the planning and organization of the two-year project. MUSE Educational Media, together with the MESL Management Committee and Project Participants, agrees to seek additional funding from public granting agencies and foundations. Some or all of the participants may also seek other funding for project activities, subject to mutual agreement. In the event that other special grants are received to support the goals of this project further, the responsibilities for fulfilling any special terms and conditions of the grants will be defined in the grant documents. Pending receipt of additional support, participants may be reimbursed for expenses associated with attending project planning meetings and, if funding permits, to help cover some expenses of project participation.

RESPONSIBILITIES OF MUSEUMS:

Museums participating in the project agree to provide selected images and accompanying information in digitized form. They agree to make the digitized images and descriptive text available to participating institutions in formats agreed upon by all the participating institutions. Museums agree to select works for inclusion in the project on the basis of a negotiated process agreed upon by all the participating institutions for the study. They agree to provide images and information conforming to the standards adopted by the project participants and reflected in project documentation for at least 500 works per year. Museums agree to provide images and accompanying documentation during the project without site licenses or royalty fees.

Should museums also wish to provide access to the test set of images and information, they agree to help define requirements and assess technological systems for network security, to withdraw other museums' digitized images and information from use after the two-year project has been completed, to provide no further access to them, and to notify the contributing museum in writing, certifying that the images have been withdrawn from use, unless subsequent licensing agreements are enacted to allow for continued use. Museums agree to monitor use patterns and collect data on uses at their institutions to help evaluate the effectiveness of images and data as educational resources and to provide evaluative information to the MESL Project Participants and Management Committee about the use of the images by museums.

The Project Coordinator will be responsible for coordination of selection of works from the museum collection and conversion to required digitized formats, involvement of the museum office which administers reproductions and rights, and participating in assessment surveys designed by project participants.

RESPONSIBILITIES OF ACADEMIC INSTITUTIONS:

Academic institutions participating in the project agree to mount test sets of digitized images and accompanying descriptive information on campus-wide networks, provide networked access to the images and text for educational purposes only and to test educational uses of the images and text. Academic institutions agree to monitor use patterns and collect data to help evaluate the effectiveness of images and data as educational resources and to provide evaluative information to the MESL Project Participants and Management Committee about the uses of the images on academic campuses.

Academic institutions agree to help define requirements and assess technological systems for network security. They agree to withdraw the museums' digitized images and information from campus use after the two-year project has been completed, to provide no further access to them, and to notify the contributing museums in writing, certifying that the images have been withdrawn from use, unless subsequent licensing agreements are entered into which allow for continued use.

The Project Coordinator will be responsible for coordination of mounting images and text on campus networks and providing access to authorized campus network users for educational purposes, and for participating in assessment surveys designed by project participants.

†As of July 1996, known as the Getty Information Institute.

(continued)

(continued)

RESPONSIBILITIES OF ALL PARTICIPATING INSTITUTIONS:

All participating institutions, both museums and academic institutions, agree to contribute staff time and technical resources in a good faith effort to accomplish the goals of the project. The Project Coordinator from each participating institution will be responsible for liaison with the MESL Management Committee, for coordinating project activities within the participating institution, and for designating project team representatives to MESL working groups. Every participating institution which makes the MESL data available on its network agrees to provide access to all project participants for the purpose of monitoring or observing the use of the data.

Project participants agree to collaborate on defining standards for security of the images and data and to cooperate on periodic assessments of the research and academic uses of the digitized materials. They agree to collaborate on defining requirements for future licensing agreements, to assess technological systems for network security and to develop a model site licensing agreement for possible future use. However, this agreement does not obligate any participating organization to offer or enter into any future license agreements after the project.

All participating institutions agree to respect the intellectual property rights of rights holders to the images and accompanying information.

Each participating institution assumes responsibility for having the rights to the images and accompanying information delivered under this agreement, or having obtained all necessary permissions for their use in the project. The participating institutions acknowledge that the images and accompanying information are the intellectual property of the contributing institution.

Each institution agrees to hold the other participating institutions harmless from claims or liability arising from the use of images and information in the project. Contributing institutions agree that during the project the images and accompanying information may be used at other participating institutions for educational purposes, including faculty research, teaching, or student projects. All participating institutions agree that neither the images nor accompanying information will be used for non-educational or commercial purposes, or redistributed for any purpose beyond the participating institutions without the prior written permission of the contributing institution. Before making any further distribution beyond the participating institutions, or engaging in any non-educational or commercial use of the materials, users must seek and obtain the written permission of the contributing institution.

Participating institutions who make the images and accompanying information available to their authorized users agree to inform these users in a manner agreed upon by the project participants of the proprietary nature of the material and the limitations on its use.

PROJECT SCHEDULE:

All participating organizations, both museums and academic institutions, agree to make their best effort to meet the project's interim deadlines to the greatest extent possible, as outlined on the workplan and agreed to by all the participants at the February 7–9, 1995 planning session and subsequent meetings.

GENERAL PROVISIONS:

Additional agreements, as established and agreed on by all the participants, addressing specific areas of the project plan and schedule which arise during the course of this project, will be appended to this agreement.

Any disputed uses of the images and accompanying documentation will be suspended until resolved by the participants. If for any reason an institution is unable to continue participating during the life of the project and must withdraw, that institution agrees that the materials it contributed up to that point will continue to be available to all participants for the duration of the project.

This Agreement sets forth the entire understanding among the parties and may not be modified or amended except by amendment in writing signed by the participating institutions.

In witness therefore, the parties listed below have entered into this agreement.

SIGNED:

Fowler Museum of Cultural History at the University of California	(date)
Print Name	(Title)
Columbia University	(date)
Print Name	(Title)
Harvard University Art Museums	(date)
Print Name	(Title)
Library of Congress	(date)
Print Name	(Title)
Museum of Fine Arts, Houston	(date)
Print Name	(Title)
National Gallery of Art	(date)
Print Name	(Title)
National Museum of American Art	(date)
Print Name	(Title)
Getty Art History Information Program†	(date)
Print Name	(Title)
American University	(date)
Print Name	(Title)

†As of July 1996, known as the Getty Information Institute.

(continued)

(continued)

George Eastman House	(date)
Print Name	(Title)
Cornell University	(date)
Print Name	(Title)
University of Illinois at Urbana–Champaign	(date)
Print Name	(Title)
University of Maryland	(date)
Print Name	(Title)
University of Michigan	(date)
Print Name	(Title)
University of Virginia	(date)
Print Name	(Title)
MUSE Educational Media	(date)
Print Name	(Title)

_drafted by Mary Levering, U.S. Copyright Office, 2/8/95;
_revised 5/10/95 (incorporating changes recommended by Christine Steiner, General Counsel for the J. Paul Getty Trust, and Jennifer Trant, Getty AHIP)†;
_reviewed and approved in principle by John Kominski, LC General Counsel, 5/19/95
_revised per discussions at MESL meeting 6/7/95
_revised per discussions with University of Maryland, Harvard University,
_National Gallery, to update indemnification language, 7/17/95

†As of July 1996, known as the Getty Information Institute.

Appendix C : Data Dictionary

MESL Data Dictionary (version 1.0)
2nd Draft, 1/23/96

Sequence #:	1
Field Name:	DATA AGREEMENT NUMBER
Type:	Non-Repeatable
Required?:	Yes
Definition:	The number given to the data dictionary and data transfer agreements governing the structure of the .DAT file.
Entry Rules:	Enter the number that identifies the version of the data dictionary which defines the .DAT file. For all data conforming to this agreement, the value of this field is "1.0".
Examples:	1.0

Sequence #:	2	
Field Name:	HOLDING INSTITUTION	
Type:	Non-Repeatable	
Required?:	Yes	
Definition:	The name of the current owner of the object.	
Entry Rules:	Enter the full name of the holding institution.	
Examples:	*FMCH:*	Fowler Museum of Cultural History, UCLA
	GEH:	International Museum of Photography at George Eastman House
	HUAM:	Harvard University Art Museums
	LC:	Library of Congress
	MFAH:	Museum of Fine Arts, Houston
	NGA:	National Gallery of Art
	NMAA:	National Museum of American Art

Sequence #:	3	
Field Name:	ACCESSION NUMBER	
Type:	Non-Repeatable	
Required?:	Yes	
Definition:	The inventory number currently assigned to the object by the holding institution.	
Entry Rules:	Enter the object's accession number as assigned by the holding institution. This is the object's current inventory number. Inventory numbers or other identifiers that may have been assigned to the object by former owners should be reported in the accompanying document "Ownership History".	
Examples:	*FMCH:*	X86.3773A,B,C
	GEH:	93:0207:0007
	HUAM:	1943.1080B
	LC:	Item in LOT 12736, no. 1388
	MFAH:	80.149.1,.2
	NGA:	1937.1.23
	NMAA:	1978.76.2

Sequence #:	4
Field Name:	ACCESSION METHOD
Type:	Non-Repeatable
Required?:	No
Definition:	The method by which the object was acquired.

Entry Rules: Enter the term(s) that indicate how an object was acquired by the holding institution.

Examples:

FMCH: Gift
GEH: Museum Collection, by exchange
HUAM: Bequest
LC: Gift, Carl Van Vechten Estate, 1966
MFAH: PURCHASE
NGA: Designated Purchase
NMAA: [NOT USED?]

Sequence #: 5
Field Name: CREDIT LINE
Type: Non-Repeatable
Required?: Yes
Definition: The minimum text which the museum requires to be displayed whenever an object's image or data appears.
Entry Rules: Enter the least amount of text that must be displayed whenever object data (image or text) appears in a MESL application. This is not the official museum credit line or donor acknowledgement text, but the display minimum that is supposed to be visible whenever an object's image and/or data appears. If the object's official credit line is present in the MESL data, it will appear as an element of the "Label".

Examples:

FMCH: FMCH UCLA X86.3773A,B,C
GEH: GEH 93.0207.0007
HUAM: HUAM 1943.1080B
LC: Carl Van Vechten Photograph Collection (Library of Congress)
MFAH: Museum of Fine Arts, Houston 80.149.1,.2
NGA: NGA 1937.1.23
NMAA: National Museum of American Art, 1978.76.2

Sequence #: 6
Field Name: LABEL
Type: Non-Repeatable
Required?: Yes
Definition: The literal text of the institutionally preferred object label.
Entry Rules: Enter the holding institution's preferred object label. This is a literal text, including line breaks and punctuation. Use the symbol ^<cr> (carat: ASCII 94, carriage return: ASCII 13) to represent carriage returns imbedded in this field (see Fowler example). The "Label" should always be available within an application; however, different than "Credit Line," there are no requirements on when it must be displayed.

Examples:

FMCH: Stirrup spout bottle. Seated figure. Height 20.2 cm.^<cr>
Two-piece mold. Height 19.6 cm.^<cr>
Chimú. North Coast Peru. AD 900 - 1430.^<cr>
This blackware stirrup spout bottle is shown with the mold that was used to manufacture its chamber. Many Chimú stirrup spout vessels have a small figure, often a monkey, at the base of the spout.^<cr>
FMCH UCLA X86.3773A,B,C. Gift of Mr. and Mrs. Herbert L. Lucas, Jr.^<cr>
Published in "Ceramics of Ancient Peru" by Christopher B. Donnan. Fowler Museum of Cultural History, UCLA. Figure 8.

GEH: from: Izaak Walton, —The Compleat Angler or The Contemplative Man's Recreation,...—, 100th Edition, edited by R.B. Marston, London: (1856-1936), active

		ca 1880s, English. A Backwater on the Lea, photograph, photogravure print, 1887. Museum Collection, by exchange
	HUAM:	1943.361 Drawing French, 19th century Gauguin, Paul (1848-1903) Terrible Words (Parau hano hano), 1892 watercolor over graphite on tan paper 157 x 219 mm (Actual) Bequest of Grenville L. Winthrop
	LC:	
	MFAH:	North German, Double Mazer Cup, c. 1475-1500, wood, copper-gilt, and champleve enamel, Museum of Fine Arts, Houston, Museum purchase with funds provided by the Laurence H. Favrot Bequest, 71.11
	NGA:	Winslow Homer, Breezing Up (A Fair Wind), 1876, oil on canvas, National Gallery of Art, Washington, Gift of the W.L. and May T. Mellon Foundation 1943.13.1
	NMAA:	Cadmus, Paul (born 1904) Aspect of Suburban Life: Public Dock, 1936 31 3/8 x 52 5/8 in. (80.5 x 133.7 cm) no medium details given Transfer from the U.S. Department of State 1978.76.2 Copyright 1995 Smithsonian Institution; Courtesy National Museum of American Art

---

Sequence #: 7
Field Name: OBJECT TYPE/OBJECT CLASS/OBJECT NAME
Type: Repeatable
Required?: Yes
Definition: The classification of the object by type.
Entry Rules: Enter the term(s) that indicate the primary classification of the object. For material culture collections, this will tend to be the object name; fine art institutions should use this field to specify object genre or format, which is the same kind of term as object name. Use a semicolon followed by an equal sign (;=) to separate multiple classification terms.

Examples:

FMCH:	Stirrup spout bottle (A);= Two-piece mold (B,C)
GEH:	photograph
HUAM:	Architectural element, Stained glass
LC:	Portrait photographs
MFAH:	DECORATIVE ART;= Double Mazer Cup with cover;= Woodwork;= Metalwork
NGA:	Decorative Art;= Ceramic;= Plate
NMAA:	graphic art

Sequence #: 8
Field Name: OBJECT TITLE/CAPTION
Type: Repeatable
Required?: Yes
Definition: A title given to the object by the creator/maker, curator, or owner or the text of a caption that appeared with the image as in prints, cartoons, and photographs.
Entry Rules: Enter a title or name of the object. Descriptive titles or names based on classification terms or object type should be provided for objects that do not have formal titles. The source of a title or name may be included here, in parentheses, if desired. If multiple titles are reported, use a semicolon followed by an equal sign (;=) to separate the titles.

Examples:

FMCH:	
GEH:	A Backwater on the Lea
HUAM:	When the Morning Stars Sang Together and All the Sons of God Shouted for Joy;= Alternate Title: Window: When the Morning Stars Sang Together
LC:	Portrait of Norman Mailer

	MFAH:	The Tale of Genji
	NGA:	Breezing Up (A Fair Wind)
	NMAA:	Aspects of Suburban Life: Public Dock

Sequence #: 9
Field Name: CREATOR/MAKER - NAME
Type: Repeatable (linked to fields 10 and 11)
Required?: Yes
Definition: The name of a person or corporate entity responsible for the design or creation of the object. Where an individual artist is unknown, this field should contain a designation by school and period or the name of the culture group responsible for the creation of the work. The name should represent the attribution currently accepted by the holding institution.
Entry Rules: Enter creator/maker name in inverted order (surname, first name(s)). Corporate names are the full legal name. For multiple artists, enter their names separated by a semicolon equal sign (;=), taking care to order data in the linked fields nationality and role.
Examples:

FMCH:	
GEH:	Emerson, P.H.
HUAM:	La Farge, John
LC:	Van Vechten, Carl
MFAH:	North German
NGA:	Franco-Flemish 15th Century
NMAA:	Cadmus, Paul

Comments: Name, nationality, and role (fields 9, 10, and 11) are subfields of the larger entity creator/maker. Because this data can repeat, it is important that it be kept in sync when multiple instances are reported. For example, an object created by three artists would have the following representation:

Creator/Maker Name: artist A;= artist B;= artist C
Creator/Maker Nationality: artist A nationality;= artist B nationality;= artist C nationality
Creator/Maker Role: artist A role;= artist B role;= artist C role
Note that when nationality or role is unavailable for a particular instance, a blank value should be generated as a placeholder. For example, if the role of artist B was unknown or not specified in the source database, the data would look like the following:
Creator/Maker Role: artist A role;= ;= artist C role
If no role data was available, the field value would be:
Creator/Maker Role: ;= ;=

Sequence #: 10
Field Name: CREATOR/MAKER - CULTURE/NATIONALITY
Type: Repeatable (linked to fields 9 and 11; see Comments for field 9)
Required?: No
Definition: The name of the culture group responsible for creation of a work that is not attributed to an individual, or the nationality of the individual creator/maker.
Entry Rules: Enter person nationality expressed as the adjectival form of an existing nation or historic geographic entity. Enter multiple nationalities for multiple artists order-keyed to the creator/maker name field and separated by a semicolon equal sign (;=).
Examples:

FMCH:	Yoruba
GEH:	English
HUAM:	French

	LC:
	MFAH:
	NGA: Franco-Flemish
	NMAA: American

Sequence #: 11
Field Name: CREATOR/MAKER - ROLE
Type: Repeatable (linked to fields 9 and 10; see Comments for field 9)
Required?: No
Definition: The role or activity performed by the creator/maker in the conception, design, or production of the object.
Entry Rules: Enter the term for the role played by the artist or technician in the creation or production of the object. Enter multiple roles for multiple artists order-keyed to the creator/maker name field and separated by a semicolon equal sign (;=).
Examples:
FMCH: [NOT USED]
GEH:
HUAM:
LC: photographer
MFAH:
NGA: painter
NMAA:

Sequence #: 12
Field Name: CREATION PLACE
Type: Repeatable
Required?: No
Definition: The geographical location in which an object was created.
Entry Rules: Enter the name for the place where the object was created. Creation place may be a landmass/continent, country, region or city. Levels of hierarchy may be placed in repeating fields (if possible) or incorporated in text (when not stored separately in source database). Separate multiple places with a semicolon followed by an equal sign (;=).
Examples:
FMCH: North Coast Peru
GEH:
HUAM:
LC:
MFAH: Japan
NGA: Deruta, or possibly Gubbio, ITA
NMAA:

Sequence #: 13
Field Name: CREATION BEGIN DATE
Type: Non-Repeatable
Required?: No
Definition: The first year of creation or the lower limit of a date range attributed to the execution of an object. Expressed as year only, the begin date may reflect a specific date, an approximate date, or the lower limit of a date range.
Entry Rules: Enter object begin date in the format YYYY. Where the date represents a BC date, enter as a negative integer. Note that this field is defined for searching purposes only: no attribution or qualifying information such as circa should be recorded here. Object display dates appear in the "Label" (field 6).

Examples: 1668
-324

Comments: In the NGA data, when the object date is unknown, the object inherits the begin and end dates of the principal artist.

Sequence #: 14
Field Name: CREATION END DATE
Type: Non-Repeatable
Required?: No
Definition: The last year of creation or the upper limit of a date range attributed to the execution of an object. Expressed as year only, the end date may reflect a specific date, an approximate date, or the upper limit of a date range. Where the object date is exact or limited to a single year, repeat begin date in this field.
Entry Rules: Enter object end date in the format YYYY. Where the date represents a BC date, enter as a negative integer. Note that this field is defined for searching purposes only: no attribution or qualifying information such as circa should be recorded here. Object display dates appear in the "Label" (field 6).
Examples: 1733
-320
Comments: In the NGA data, when the object date is unknown, the object inherits the begin and end dates of the principal artist.

Sequence #: 15
Field Name: CREATION TECHNIQUE/METHOD/PROCESS
Type: Repeatable
Required?: No
Definition: A term describing how the object was created.
Entry Rules: Enter the term(s) that describe how the object was created. Terms used here should be in the AAT. Separate multiple terms with a semicolon followed by an equal sign (;=). Hierarchy or qualification within a term may be expressed with various forms of punctuation.
Examples:
FMCH: press molded;= slip;= burnished;= smudge fired;= molded from mold matrix
GEH:
HUAM:
LC: Silver gelatin prints
MFAH:
NGA: etching, aquatint
NMAA: LITHOGRAPH

Sequence #: 16
Field Name: MATERIAL/MEDIUM
Type: Repeatable
Required?: No
Definition: The substance(s) of which the object is made.
Entry Rules: Enter the term(s) that describe the media or material of which the object is made. Terms used here should be in the AAT. Separate multiple terms with a semicolon followed by an equal sign (;=). Hierarchy or qualification within a term may be expressed with various forms of punctuation.
Examples:
FMCH: leather;= rawhide;= iron nails;= glass beads
GEH:
HUAM: watercolor
LC:

	MFAH:	
	NGA:	metal, bronze
	NMAA:	paper

Sequence #: 17
Field Name: SUPPORT
Type: Repeatable
Required?: No
Definition: The material on which a two-dimensional work of art has been executed.
Entry Rules: Enter the term(s) that describe the support on which a two-dimensional work of art has been executed. Terms used here should be in the AAT. Separate multiple terms with a semicolon followed by an equal sign (;=). Hierarchy or qualification within a term may be expressed with various forms of punctuation.
Examples:

FMCH:	[NOT USED]
GEH:	
HUAM:	paper
LC:	
MFAH:	
NGA:	wood, cradled
NMAA:	

Sequence #: 18
Field Name: DIMENSION/EXTENT-QUANTITY-UNIT
Type: Repeatable
Required?: No
Definition: Measurements associated with any particular dimension of the object.
Entry Rules: Enter object measurements in metric or U.S. units. The structure of this field is measurement extent (e.g., height, width, depth, etc.), number, and unit of measure without internal punctuation. Use a semicolon followed by an equal sign (;=) to separate multiple measurements.
Examples:

FMCH:	Height 20.2 cm (bottle);= Height 19.6 cm (mold)
GEH:	
HUAM:	Height 34 1/2 in;= Width 24 1/4 in (Actual measurement)
LC:	
MFAH:	
NGA:	height painted surface 52.0 cm;= width painted surface 36.6 cm
NMAA:	height 477 mm;= width 483 mm;= depth 251 mm

Sequence #: 19
Field Name: PARTS/PIECES
Type: Repeatable
Required?: No
Definition: The names of parts of the object and the number of each, or designation of pieces.
Entry Rules: Specify by name and number the component parts that constitute the whole object. Leave this field blank if the object documented is a single item. Objects with components should have each component listed if possible, if not, the total number of components should be indicated. Use a semicolon followed by an equal sign to separate numbers of items set apart by type. This field is not for related objects.
Examples:

FMCH:	bottle (1);= mold (2 halves)
GEH:	
HUAM:	

LC:
MFAH:
NGA: [NOT USED]
NMAA: lid

Sequence #: 20
Field Name: MARKS/INSCRIPTIONS
Type: Repeatable
Required?: No
Definition: Any signatures, dates, annotations, makers marks, collectors marks or other distinguishing inscriptions, along with reference to their location.
Entry Rules: Enter here the transcription of all signatures, dates, numbers, and annotations by any hand, whether written on or printed in a work, optimally giving author if other than the artist, location on the object, and medium. When two or more discrete inscriptions appear on a work they should be separated from one another by a semicolon followed by an equal sign (;=).
Examples: *FMCH:* [NOT USED]
GEH:
HUAM:
LC:
MFAH:
NGA: upper right: HOMER 1876;= lower left: HOMER
NMAA: signed lower right in oil: cadmus

Sequence #: 21
Field Name: EDITION/STATE
Type: Repeatable
Required?: No
Definition: A term denoting the stage in a production process or the named production run to which an object belongs.
Entry Rules: Enter the name of the specific edition to which an object belongs and/or edition size expressed as the total number of impressions in an edition plus the number of proofs. This field may also be used to record the identifying number or name assigned to the specific state or stage of development of a work that exists in more than one form. While largely used in print related processes, the concept applies to casting and manufacturing techniques as well; note that the language is not standardized. Separate multiple values with a semicolon followed by an equal sign (;=).
Examples: *FMCH:* [NOT USED]
GEH:
HUAM:
LC:
MFAH:
NGA: 5/22;= 50: 22 HC
NMAA: 30/46

Sequence #: 22
Field Name: ASSOCIATED EVENTS, PEOPLE, ORGANIZATIONS, PLACES
Type: Repeatable
Required?: No

Definition: The name of a generic or specific event with which the object is associated, a person or organization associated with an object other than in the process of creation, or a place associated with the discovery or use of an object.

Entry Rules: Enter the name of an event, person, or place that is associated with the object and is not otherwise recorded. Proper names should be entered in normal (forward) word order. Associated events are typically only found with material culture objects or commissioned works; the relationship may be specified or not. Do not use this field for recording the place where the object was created or published (see field 12). Similarly, do not use this field for terms describing object subject matter (see field 23). Separate multiple values with a semicolon followed by an equal sign (;=).

Examples:
FMCH: [NOT USED]
GEH:
HUAM:
LC:
MFAH:
NGA: [NOT USED]
NMAA:

Sequence #: 23
Field Name: CONCEPTS/SUBJECT
Type: Repeatable
Required?: No
Definition: The content or subject matter of the object.
Entry Rules: Enter the word or string of words that describes the subject content of the object. Use a semicolon followed by an equal sign (;=) as the break character between multiple terms. Hierarchy or qualification within a term may be expressed with various forms of punctuation.
Examples:
FMCH: Seated figure;= anthropomorphic monkey on spout
GEH:
HUAM:
LC: United States—Rhode Island—Providence
MFAH:
NGA: genre, amusement;= Boating
NMAA: travel;= Air;= Airplane

Sequence #: 24
Field Name: CONCEPTS/STYLE-PERIOD
Type: Repeatable
Required?: No
Definition: A term identifying a style or period in the history of art.
Entry Rules: Enter the term(s) identifying a style or period whose characteristics are represented by the object. These terms will probably be in the AAT, except where the AAT is too Western Art centric. Use a semicolon followed by an equal sign (;=) as the break character between multiple terms.
Examples:
FMCH: Period of Regional States
GEH:
HUAM:
LC:
MFAH: North German;= Late Gothic
NGA: Franco-Flemish;= Renaissance
NMAA:

Sequence #: 25
Field Name: CONCEPTS/FUNCTION
Type: Repeatable
Required?: No
Definition: A term describing the role the object played.
Entry Rules: Enter a term that describes object function. Much art, seen as valuable in itself, will have no terms associated with it here. Use a semicolon followed by an equal sign (;=) as the break character between multiple terms.
Examples:
FMCH: [NOT USED]
GEH:
HUAM:
LC:
MFAH:
NGA: [NOT USED]
NMAA:

Sequence #: 26
Field Name: DESCRIPTION
Type: Non-Repeatable
Required?: No
Definition: Any descriptive text, remarks and comments documenting the object or commenting on it from an interpretive/curatorial perspective.
Entry Rules: Enter comments describing the object from an interpretive/curatorial perspective. This could be a full entry from a published catalog, or a multiple page essay.
Examples:
FMCH: Stirrup spout bottle with the mold that was used to manufacture its chamber.
GEH:
HUAM:
LC:
MFAH: This piece consists of two roughly spherical cups made of mazer, a knotty wood that was thought to absorb and neutralize any poison poured into it. Both the body and cover of the cup are supported by mounts of copper-gilt. The body, with incised foliate ornament, is coupled with a handle in the form of a small fortified chapel on which are mounted crockets, finials, and a trumpeting angel.
NGA: [NOT USED N.B. this information is extracted as the accompanying document "Curatorial Notes"]
NMAA:

Sequence #: 27
Field Name: ACCOMPANYING IMAGE - FILE NAME
Type: Repeatable (linked to fields 28 and 29)
Required?: Yes
Definition: The name of a file containing an image of the object. Every object must have at least one (1) accompanying image.
Entry Rules: Enter the name(s) of the file(s) containing images of the object including path name. Image files should be uniquely identified and use dot-three naming conventions identifying the format in which they are stored. If more than one image exists, enter their names separated by a semicolon equal sign (;=), taking care to order data in the linked fields caption and capture data.

Examples:
FMCH:
GEH:
HUAM:
LC:
MFAH:
NGA: NGA\a000046a.jpg
NMAA:

Comments: Image file name, caption and capture data (fields 27, 28 and 29) are subfields of the larger entity accompanying image. Because this data can repeat, it is important that it be kept in sync when multiple images are provided for a single object. Examples of synchronizing repeating data can be found in Comments for field 9.

Sequence #: 28
Field Name: ACCOMPANYING IMAGE - CAPTION
Type: Repeatable (linked to fields 27 and 29; see Comments for field 27)
Required?: No
Definition: A list of captions to be associated with the image files listed in the previous field.
Entry Rules: Enter captions for the images files referenced in the previous field. Leave this field blank if the object label and image caption are one and the same. Enter multiple captions for multiple images order-keyed to the file name field and separated by a semicolon equal sign (;=).
Examples:
FMCH: View of ceramic vessel;= Drawing of design on vessel
GEH:
HUAM:
LC:
MFAH: general view A;= general view B;= detail view: top of handle;= detail view: coat of arms on lid
NGA:
NMAA:

Sequence #: 29
Field Name: ACCOMPANYING IMAGE - CAPTURE DATA
Type: Repeatable (linked to fields 27 and 28; see Comments for field 27)
Required?: No
Definition: This field contains information regarding the methods and circumstances under which the image information associated with the record was captured.
Entry Rules: Enter capture data for the image files referenced in the image file name field. If possible, include degree of compression for JPEG images. Enter multiple instances of capture data for multiple images order-keyed to the image file name field and separated by a semicolon equal sign (;=).
Examples:
FMCH: 4x5 transparency duplicated as 35 mm slide which was scanned onto PhotoCD
GEH:
HUAM: Scanned at 300dpi from an 8x10 transparency. Reduced to fit within 1024x768, minimal color correction
LC: Scanned from film intermediate, uncorrected (see also Technical Note on the Van Vechten Digital Images)
MFAH: from 35mm slides scanned onto Kodak writable CD
NGA: 24 bit color, corrected
NMAA: PCD->UR->TIF

Sequence #: 30
Field Name: ACCOMPANYING DOCUMENT - FILE NAME
Type: Repeatable (linked to field 31)
Required?: No
Definition: The name of a file containing an electronic document (other than an image) which is related to the object.
Entry Rules: Enter the name(s) of the file(s) containing documents related to the object including the name of the path in which the files are located. Document files should be uniquely identified and use dot-three naming conventions identifying the format in which they are stored. All text files should have .TXT extensions in their name. Other files listed here may include sound files and multi-media documents such as interactives, games, or full-motion video with or without sound. If an object has more than one accompanying document, enter their names separated by a semicolon equal sign (;=), taking care to order data in the linked field accompanying document type.
Examples:
FMCH:
GEH:
HUAM:
LC:
MFAH:
NGA: NGA\C0000031.TXT;= NGA\E0000031.TXT;= NGA\O0000031.TXT;= NGA\P0000031.TXT
NMAA:

Sequence #: 31
Field Name: ACCOMPANYING DOCUMENT - TYPE
Type: Repeatable (linked to field 30)
Required?: Yes if data is provided in field 30
Definition: A list of types of other electronic documents which relate to the object, correlated to the file list in the previous field.
Entry Rules: Enter the word or words that identify the type of the file(s) referenced in the previous field. Legal values for constructed document types are: Publication History; Exhibition History; Conservation History; Research History; Ownership History; Field Collection Notes; Related Object Notes; and Curatorial Notes. Terms for describing other document types such as sounding recordings, digitized video, and published texts are not prescribed by MESL. Enter multiple values for multiple documents order-keyed to the file names in field 30 and separated by a semicolon equal sign (;=).
Examples:
FMCH: Published text
GEH:
HUAM: Authorities;= Detail Notes
LC:
MFAH:
NGA: Curatorial Notes;= Exhibition History;= Ownership History;= Publication History
NMAA:

Sequence #: 32
Field Name: VERSION IDENTIFICATION
Type: Non-Repeatable
Required?: No
Definition: This field contains data which the content provider considers necessary to uniquely identify the version of the object information represented.

Entry Rules: Enter version identification information. This field may contain an arbitrary number or the date of creation of the electronic data set, or it may point to any internal version control information needed by the content provider. This data has meaning for the content providers only.

Examples:

FMCH: 7/15/95
GEH:
HUAM: 12/18/95
LC:
MFAH: 6/27/95
NGA: 07/05/1995 01/05/1995
NMAA: Thursday, August 24, 1995: OMNIMARK SCRIPTS RUNMESL1, RUNMESL2 and RUNMESL3

Appendix D : Chart of MESL Field Usage

Field Number	Field Name	Fowler Museum of Cultural History	George Eastman House	Harvard University Art Museums	The Museum of Fine Arts, Houston	Library of Congress	National Gallery of Art	National Museum of American Art
1	Data Agreement Number	fixed content	fixed content	fixed content	fixed content	fixed content	fixed content	fixed content
2	Holding Institution	fixed content	fixed content	fixed content	fixed content	fixed content	fixed content	fixed content
3	Accession Number	yes	yes	yes	yes	inventory number or call number	yes	yes
4	Accession Method	yes	yes	yes	yes	no	yes	not supplied; used for administrative purposes
5	Credit Line	yes	yes	yes	yes	yes	yes	yes
6	Label	yes	yes	yes	yes	aggregated	yes	yes
7	Object Type	yes	yes	yes	yes	yes	yes	yes
8	Object Title	yes	yes	yes	yes	yes	yes	yes
9	Creator	yes	yes	yes	yes	yes	yes	yes
10	Creator-Culture/ Nationality	yes	yes	yes	yes	no	yes	yes
11	Creator-Role	no data	yes	no data	yes	no	yes	used only for multiple artist works
12	Creation Place	yes	yes	yes	yes	no	yes	no data
13	Begin Date	yes	yes	yes	yes	yes	yes	yes
14	End Date	yes	yes	yes	yes	no	yes	yes
15	Creation Technique	yes	yes	yes	yes	yes	yes	yes
16	Material/Medium	yes	no data	yes	yes	no	yes	yes
17	Support	D2: no data	no data	yes	yes	no	yes	yes
18	Dimensions	yes	yes	yes	yes	yes	yes	yes
19	Parts	yes	no data	no data	yes	no	yes	not relevant to objects provided

(continued)

Field Number	Field Name	Fowler Museum of Cultural History	George Eastman House	Harvard University Art Museums	The Museum of Fine Arts, Houston	Library of Congress	National Gallery of Art	National Museum of American Art
20	Marks	no data	yes	yes	yes	no	yes	yes
21	Edition/State	no data	no data	yes	no data	no	yes	yes
22	Assoc. Events, etc.	D2: no data	no	no data	no data	no	no data	no data
23	Concepts/Subject	D2: no data	yes	no data	yes	yes	yes	yes
24	Concepts/Style	yes	no data	no data	yes	no	yes	no data except for a small number of decorative arts pieces
25	Concepts/ Function	D1: no data	no	no data	yes	no	no data	no data
26	Description	yes	no data	yes	yes	yes	yes	no data
27	Accompanying Image File	yes	yes	yes	yes	yes	yes	yes
28	Accompanying Image Caption	yes	yes	yes	yes	no	yes	no data
29	Capture Data	yes	no data	yes	yes	yes	yes	yes
30	Accompanying Documents	D2: no data	no data	yes	no data	collection level notes	yes	no data
31	Accompanying Document Type	D2: no data	no data	yes	no data	yes	yes	no data
32	Version Identification	fixed content	fixed content	fixed content	fixed content	fixed content	fixed content	fixed content
	Coll Management	Questor	in house	in house (now EmbARK)	Quixis		in house	in house
	External Authorities	yes	yes	yes - AAT	none	LC Name, LCSH, LC Graphics	none	none

Appendix E : Instructor/Student Surveys

Instructor Preliminary Questionnaire
Museum Educational Site Licensing Project

The purpose of this survey is to gather information about the use of digital images from the Museum Educational Site Licensing (MESL) project. We would greatly appreciate any information and insights you would be willing to share about your experience.

I. Personal Information

1. **Name:** ______________________________
2. **Course #:** ___________________________ 4. **Course Title:** ______________________________
3. **Department:** _________________________ 5. **College:** __________________________________

6. **Institution:** *(Circle one)*
   1) American University
   2) Columbia University
   3) Cornell University
   4) University of Illinois
   5) University of Maryland
   6) University of Michigan
   7) University of Virginia

7. **Status:** *(Circle One)*
   1) Professor
   2) Associate Professor
   3) Assistant Professor
   4) Lecturer
   5) Adjunct Faculty
   6) Master's & Teaching / Research Assistant
   7) Ph.D. & Teaching / Research Assistant
   8) Other ____________________________ ***(please specify)***

8. **Gender:** *(Circle one)* 1) Male 2) Female

Optional

9. **Race/ethnicity:** *(Circle all that apply)*
   1) White
   2) Asian
   3) Native American
   4) African-American
   5) Hispanic
   6) Other ______________________________ ***(please specify)***

II. Technology Background

1. For each of the following categories of computer applications please indicate your level of experience.

Check the appropriate box	**No Experience**	**Low Experience**	**Average Experience**	**Above Average**	**High Experience**
1) Word Processing (e.g., Word)	1	2	3	4	5
2) Spreadsheet (e.g., Excel)	1	2	3	4	5
3) Desktop Publishing (e.g., PageMaker)	1	2	3	4	5
4) Presentation Software (e.g., PowerPoint)	1	2	3	4	5
5) Databases (e.g., FileMaker Pro)	1	2	3	4	5
6) Email (e.g., Eudora, Pine)	1	2	3	4	5
7) Internet (e.g., World Wide Web, Gopher)	1	2	3	4	5

(continued)

8) Web (HTML) Authoring (e.g., Web Weaver)	1	2	3	4	5
9) Programming (e.g., CGI scripting, Java, Perl)	1	2	3	4	5
10) Image Scanning (e.g., Pictures, Text)	1	2	3	4	5
11) Image Editing (e.g., Photoshop)	1	2	3	4	5
12) Digital Video Editing (e.g., Premiere)	1	2	3	4	5
13) 3-D Graphic Design (e.g., VRML)	1	2	3	4	5
14) Other technologies ____________ *(please specify)*	1	2	3	4	5

2. For each of the following categories of computer applications please indicate if you or your students have used these to prepare or complete assignments in your course.

Check the appropriate box	**Class Presentations**	**Exam Review**	**Student Projects**	**Research**	**Other**
1) Word Processing (e.g., Word)	1	2	3	4	5
2) Spreadsheet (e.g., Excel)	1	2	3	4	5
3) Desktop Publishing (e.g., PageMaker)	1	2	3	4	5
4) Presentation Software (e.g., PowerPoint)	1	2	3	4	5
5) Databases (e.g., FileMaker Pro)	1	2	3	4	5
6) Email (e.g., Eudora, Pine)	1	2	3	4	5
7) Internet (e.g., World Wide Web, Gopher)	1	2	3	4	5
8) Web (HTML) Authoring (e.g., Web Weaver)	1	2	3	4	5
9) Programming (e.g., CGI scripting, Java, Perl)	1	2	3	4	5
10) Image Scanning (e.g., Pictures, Text)	1	2	3	4	5
11) Image Editing (e.g., Photoshop)	1	2	3	4	5
12) Digital Video Editing (e.g., Premiere)	1	2	3	4	5
13) 3-D Graphic Design (e.g., VRML)	1	2	3	4	5
14) Other technologies ____________ *(please specify)*	1	2	3	4	5

(continued)

(continued)

III. Use of the MESL Images

1. Have you used the MESL images? *(Circle One)* 1) Yes 2) No

2. Please describe how you use or intend to use the MESL images. ***(Circle all that apply)***

    1) To search / browse the MESL collection to determine its contents.
    2) To select images for class.
    3) Display the images in class.
    4) Incorporate the images into an electronic (Web) page.
    5) To create assignments for student projects.
    6) To use images for research.

3. For each of the following phrases, please indicate your opinions about using technology and how the MESL digital images will help or impede your instruction, your research, and your students.

Check the appropriate box	**Strongly Disagree**	**Disagree**	**Agree**	**Strongly Agree**
1) Students will be able to view images from a remote location.	1	2	3	4
2) Students can easily integrate images into their papers and/or projects	1	2	3	4
3) Students can access art works (images) not otherwise available.	1	2	3	4
4) Using images online involves extra work (studying the slides, the textbook, and the digital images).	1	2	3	4
5) MESL images will provide an additional perspective on a given concept.	1	2	3	4
6) MESL images will complement slides, the textbook, photographs or prints.	1	2	3	4
7) MESL images will be used to design assignments that are not possible with slide/print images.	1	2	3	4

4. Please comment on how often you use visual resources.

Check the appropriate box	**Never**	**Rarely** (1–5 times per term)	**Sometimes** (6–10 times per term)	**Regularly** (11–20 times per term)	**Often** (more than 20 times per term)
1) How often do you use slides to discuss visual materials?	1	2	3	4	5
2) How often do you use a textbook, prints, or photographs to discuss visual material?	1	2	3	4	5
3) How often do you use digital images in any of your classes?	1	2	3	4	5

(continued)

6. For each of the following phrases, please indicate your level of agreement.

Check the appropriate box	**Strongly Disagree**	**Disagree**	**Agree**	**Strongly Agree**
1) I am comfortable using computer technology as part of my daily work.	1	2	3	4
2) I am comfortable using computer technology in the classroom.	1	2	3	4
3) I am familiar with using computer technology to develop my course material.	1	2	3	4
4) It is difficult to get help on campus to learn how to use computer technology.	1	2	3	4
5) My department provides access to computer technology that would enable me to use MESL images.	1	2	3	4
6) Students in my classes have easy access to a computer lab to access good quality MESL images.	1	2	3	4
7) Classrooms for using MESL images are conveniently located.	1	2	3	4

7. There is a computer in my office from which I can access MESL images. ***(Circle one)***

1) Yes 2) No

8. How do you think digital images will affect your instruction, your research, and your students' research?

9. What will be the advantages and disadvantages of using MESL in this course?

1) Advantages

2) Disadvantages

(Optional)

If you would be willing to participate in a follow-up interview, please include your name and email address:

Name: ______________________ email: ______________________

(please print)

THANK YOU FOR TAKING THE TIME TO COMPLETE THIS SURVEY

STUDENT PRELIMINARY QUESTIONNAIRE
Museum Educational Site Licensing Project

The purpose of this survey is to gather preliminary information about your use of digital images from the Museum Educational Site Licensing (MESL) project, as part of this course. We would greatly appreciate any information and insights you would be willing to share about your experience.

I. PERSONAL INFORMATION

1. Student Code: ______________
(Last 4 digits of your Social Security Number or an assigned unique number)

2. Course #: ______________________ **3. Course Title:** ______________________

Please circle the code number for your answer.

4. Institution: *(Circle one)*
1) American University
2) Columbia University
3) Cornell University
4) University of Illinois
5) University of Maryland
6) University of Michigan
7) University of Virginia

5. Status: *(Circle one)*
1) Freshman
2) Sophomore
3) Junior
4) Senior
5) Master's
6) Ph.D.
7) Master's & Teaching / Research Assistant
8) Ph.D. & Teaching / Research Assistant
9) Non-Degree

6. Major: *(Circle one)*
1) Fine Arts
2) Humanities
3) Social Science
4) Science/Professional
5) Undeclared / Other ______________ *(please specify)*

7. Gender: ***(Circle one)*** 1) Male 2) Female

8. Main reason for taking the course: *(Circle one)*
1) Major
2) General Requirement
3) Personal Interest
4) Other ______________ *(please specify)*

Optional

9. RACE/ETHNICITY: *(Circle all that apply)*
1) White
2) Asian
3) Native American
4) African-American
5) Hispanic
6) Other ______________ *(please specify)*

II. TECHNOLOGY BACKGROUND

1. For each of the following categories of computer applications please indicate your level of experience.

Check the appropriate box	**No Experience**	**Low Experience**	**Average Experience**	**Above Average**	**High Experience**
1) Word Processing (e.g., Word)	1	2	3	4	5
2) Spreadsheet (e.g., Excel)	1	2	3	4	5
3) Desktop Publishing (e.g., PageMaker)	1	2	3	4	5
4) Presentation Software (e.g., PowerPoint)	1	2	3	4	5
5) Databases (e.g., FileMaker Pro)	1	2	3	4	5
6) Email (e.g., Eudora, Pine)	1	2	3	4	5

(continued)

7) Internet (e.g., World Wide Web, Gopher)	1	2	3	4	5
8) Web (HTML) Authoring (e.g., Web Weaver)	1	2	3	4	5
9) Programming (e.g., CGI scripting, Java, Perl)	1	2	3	4	5
10) Image Scanning (e.g., Pictures, Text)	1	2	3	4	5
11) Image Editing (e.g., Photoshop)	1	2	3	4	5
12) Digital Video Editing (e.g., Premiere)	1	2	3	4	5
13) 3-D Graphic Design (e.g., VRML)	1	2	3	4	5
14) Other technologies ________ *(please specify)*	1	2	3	4	5

III. Use of the MESL Images

1. Have you used the MESL images? ***(Circle One)*** 1) Yes 2) No

2. Please describe how you <u>use or intend to use</u> the MESL images and text information. ***(Circle all that apply)***

   1) To write a paper in which I analyze MESL images.
   2) Incorporate the MESL images into an electronic (Web) page.
   3) Edit and change the MESL images to incorporate them into a project.
   4) Search the MESL collection to examine the images.

3. For each of the following phrases, please indicate <u>your opinion</u> about technology and what you hope it will enable you to do with the MESL images.

Check the appropriate box	**Strongly Disagree**	**Disagree**	**Agree**	**Strongly Agree**
1) I will be able to view images from a remote location.	1	2	3	4
2) It will be less convenient than using slides or books.	1	2	3	4
3) It will allow me to easily integrate images of art into my papers and projects.	1	2	3	4
4) It will give me access to art works not otherwise available.	1	2	3	4
5) Using images online involves extra work (studying slides, textbook, and the digital images).	1	2	3	4
6) I am comfortable using computer technology as part of coursework.	1	2	3	4
7) It is difficult to get help on campus to learn how to use computer technology.	1	2	3	4
8) I have access to computer technology on campus that would enable me to use MESL images.	1	2	3	4

(continued)

(continued)

4. I have a computer (in my office, dorm, or at home) that I can use to access the MESL images. ***(Circle one)***

1) Yes 2) No

5. Please indicate your current use of visual resources.

Check the appropriate box	**Never**	**Rarely** (1–5 times per term)	**Sometimes** (6–10 times per term)	**Regularly** (11–20 times per term)	**Often** (more than 20 times per term)
1) How often do you use slides to discuss visual materials?	1	2	3	4	5
2) How often do you use a textbook, photographs, or prints to study visual materials?	1	2	3	4	5
3) How often do you use digital images to study visual materials?	1	2	3	4	5

6. In what additional ways do you think using MESL images will affect your work?

7. **For Master's Degree and Ph.D. Students:** How do you think using MESL images will affect your research and your teaching?

(Optional)
If you would be willing to participate in a follow-up interview, please include your name and email address.
Name: ______________________ email: ______________________
(please print)

THANK YOU FOR TAKING THE TIME TO COMPLETE THIS SURVEY

INSTRUCTOR POST QUESTIONNAIRE
Museum Educational Site Licensing Project

The purpose of this survey is to gather information about the use of digital images from the Museum Educational Site License (MESL) project. We would greatly appreciate any information and insights you would be willing to share about your experience.

I. PERSONAL INFORMATION

1. **Name:** ______________________________
2. **Course #:** ______________________________ 4. **Course Title:** ______________________________
3. **Department:** ______________________________ 5. **College:** ______________________________
4. **Institution:** ______________________________

II. USE OF THE MESL IMAGES

This section applies to the use of the MESL database by faculty to support instruction and research.

1. From where did you access the MESL materials? ***(Circle all that apply)***

   1) Lab 3) Classroom 5) Office
   2) Library 4) Off campus 6) Other ______________________________ *(please specify)*

2. Estimate how often you used MESL images during the term. ***(Circle one)***

   1) Once 2) 2–10 times 3) 11–20 times 4) more than 20 times

3. Use of the MESL collection(s). ***(Circle all that apply)***

Collection you intended to use	**Collection you actually used**
1) National Gallery of Art	1) National Gallery of Art
2) Museum of Fine Arts, Houston	2) Museum of Fine Arts, Houston
3) Harvard University Art Museums	3) Harvard University Art Museums
4) National Museum of American Art	4) National Museum of American Art
5) Fowler Museum of Cultural History	5) Fowler Museum of Cultural History
6) George Eastman House	6) George Eastman House
7) Library of Congress	7) Library of Congress

4. Which of these phases describes your best use of the MESL images? ***(Circle one)***

1) Used the images for a project or assignment for this class
2) Used in class to accompany lectures
3) Used it for projects outside this class
4) Used the text information for factual research about the image or artist
5) Used it for my research
6) Other ______________________________ *(please specify)*

5. How many times (semesters) have you used MESL in the class? What was different?

(continued)

(continued)

6. How do you think using MESL assisted you in teaching ?

Circle the appropriate number	Strongly Disagree	Disagree	Agree	Strongly Agree
1) I used MESL images to provide an additional perspective on a given concept	1	2	3	4
2) I used MESL images to complement the slides and images in the textbook.	1	2	3	4
3) I used MESL images to design assignments that are not possible with slide/print images.	1	2	3	4

7. For each of the following phrases, please indicate your opinions about how technology and the MESL digital images affected your work in this class.

Circle the appropriate number	Strongly Disagree	Disagree	Agree	Strongly Agree
1) It was advantageous to view images from remote location(s).	1	2	3	4
2) Using MESL images was less convenient than using slides or books.	1	2	3	4
3) Students could integrate images into papers and projects.	1	2	3	4
4) It gave me access to images not otherwise available.	1	2	3	4
5) Using images involved extra work (using slides, textbook, and the digital images)	1	2	3	4
6) The MESL database was easy to use.	1	2	3	4
7) I can get access to a better selection of images than MESL.	1	2	3	4
8) Digital images make the study of art more interesting than using slides, prints, and textbooks.	1	2	3	4
9) I could not have achieved the same objectives in my class by using textbook, prints, and slides.	1	2	3	4
10) The selection of images was adequate for my use.	1	2	3	4
11) The classroom setup was convenient and easy for using MESL images.	1	2	3	4

8. Rate the usefulness of various parts of the MESL database.

Circle the appropriate number	Not at all Useful	Not too Useful	Somewhat Useful	Very Useful
1) Search capability	1	2	3	4
2) Thumbnail images	1	2	3	4
3) Screen-size images	1	2	3	4
4) Highest resolution images	1	2	3	4
5) Text information describing the image	1	2	3	4
6) Curatorial information and additional text	1	2	3	4

(continued)

9. Rate the quality of the images for student viewing when you viewed them on a computer screen.

Circle the appropriate number	Poor	Fair	Good	Excellent	Not Applicable
1) Color	1	2	3	4	5
2) Detail	1	2	3	4	5
3) Clarity / Resolution	1	2	3	4	5
4) Size	1	2	3	4	5
5) Time to download images	1	2	3	4	5

10. Rate the quality of the images for student viewing when you viewed them with classroom projection equipment.

Circle the appropriate number	Poor	Fair	Good	Excellent	Not Applicable
1) Color	1	2	3	4	5
2) Detail	1	2	3	4	5
3) Clarity / Resolution	1	2	3	4	5
4) Size	1	2	3	4	5
5) Time to download images	1	2	3	4	5

11. What kinds of functions and information do you think it is important to include in a **future image** database like MESL? ***(Circle all that apply)***

1) More images
2) More artist(s)
3) More culture(s)
4) More genres (e.g., portraits, landscapes)
5) More styles (e.g., gothic, impressionism)
6) Higher resolution images
7) More text information about the images
8) More information about artists
9) High quality printing capability
10) Zooming in and out to view details
11) Image editing tools (crop, rotate, sharpen)
12) Easy export of images to other software
13) Search for images by: artist's name
14) Search for images by: culture
15) Search for images by: style
16) Search for images by: genre
17) Search for images by: geographic place
18) Search for images by: date
19) Save search results
20) Sort and mark sets of images for later use
21) Ability to annotate images with my comments
22) Ability to post my notes to a shared database
23) Engage in online chat with others about images
24) Ability to ask museums questions about images
25) Browse online museum catalogs and / or request images
26) Display and compare two or more images on screen
27) Other: ____________________ ***(please specify)***

12. In what ways did you ask students to use MESL images in the class?

13. Did the use of MESL images change the students' assignments for this course? Please describe.

(continued)

(continued)

14. Describe what changes you had to make as a result of using the MESL images for your course.

15. Did you have assistance to develop MESL for the class?

16. What kind of ongoing support do you need to incorporate digital images into your teaching?

17. In what innovative ways can digital images be used in instruction?

18. Would you use MESL again? Please comment.

(Optional)
If you are willing to participate in a follow-up interview, please indicate your name and email address below:

Name: ______________________________ email: ______________________

THANK YOU FOR TAKING THE TIME TO COMPLETE THIS SURVEY.

STUDENT POST QUESTIONNAIRE
Museum Educational Site Licensing Project

The purpose of this survey is to gather information about your use of digital images from the Museum Educational Site Licensing (MESL) project. We would greatly appreciate any information and insights you would be willing to share about your experience.

I. PERSONAL INFORMATION

1. Student Code: ______________

(Last 4 digits of your Social Security Number or an assigned unique number)

2. Course #: ____________________ **3. Course Title:** ______________________________

Please circle the code number for your answer.

4. Institution: *(Circle one)*
1) American University
2) Columbia University
3) Cornell University
4) University of Illinois
5) University of Maryland
6) University of Michigan
7) University of Virginia

5. Status: *(Circle one)*
1) Freshman
2) Sophomore
3) Junior
4) Senior
5) Master's
6) Ph.D.
7) Master's & Teaching / Research Assistant
8) Ph.D. & Teaching / Research Assistant
9) Non-Degree

6. Major: *(Circle one)*
1) Fine Arts
2) Humanities
3) Social Science
4) Science/Professional
5) Undeclared / Other ______________ *(please specify)*

7. Gender: ***(Circle one)*** 1) Male 2) Female

8. Main reason for taking the course: *(Circle one)* 1) Major 2) General Requirement 3) Personal Interest 4) Other ______________ *(please specify)*

Optional

9. RACE/ETHNICITY: *(Circle all that apply)*
1) White
2) Asian
3) Native American
4) African-American
5) Hispanic
6) Other ______________ *(please specify)*

II. TECHNOLOGY BACKGROUND

1. Please indicate which of the following technologies you used in conjunction with this course that were new to you.

(Circle all that apply)
1) Word Processing (e.g., Word)
2) Spreadsheet (e.g., Excel)
3) Desktop Publishing (e.g., PageMaker)
4) Presentation (e.g., PowerPoint)
5) Databases (e.g., FileMaker Pro)
6) Email (e.g., Eudora, Pine)
7) Internet (e.g., World Wide Web)
8) Web (HTML) Authoring (e.g., Web Weaver)
9) Web Programming (e.g., CGI scripting, Java, Perl)
10) Image Scanning (e.g., Pictures, Text)
11) Image Processing & Editing (e.g., Photoshop)
12) Digital Video Editing (e.g., Premiere)
13) 3-D Graphic Design (e.g., VRML)
14) Other technologies: ____________________ *(please specify)*

(continued)

(continued)

III. Use of the MESL Images

Please answer each of the following questions by circling the appropriate response.

1. Do you have a computer with modem to access the Web from a residence or a dormitory?
   1) Yes 2) No

2. Did you use digital images other than the MESL images during this term for this or any other course?
   1) Yes 2) No

3. Did you view MESL images for this course? 1) Yes 2) No
   (If No, Skip to Question # 14)

If you answered yes, please continue with the following questions in Part III.

4. From where did you access the MESL materials the most? ***(Circle all that apply)***

   1) Lab 3) Classroom 5) Residence Hall
   2) Library 4) Home 6) Other ________________________
   (please specify)

5. Estimate how often you used MESL images during this term. ***(Circle one)***

   1) Once 2) 2–10 times 3) 11–20 times 4) more than 20 times

6. Which of these phrases describes how you used the MESL images?

Check the appropriate box	**Never**	**Rarely** (1–5 times per term)	**Sometimes** (6–10 times per term)	**Regularly** (11–20 times per term)	**Often** (more than 20 times per term)
1) Did a side-by-side image comparison for formal (visual) analysis.	1	2	3	4	5
2) Used the text information for factual research about the image or artist.	1	2	3	4	5
3) Used the images to review for tests.	1	2	3	4	5
4) Attended lectures where MESL images were used.	1	2	3	4	5
5) Incorporated the MESL images into research about the image or artist.	1	2	3	4	5
6) Edited and changed the MESL images to incorporate them into a multimedia presentation.	1	2	3	4	5
7) Created a database from which MESL images could be searched and retrieved.	1	2	3	4	5

7. Did you use MESL images in any other ways? Please describe.

(continued)

8. For each of the following phrases, please indicate your opinions about how technology and the MESL digital images affected your work in this class.

Check the appropriate box	Strongly Disagree	Disagree	Agree	Strongly Agree
1) It was advantageous to be able to view images from remote location(s).	1	2	3	4
2) Using MESL images was less convenient than using slides or books.	1	2	3	4
3) It was useful to integrate images into my papers and projects.	1	2	3	4
4) It gave me access to images not otherwise available.	1	2	3	4
5) Using images online involved extra work (studying the slides, textbook, and the digital images).	1	2	3	4
6) I am comfortable using computer technology for class.	1	2	3	4
7) The MESL database was easy to use.	1	2	3	4
8) I can get access to a better selection of images than MESL.	1	2	3	4
9) I could do things with MESL images that I cannot do with slides, prints, or textbooks.	1	2	3	4
10) The MESL images were presented with enthusiasm in class.	1	2	3	4
11) MESL images were discussed frequently.	1	2	3	4
12) Digital images make the study of art more interesting than using slides, prints, and textbooks.	1	2	3	4

9. Rate the usefulness of various parts of the MESL database.

Check the appropriate number	Not at all Useful	Not too Useful	Somewhat Useful	Very Useful
1) Search capability (e.g., artist, title, object type)	1	2	3	4
2) Thumbnail images	1	2	3	4
3) Screen-size images	1	2	3	4
4) Highest resolution images	1	2	3	4
5) Text information describing the image	1	2	3	4
6) Curatorial information and additional text	1	2	3	4

10. Rate the quality of the MESL images when you viewed them on a computer screen.

Check the appropriate box	Poor	Fair	Good	Excellent	Not Applicable
1) Color	1	2	3	4	5
2) Detail	1	2	3	4	5
3) Clarity / Resolution	1	2	3	4	5
4) Size	1	2	3	4	5
5) Time to load images	1	2	3	4	5

(continued)

(continued)

11. Rate the quality of the MESL images when you viewed them with classroom projection equipment.

Circle the appropriate number	**Poor**	**Fair**	**Good**	**Excellent**	**Not Applicable**
1) Color	1	2	3	4	5
2) Detail	1	2	3	4	5
3) Clarity / Resolution	1	2	3	4	5
4) Size	1	2	3	4	5
5) Time to load images	1	2	3	4	5

12. Please add any additional comments you may have about the quality of images compared to slides, textbooks, and prints.

13. Please comment further on how you think the use of digital images has affected your work in this class.

14. What kinds of functions and information do you think it is important to include in a **future image** database like MESL? ***(Circle all that apply)***

    1) More images
    2) More artist(s)
    3) More culture(s)
    4) More genres (e.g., portraits, landscapes)
    5) More styles (e.g., gothic, impressionism)
    6) Higher resolution images
    7) More text information about the images
    8) More information about artists
    9) High quality printing capability
    10) Zooming in and out to view details
    11) Image editing tools (crop, rotate, sharpen)
    12) Easy export of images to other software
    13) Search for images by: artist's name
    14) Search for images by: culture
    15) Search for images by: style
    16) Search for images by: genre
    17) Search for images by: geographic place
    18) Search for images by: date
    19) Save search results
    20) Sort and mark sets of images for later use
    21) Ability to annotate images with my comments
    22) Ability to post my notes to a shared database
    23) Engage in online chat with others about images
    24) Ability to ask museums questions about images
    25) Browse online museum catalogs and / or request images
    26) Display and compare two or more images on screen
    27) Other: ______________________________
    (please specify)

(Optional)
If you would be willing to participate in a follow-up interview, please include your name and email address:
Name: ______________________________ mail: ______________________________

THANK YOU FOR TAKING THE TIME TO COMPLETE THIS SURVEY

Appendix F: Casual User Survey

Thank You for Looking at MESL!

We are no longer offering a poster or cash for participating in our survey. **However**, if you would still like to send us your comments to help us improve the site, please fill out the survey below.

Thank you very much!

---

0) Which university MESL site are you evaluating?

[**MESL Site ...**]

1) Where did you learn about the MESL web site? (Check all that apply)

❑ Class assignment

❑ Friend's recommendation

❑ Found using a web search tool

❑ Saw it mentioned on an electronic mailing list

❑ Link from another web site. Which? [ ]

❑ Other [ ]

2) Approximately how many total times have you visited the MESL web site?

[**Frequency ...**]

3) What is the main reason you visited the MESL web site this time?

❍ Class assignment

❍ Research

❍ Entertainment

❍ Curiosity

❍ Other [ ]

(continued)

(continued)

4) Please rate the following aspects of the MESL web site:

	Scale: Excellent (5) to Poor (1) or Not Applicable					
Overall appeal	❍ 5	❍ 4	❍ 3	❍ 2	❍ 1	❍ NA
Clarity of written information	❍ 5	❍ 4	❍ 3	❍ 2	❍ 1	❍ NA
Appeal of screens (icons, layout, etc.)	❍ 5	❍ 4	❍ 3	❍ 2	❍ 1	❍ NA
Ease of browsing	❍ 5	❍ 4	❍ 3	❍ 2	❍ 1	❍ NA
Ease of searching	❍ 5	❍ 4	❍ 3	❍ 2	❍ 1	❍ NA
Effectiveness of searching	❍ 5	❍ 4	❍ 3	❍ 2	❍ 1	❍ NA
Speed of delivery	❍ 5	❍ 4	❍ 3	❍ 2	❍ 1	❍ NA
Quality of written information	❍ 5	❍ 4	❍ 3	❍ 2	❍ 1	❍ NA
Quality of images	❍ 5	❍ 4	❍ 3	❍ 2	❍ 1	❍ NA

5) What were you looking for? (Optional) [ ]

6) Did you find what you were looking for? (Check all that apply.)

❑ I found what I was looking for.

❑ I found something that interests me.

❑ I was unable to find what I was looking for.

❑ I was just browsing.

6a) What will you do with the information that you found? (Check all that apply.)

❑ Use it in a report, research, etc.

❑ Copy and paste it in another program

❑ Print it out

❑ Refer / link other users to it

❑ Nothing

❑ Other [ ]

7) Before MESL and other World Wide Web resources brought digital images to your computer, how frequently did you use images in your class assignments or research?

[Frequency ...]

(continued)

8) Tell us about you.

- **Institution ...**
- **Status ...**
- **Major field of study ...**
- **Age ...**
- **Gender ...**

9) Overall, please rate the value of this web site?

❍ Excellent ❍ Good ❍ Satisfactory ❍ Unsatisfactory ❍ Poor

10) Please enter additional comments here. We are particularly interested in learning if MESL helps you use digital images in new or different ways.

Optional User Information

E-mail address:

Name:

Affiliation:

Can we contact you by e-mail for further information?

❍ Yes ❍ No

Submit **Clear**

Thank you!

Return links to MESL Sites

National MESL Site	American University	Columbia University	Cornell University
University of Illinois	University of Maryland	University of Michigan	University of Virginia

Created by the Interactive Multimedia Group at Cornell University.
Comments should be emailed to (rrp8@cornell.edu)
Last Updated 5/23/97.

About the Contributors

HOWARD BESSER is Adjunct Associate Professor at the School of Information Management and Systems of the University of California–Berkeley, where he teaches courses on image databases, Web design, and the social and cultural effects of new information technology. He publishes articles on image databases, frequently speaks at conferences, and consults for museums, libraries, and arts organizations. He has been on the MESL Management Committee since its inception.

ROBIN DOWDEN is Manager of Integrated Information Resources at the Walker Art Center in Minneapolis (as of October 1997). She is responsible for the development and implementation of the Integrated Arts Information Access Project, a joint project of the Walker Art Center and The Minneapolis Institute of the Arts. During the MESL project, Robin was in charge of the collection information systems and Web site of the National Gallery of Art, and served as co-chair of the MESL Documentation and Distribution Working Group.

GERALDINE GAY is Associate Professor of Communication at Cornell University, where she also directs the Interactive Media Group (IMG). The IMG is a research and development team that designs and investigates the use of computer-mediated learning environments. Professor Gay's research interests focus on cognitive and social issues for the design of interactive communication technologies.

MARY LEVERING is the Associate Register for National Copyright Programs in the U.S. Copyright Office, a service unit of the Library of Congress. She is a copyright lawyer and is currently responsible for representing the U.S. Copyright Office on major national issues with copyright implications, including intellectual property rights and the development of information networks, collective administration of rights, digital library matters, and the evolution of new media of communications.

MELISSA SMITH LEVINE is the Legal Advisor to the Library of Congress's National Digital Library Program. She provides legal review of Library collections for issues such as copyright management, publicity, and privacy prior to release on the Internet. She also works with library staff, the U. S. Copyright Office, and the Office of General Counsel on a wide range of legal, policy, and contractual matters relating to the Internet. Formerly, she worked at the Smithsonian Institution.

CLIFFORD LYNCH is the newly appointed (July 1997) Executive Director of the Coalition for Networked Information (CNI). Previously, he served as the Director of Library Automation at the University of California, where he led the development and implementation of the Melvyl online library catalog that links all of the UC campuses. He also served as a member of the MESL project Management Committee.

PATRICIA MCCLUNG is a consultant to libraries and museums on digital initiatives and has served as manager of the MESL project since 1995. Prior to that she managed collaborative projects and was Director of Member Services at The Research Libraries Group.

ANDREA NOTMAN is Associate Registrar for Collections Management at the Harvard University Art Museums, where she has supervised the collections database project since its inception in 1983. In addition, she coordinates special projects on traditional and creative uses of museum information.

ROBERT RIEGER is the Assistant Director of the Interactive Media Group in the Department of Communication at Cornell University. With students and faculty colleagues, he investigates the use of computer and multimedia technologies in education and communication.

BETH SANDORE is the Assistant Director for Imaging Projects of the Digital Imaging Initiative program and Associate Professor at the University of Illinois at Urbana–Champaign Library. Her work and research focus on technology development and evaluation in libraries, including experimental work with image and multimedia databases.

NAJMUDDIN SHAIK is a Ph.D. student at the University of Illinois at Urbana–Champaign and is also a member of the Digital Imaging Initiative program. He has worked with several collaborative projects at the University, including MESL, for which he provided faculty support. His current research interest is design and evaluation of distributed collaborative interactive tutoring systems.

CHRISTIE STEPHENSON is the newly appointed Librarian for Digital Collections at the New York University Libraries. Previously, she worked for 18 years at the University of Virginia Libraries, most recently as coordinator of the Digital Image Center. She became the MESL Project Director in the fall of 1996, after having served as the University of Virginia's MESL Project Coordinator.

AMANDA STURGILL is an instructor in journalism at Baylor University and a research associate with the Interactive Media Group at Cornell University. Her research efforts concentrate on the impacts of communication technologies in various educational domains.

ROBERT YAMASHITA is Assistant Professor in interdisciplinary studies in science and society at California State University at San Marcos. His work focuses on the social and cultural impact of new technology; his research includes studies of the new genetic technologies, and the use of new technology for evaluating qualitative data (text, voice, and image). He is the coordinator of the Mellon Study that is investigating the social economics of digital and analog information.

Project Team Members

Editors' note: These lists were provided by the Project Coordinators at the end of the project. In some cases, they represent the list of institutional participants at the project's end; in other cases, they are comprehensive over the course of the project. Apologies to any whose names are omitted.

Fowler Museum of Cultural History
Don McClelland
Doran Ross
Sarah Kennington
Roy Hamilton
Donna McClelland
Virginia Hetrick
Ledda Macera
Eric Anderson
Bata Unkovic

George Eastman House
Roger Bruce
Andrew Eskind
Marianne Fulton
Therese Mulligan
David Wooters

Harvard University Art Museums
Andrea Notman
Frances Beane
Marjorie Cohn
Elizabeth Gombosi
Sarah Kianovsky
Henry Lie
Lee Mandell
Miriam Stewart
Meg Howland

Library of Congress
Carl Fleischhauer
Mary Levering
Meslissa Smith Levine
Helena Zinkham
Phil Michel
Brett Carnell

The Museum of Fine Arts, Houston
Jeannette Dixon
Gwen Goffe
Beth Schneider
Charles Carroll
Marty Stein
Misty Moye
Margaret Stone
Lih Kai
Barbara Michels

National Gallery of Art
Ric Snyder
Robin Dowden
Ric Foster
Nancy Breuer
Marilyn Shaw
Ruth Perlin

National Museum of American Art
Rachel Allen
Steve Dietz
Woody Dowling
Mary Ellen Guerra
Mike Briggs
Thornton Staples

American University
Diana Vogelsong
Kathe Albrecht
Greg Welsh
Teresa Fernandez
Alicia Abramson
Melissa Becher
Brian Kehs
Karthic Lakshamanan
Chris Lewis
Dhiren Shah
Alan Callander
Norma Broude
Jean-Christophe "Max" Hyacinthe
Helen Langa
Patricia Meilman
Ann Zelle

Columbia University
Angela Giral
David S. Millman
Robert Cartolano

Stephen Davis
Janet Gertz
Katie Keller
Carol Mandel
Robert O. McClintock
Linda Ellen Strauss
Robert Wolven

Cornell University

H. Thomas Hickerson
Peter Hirtle
Noni Korf Vidal
Claudia Lazzaro
Laura Meixner
Geri Gay
Marcy Rosenkrantz
Carol Denatale
Elaine Engst
Jean Locey
Laurie McEvoy
Barbara Prior
Sheryl Reiss
Margaret Webster

University of Illinois

Beth Sandore
Jane Block
Robert Wedgeworth
William Mischo
Linda Duke
Robert A. Jones
Jane Goldberg
Jane Darcovich
Katherine Manthorne
Tim Cole
Charles Bauer
Merri Beth Lavagnino
Najmuddin Shaik

University of Maryland

Sally M. Promey
Catherine Hays
Ellen Borkowski
C.S. Chang
James Douglas Farquhar
Sharon E. Gerstel
Walter Gilbert
Terry Gips
Susan Jenson
Sarah Miller
Kathy Russell
Adele Seeff
Lynn Woodruff
Amy Decker
Quint Gregory

University of Michigan

Wendy P. Lougee
John Weise
Allison Colborne
Sandy Colombo
Peggy Daub
C. Olivia Frost
Zoe Gurevich
Diane Kirkpatrick
Gail Lift
Michael D. Miller
John Price-Wilkin
Karen Sayer
Deirdre Spencer

University of Virginia

Judith Thomas
Lara Ashmore
Kaylyn Hipps
Christie Stephenson
Jeph Herrin
Thornton Staples
Johanna Bauman
April Oettinger

▶ Management Committee

Maxwell Anderson
David Bearman
Howard Besser
Clifford Lynch
Patricia McClung
Geoff Samuels*
Christie Stephenson
Jennifer Trant

*Geoff Samuels served for the first year of the project.

Credits

The reproductions of the computer display screens in this volume were produced in Adobe Illustrator 6.0 to improve their clarity and legibility in the printing process. The images in the screen shots were derived from the highest quality digital files supplied by the MESL participating museums. They were resized, converted to halftones, and then imported into the Illustrator files. The images on pages 15 and 16, reproducing the images manipulated by students as part of their assignments, are resized versions of the actual screen resolution images.

The Netscape Navigator and Apple logos are used with special permission.

Netscape:

Portions © Netscape Communications Corporation, 1997. All Rights Reserved. Netscape, Netscape Navigator, and the Netscape N logo are registered trademarks of Netscape in the United States and other countries.

Apple:

System Software Mac OS 8.1 © 1983–1997 Apple Computer, Inc. All Rights Reserved. Apple® and the Apple logo are registered trademarks of Apple Computer, Inc.

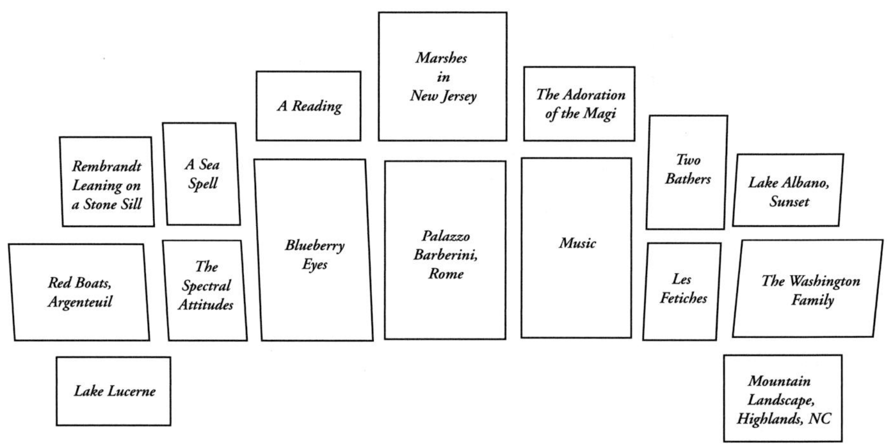

Cover, background image:

Johann Heinrich Ramberg, *The Exhibition of the Royal Academy in 1787*, engraved by Pietro Martini, 1787, © The British Museum. Negative from which the image was manipulated, © The Courtauld Institute.

Cover, inset images:

Carroll Beckwith (1852–1917), *Palazzo Barberini, Rome*, ca. 1910, oil on wood, 1974.69.6, © 1995 Smithsonian Institution; courtesy National Museum of American Art, transfer from S.I., Cooper-Hewitt Museum of Decorative Arts and Design.

Albert Bierstadt (1830–1902), *Lake Lucerne,* 1858, oil on canvas, National Gallery of Art, Washington, D.C., 1990.50.1, gift of Richard M. Scaife and Margaret R. Battle, in honor of the 50th anniversary of the National Gallery of Art.

Elmer Bischoff (1916–1991), *Two Bathers,* 1960, oil on canvas, 1968.52.7, © 1995 Smithsonian Institution, courtesy National Museum of American Art, gift of S.C. Johnson & Son, Inc.

Sandro Botticelli (1444/1445–1510), *The Adoration of the Magi,* early 1480s, tempera and oil on panel, National Gallery of Art, Washington, D.C., Andrew W. Mellon Collection, 1937.1.22.

Thomas Wilmer Dewing (1851–1938), *Music,* ca. 1895, oil on canvas, 1929.6.32, © 1995 Smithsonian Institution; courtesy National Museum of American Art, gift of John Gellatly.

Thomas Wilmer Dewing (1851–1938), *A Reading,* 1897, oil on canvas, 1948.10.5, © 1995 Smithsonian Institution, courtesy National Museum of American Art, bequest of Henry Ward Ranger through the National Academy of Design.

George Inness (1825–1894), *Lake Albano, Sunset,* ca. 1874, oil on canvas, National Gallery of Art, Washington, D.C., 1962.2.1, gift of Alice Dodge in memory of her father, Henry Percival Dodge.

Lois Mailou Jones (born 1905), *Les Fetiches,* 1938, oil on linen, 1990.56, © 1995 Smithsonian Institution, courtesy National Museum of American Art, museum purchase made possible by Mrs. N.H. Green, Dr. R. Harlan, and Francis Musgrave.

Gerome Kamrowski (born 1914), *The Spectral Attitudes,* 1941, oil on canvas, 1986.92.62, © 1995 Smithsonian Institution, courtesy National Museum of American Art, gift of Patricia and Phillip Frost.

Franz Kline (1910–1962), *Blueberry Eyes,* 1959–1960, oil on paperboard, 1982.57, © 1995 Smithsonian Institution, courtesy National Museum of American Art, gift of the Woodward Foundation.

Claude Monet (1840–1926), *Red Boats, Argenteuil,* 1875, oil on canvas, courtesy of the Fogg Art Museum, Harvard University Art Museums, 1951.54, bequest of Collection of Maurice Wertheim, Class of 1906.

Rembrandt Harmensz van Rijn (Leiden, 1606–1669, Amsterdam), *Rembrandt Leaning on a Stone Sill,* 1639, etching on paper, courtesy of the Fogg Art Museum, Harvard University Art Museums, M12899, gift of Arnold Knapp.

Dante Gabriel Rossetti (1828-1882), *A Sea Spell,* 1875–1877, oil on canvas, courtesy of the Fogg Art Museum, Harvard University Art Museums, 1939.92, gift of Grenville L. Winthrop.

Edward Savage (1761–1817), *The Washington Family,* 1789–1796, oil on canvas, National Gallery of Art, Washington, D.C., Andrew W. Mellon Collection, 1940.1.2.

Henry Ossawa Tanner (1859 USA–1937 France), *Mountain Landscape, Highlands, NC,* 1889, watercolor, pencil, and colored pencil on paper mounted on paperboard, 1983.95.25, © 1995 Smithsonian Institution, courtesy National Museum of American Art, gift of Mr. and Mrs. Norman B. Robbins.

Henry Ossawa Tanner (1859 USA–1937 France), *Marshes in New Jersey,* 1895, pastel and pencil on paper mounted on paperboard, 1984.149.3, © 1995 Smithsonian Institution, courtesy National Museum of American Art, gift of Mr. and Mrs. Alfred T. Morris, Jr.

PAGE 77:

TOP ROW, LEFT TO RIGHT: George Bellows, *Haystacks and Barn,* 1909, oil on canvas, The Museum of Fine Arts, Houston, Wintermann Collection of American Art, 85.154, gift of Mr. and Mrs. David R. Wintermann. Pierre Bonnard, *Landscape with Two Haystacks,* ca. 1892, oil on pulpboard panel, The Museum of Fine Arts, Houston, 91.1601, gift of Virginia and Ira Jackson. P.H. Emerson (1856–1936), *Stacking (Hay),* 1886, platinum print photograph, George Eastman House, Museum Collection, 81:1285:0034.

BOTTOM ROW, LEFT TO RIGHT: Paul Gauguin (French, 1848–1903), *Haystacks in Brittany,* 1890, oil on canvas, © 1998 Board of Trustees, National Gallery of Art, Washington, D.C., 1972.9.11, gift of the W. Averell Harriman Foundation in memory of Marie N. Harriman. Henry R. Robinson, *A Very Bad Man,* 1833, lithograph on wove paper, Library of Congress (the print was deposited for copyright on July 18, 1833 by New York publisher Henry Robinson & Company, from the collection of American Political Prints, Prints and Photographs Division). John Henry Twachtman (1853–1902), *Haystacks at Edge of Woods,* ca. 1895, pastel on paperboard, 1929.6.139, © 1995, Smithsonian Institution, courtesy National Museum of American Art, gift of John Gellatly.

PAGE 78:

TOP: Paul Gauguin (French, 1848–1903), *Haystacks in Brittany,* 1890, oil on canvas, © 1998 Board of Trustees, National Gallery of Art, Washington, D.C., 1972.9.11, gift of the W. Averell Harriman Foundation in memory of Marie N. Harriman.

BOTTOM: John Henry Twachtman (1853–1902), *Haystacks at Edge of Woods,* ca. 1895, pastel on paperboard, 1929.6.139, © 1995, Smithsonian Institution, courtesy National Museum of American Art, gift of John Gellatly.

PAGE 80:

TOP TO BOTTOM: Fernand Leger (French, 1881–1955), *France Reborn, from the United Nations series,* 1945, watercolor, gouache, and pencil on paper mounted on paperboard, 1984.124.173, © 1995 Smithsonian Institution, courtesy National Museum of American Art, gift of Container Corporation of America.

Daniel Chester French (1850–1931), *Concord Minute Man of 1775,* bronze, 1889/cast 1917, 1991.193, © 1995 Smithsonian Institution, courtesy National Museum of American Art, museum purchase.

Pierre-Auguste Renoir *Still Life with Bouquet,* 1871, oil on canvas, The Museum of Fine Arts, Houston, The Robert Lee Blaffer Memorial Collection, 51.7, gift of Sarah Campbell Blaffer.

François Bonvin, *Still Life,* 1858, oil on canvas, The Museum of Fine Arts, Houston, museum purchase, 85.286.

PAGE 81:

TOP TO BOTTOM: Daniel Chester French (1850–1931), *Concord Minute Man of 1775,* bronze, 1889/cast 1917, 1991.193, © 1995 Smithsonian Institution, courtesy National Museum of American Art, museum purchase. Edouard Manet (French, 1832–1883), *Flowers in a Crystal Vase,* ca. 1882, oil on canvas, © 1998 Board of Trustees, National Gallery of Art, Washington, D.C., 1970.17.37, Ailsa Mellon Bruce Collection. Paul Cézanne (French, 1839–1906), *Flowers in a Rococo Vase,* ca. 1876, oil on canvas, © 1998 Board of Trustees, National Gallery of Art, Washington, D.C., 1963.10.105, Chester Dale Collection.

Selected Bibliography

About MESL

Albrecht, Kathe Hicks. "Digital Imaging on Campus: An Early Look at the Museum Educational Site Licensing Project." *VRA Bulletin* 22, no. 4 (Winter 1995): 12.

Albrecht, Kathe Hicks. "Educational Use of Networked Museum Information." *Spectra* 25, no. 2 (Winter 1997–98): 33–39.

Bearman, David, and Jennifer Trant. "Museums and Intellectual Property: Rethinking Rights Management for a Digital World." *Visual Resources* 12, no. 3–4: 269–279.

Besser, Howard, et al. *The Costs of Digital Image Distribution* (reports on the Mellon Foundation Grant). *http://www.sims.berkeley.edu/research/mellon/*

Besser, Howard. "Comparing Five Implementations of the Museum Educational Site Licensing Project: 'If the Museum Data's the Same, Why's It Look so Different?'" *Proceedings of the Fourth International Conference on Hypermedia and Interactivity in Museums* (Paris, France, 3–5 September 1997). Pittsburgh: Archives and Museum Informatics: 317–325.

Besser, Howard, and Christie Stephenson. "The Museum Educational Site Licensing Project: Technical Issues in the Distribution of Museum Images and Textual Data to Universities," in James Hemsley (ed.) *EVA '96 Electronic Imaging and the Visual Arts.* Hampshire, UK: Vasari Ltd., 1996: 5-1–5-15. (*http://www.gii.getty.edu/mesl/about/docs/EVA.html*)

Giral, Angela, and Jeannette Dixon. "The Virtual Museum Comes to Campus: Two Perspectives on the Museum Educational Site Licensing Project." *Art Libraries Journal* 21, no. 1 (1996): 14–17.

Lebowitz, Lisa. "MESL Brings Museum Images to Universities." *Information Technology Digest: University of Michigan* 4, no. 8: 1–4.

Museum Educational Site Licensing Project. Project Web Site. *http://www.gii.getty.edu/mesl*

Promey, Sally, and Miriam Stewart. "Digital Art History: A New Field for Collaboration." *American Art* 11, no. 2 (Summer 1997): 36–41.

Samuels, Geoff. "The Site Licensing Solution." *Museum News* 75, no. 3: 54.

Trant, Jennifer. "Exploring New Models for Administering Intellectual Property: The Museum Educational Site Licensing Project." *Digital Image Access & Retrieval.* Urbana–Champaign: GSLIS, University of Illinois, 1997: 29–41.

Trant, Jennifer. "The Museum Educational Site Licensing Project." *Spectra* 22, no. 2 (Winter 1994–95): 19–21.

Trant, Jennifer. "The Museum Educational Site Licensing (MESL) Project: An Update." *Spectra* 23, no. 1 (Spring 1996): 32–34.

Other Cited Works and Selected Additional Resources

Art Museum Image Consortium (AMICO) Web Site. *http://www.amico.net*

"Copyright and Fair Use, the Great Image Debate." Special Issue, *Visual Resources* 12, no. 3–4 (1997).

Ester, Michael. "Image Quality and Viewer Perception." *Leonardo* 23:1 (1990): 51–63.

Ester, Michael. "Digital Images in the Context of Visual Collections and Scholarship." *Visual Resources* X:1 (1994): 11–24.

Jones-Garmil, Katherine (ed.). *The Wired Museum: Emerging Technology and Changing Paradigms.* Washington, D.C.: American Association of Museums, 1997.

LIBLICENSE-L List Archives. *http://www.library.yale.edu/~llicense/ListArchives*

Museum Digital Licensing Collective (MDLC) Web Site. *http://www.museumlicensing.org*

National Initiative for a Networked Cultural Heritage (NINCH). *Copyright, Fair Use & Licensing In A Digital World. http://www-ninch.cni.org/ISSUES/COPYRIGHT.html*

The Research Libraries Group. REACH Project Web Site. *http://www.rlg.org/reach.html*

Steiner, Christine. "The Double-Edged Sword: Museums and the Fair Use Doctrine." *Museum News* 76, no. 5 (Setember/October 1997): 32–35.

Trant, Jennifer. "Framing the Picture: Standards for Imaging Systems." *http://www.io.org/~jtrant/papers/ichim/ichim.1.intro.html*

U.S. Patent and Trademark Office. The Conference on Fair Use. *Report to the Commissioner on the Conclusion of the First Phase of the Conference on Fair Use* (September 1997). *http://www.uspto.gov/web/offices/dcom/olia/confu/conclutoc.html*